MW00564045

WRITERS REPUBLIC

THE GREATEST STORY NEVER TOLD

ORAL TRADITION AND THE DEVELOPMENT OF MESSAGES IN THE BOOK OF GENESIS

VINCENT KRIVDA

WRITERS REPUBLIC L.L.C.
515 Summit Ave. Unit R1
Union City, NJ 07087, USA

Website: *www.writersrepublic.com*
Hotline: *1-877-656-6838*
Email: *info@writersrepublic.com*

Ordering Information:
Quantity sales. Special discounts are available on quantity purchases by corporations, associations, and others. For details, contact the publisher at the address above.

Library of Congress Control Number: 2021917351
ISBN-13: 978-1-63728-759-0 [Paperback Edition]
978-1-63728-760-6 [Hardback Edition]
978-1-63728-761-3 [Digital Edition]

Rev. date: 09/07/2021

To Coty, the moment I saw you, the sight of you pierced my soul. It was then that I knew that I loved you!

—∞—

To Joseph, Lydia, and all those embarking on a journey to hear the greatest story never told; I offer two bits of advice which I regularly share with my class: (1) Never bite at the first apple (Gen. 3:6) and (2) It is never about the murder! (Gen. 4:8). May our names be written in the Book of Life.

—∞—

Special Appreciation

Jeffrey Burghauser, Dr. Russell Elam, Dr. Rebecca Morrison, & the entire Oakstone Academy family. Dare to be a Daniel! (Dan. 1:8-9)

INTRODUCTION

The Torah is the Hebrew name for the first five books of the Bible. Translated, it means, "to teach." Christians and Jews turn to the Torah for teaching. It is fair to ask exactly what it teaches?

In the New Testament's book of Matthew, Jesus restates six separate commands from the Torah:

> You have heard that it was said to those of old "You shall not murder," and whosover murders will be in danger of the judgment. But I say to you... (Matt. 5:21–22a)
>
> You have heard that it was said to those of old, "You shall not commit adultery." But I say to you... (Matt. 5:27–28a)
>
> Furthermore it has been said, "Whoever divorces his wife, let him give her a certificate of divorce"...But I will say to you... (Matt. 5:31–32a)
>
> Again you have heard that it was said to those of old, "You shall not swear falsely..." But I say to you... (Matt. 5:33–34a)
>
> You have heard that it was said "An eye for an eye and a tooth for a tooth." But I tell you... (Matt. 5:38–39a)
>
> You have heard that it was said "You shall love your neighbor and hate your enemy." But I say to you, love your enemies... (Matt 5:43–44a)

A peculiar problem is highlighted when we consider these words of Jesus. What was the methodology and transmission in our historical past of the Torah? If we can trust the account related in Matthew, Jesus suggested that people in the first-century AD still received their Torah instruction in a verbal unwritten format. Listen to the words: "You have heard that it was said …But I say to you…" He did not say, "You have read…but I write unto you."

Alongside the issue of the method of transmission of the message one must ask: were the messages being transmitted as originally intended? The Masoretic Hebrew text passed down to us includes both vowels and diacritic marks to preserve the oral tradition of antiquity.[1] The vowel system facilitated word pronunciation in order to ensure that the messages were not lost.

The great stories of the Bible arose from the oral tradition, yet in this age, we encourage people to read the Bible stories. Talking about the stories seems old-fashioned. Families and friends would to gather and enjoy a meal and sit and talk. With the hustle and bustle of modernity, we rarely have time for such a luxury. In fact, the art of family talk is disappearing from the cultural landscape. The solitude of reading dominates the structure of how information is received.

Left unanswered are important questions: how should one read the Bible if it was intended for an oral transmission? Some argue the Bible remains the single most interpretable text known to man. Is it an open text subject to various interpretations? Or is there a right way to read the Bible and a wrong way to read the Bible?

If there is a point to this book, then it can be revealed by considering those questions. Yet here is the problem: scholars admit that the stories of the book of Genesis originated out of an oral tradition, not a written tradition.

This book therefore asks questions, but in a different way.

1) What is the nature of the stories in the Torah?
2) Are the stories as told different from what we have been informed they mean when read as a text?

---

1. Joel L. Hoffman, *In the Beginning: A Short History of the Hebrew Language* (New York: University Press, 2004), 76.

3) How would the original audience have heard (sic understood) those stories?

Of the translated Hebrew text, it is accepted that there are thirty-nine books that comprise the Protestant Bible and forty-six books in the Catholic canon. It is also accepted that there are many authors of the Bible. The position of this book differs in the practical application of understanding the meaning of the Torah portions (first five books). Some scholars generally attribute Moses as the author of the Torah. Other scholars broadly adhere to a format of multiple authorship of the Torah.

Could it be that the first five books were edited from oral traditions often in conflict with various existing proliferated versions? If so, how did those conflicts come to be? In short, they were handed down through stories from generation to generation. In that genre, the oral tradition offered different versions of the same story. They were the product of family gatherings and conversations. Those differing stories had a purpose. They connected generations by teaching moral lessons.

Ancient Semitic traditions and religions were homespun family affairs. Religion in Palestine during the first millennia BCE was not a take-it-or-leave-it commodity. Religion in our postmodern world is vastly different, characterized by brick-and-mortar institutions. We can be born as Lutherans; and if that does not meet our fancy, we can leave that church and become something else, like a Pentecostal. Both denominations are Christian in faith yet strongly different in ideological underpinnings.

Our first rule is now introduced. We must be willing to change the lens of our evaluation to accommodate the origin of these family stories. There were no church creeds in ancient Palestine. There were no doctrinal statements imposed under a unified temple. Each successive generation learned what was moral and proper from stories passed down over time. Those stories entertained the family.

Judaism in the ancient world was not a monolithic religion. But when we recreate the story, even recreating it from the simple written text, we treat the story as if it were part of a broader established religion. Nothing could have been further from the truth. These stories were told not to establish orthodoxy but instead promote discussions about right and wrong. Modern readers err by attempting to use the episodes set forth in the Bible as a law book. Following that law book to the letter produces failed conclusions.

This approach toward reading the Bible includes some potential reductionism. If one reads the Bible under the model outlined in this book, does that interpretation preclude other interpretations? In Genesis chapter 1, God created male and female humans. In creating man, the Hebrew word *tzacar* is used instead of the traditional word for "man," *ish*. Absent any attached vowels, the word tzacar could be translated as 'male' or 'remember.' A very reasonable discussion would have then followed: "What does God want man to remember?" That would segue into practical family and social issues. It is now obvious we are not concerned with how a word is translated. We will be concerned with the messages and give and take inherent in dialogue and discussions.

This book is broken down into three parts, conveniently labeled Part I, Part II, and Part III. Part I serves to introduce the historical flow of the ancient Near East. Part II includes episodic stories that utilize a creation format as a backdrop. Part III breaks down the various stories circulating involving the figure of Abraham. By its nature, both Parts II & III will appear to be disjointed commentary, if one is looking for a 'standard' bible commentary. It is commentary, but commentary on the oral tradition.

The first chapters in the Bible seemingly address cosmogony. *Cosmogony* is a fancy word for the study of origins. Of course, nothing is off the table. We will question whether the first book of the Bible, Genesis, is even relatable to cosmogony.

After that we will introduce the Sumerian/Akkadian migrant, celebrated in tradition as Abraham. We will break down each of the Twenty-one Abraham episodes contained in the book of Genesis. We will discover that in some cases he is a heroic protagonist. In other cases, we will close our eyes. Abraham will not be a person that we will even like! These portrayals are purposeful, and they teach. Through contrast, they teach unmistakable life lessons.

The goal of this book is to not convince you the reader to accept my view or my interpretation or translation. If you read this book and violently disagree but curiously reread the book of Genesis, then the goal has been accomplished. The Bible is a lamp unto our feet. It is a light unto our path.

Our task challenges established interpretations of the numerous episodes contained in the book of Genesis. That is a fair endeavor. It will not threaten the text itself, instead reevaluate how the text is understood. The book of Genesis is not the construction of a single author, nor is it per se the product of multiple authors. Instead, it is the redacted surviving account(s) of multiple oral traditions that were naturally transformed over hundreds of years, thousands of years ago. Our goal is to reveal the lessons that might have been told. That perspective must be considered.

PART I

I don't speak because I have the power to speak: I speak because I don't have the power to remain silent.

Abraham Isaac Kook

CHAPTER 1

WHAT IS ORAL TRADITION?

What is oral tradition? Oral tradition is the entire sum of stories preserved by the Israelites over a time period before they were written and codified in the Bible as text. Do we sometimes get the oral transmission wrong? As a young undergraduate student at Lee University in Cleveland, Tennessee, I was introduced to oral tradition. It was described as a careful process. The Israelite community preserved oral stories with a varnished coat of sacredness. Why would they do this? They did it because those words were believed to have been the exact words of God. Those words were carefully handed down from generation to generation, unchanged. The preservation of the oral tradition was a miracle. It demonstrated God's ability to preserve words within a tradition. Those were holy words. To the extent they were God's words, their care received all the more attention.

But just how careful was this process? Re-examining the words of Jesus, one can observe glaring inconsistent contradictions between the written and oral traditions. For example:

> You have heard that it was said "You shall love your neighbor and hate your enemy." But I say to you, love your enemies… (Matt. 5:43–44a)

Was this oral tradition as carefully preserved as some think? What exactly does the Torah text state that was misquoted by Jesus?

> You shall not take vengeance, nor bear any grudge against the children of your people, but you shall love your neighbor as yourself: I am the Lord. (Lev. 19:18)

Clearly, the Torah did not require the Israelites to love their neighbor and hate their enemy. How could Jesus have been so confused about the Law of God? Can we accept as an introducing thought that there are differences between the oral tradition and the written Torah? If we do, we then bring into question the preservation process under which the written text eventually emerged.

Jesus was not confused. Instead, Jesus was perhaps quoting popular sayings of his day. Most likely the enemy was a reference to the Roman military occupation of Palestine. Jesus lived in a world of context peculiar to his day. His words addressed that context. Principles and morals were communicated in that language with those specific words.

What lesson(s) can we take from this analysis? The Bible stories emerged from oral tradition. They were later reduced to a written text. Dominating the method of religious messaging during Jesus's own day was the oral tradition. The written tradition corrupted the oral tradition. Why is that important to recognize? The oral tradition Jesus related was much different than the written tradition. If the oral tradition was not the same tradition as the written text, then perhaps we can rediscover the messages of the Torah by listening to those messages. The individual stories and separate episodes were not history lessons; they were context points to begin discussions, not answer questions. Is this a reasonable approach? If we compare Jesus's quote, we need only let that conclusion speak for itself.

This book was not written to convince you the reader that I have any special insight into the Bible. In fact, I do not. This particular work originated one day when I found myself laughing while I was reading the Torah in Hebrew. I realized that if I was listening to the story, instead of reading it, both the mood and demeanor of the story line would completely change. Reviewing stories in the Torah then began to unfold under a whole new light. The verse I was reading in English was not funny at all. All the previous readings of this verse over forty years caused me to just gloss over the text. The story I found to be funny was recorded in Genesis 17:20. The Lord God is recorded as saying, "And as for Ishmael, I have heard you." Later in Chapter 8, we will explore why that might be a "funny" line within an oral setting.

This book opens the various episodic stories of the Bible. We use the term *episodic* to relate a concept. Each episode contained its own specific teaching or moral lesson. It is essential to look at how those messages and story lines were understood by their original audience(s). The ancient world gave birth to the Bible. Expectations in the reading process must be set. Those expectations need to be derived from how the text contextually sounded and what they would have meant to an audience.

Exploring truth is an essential function of theology. Yet generation after generation seems to be engaged in an endless quest for meaning. As an undergraduate student, I recall a sign posted over the door of the psychology professor's office: "Having abandoned my quest for truth I am now in search of a good fantasy to believe in!" Wow! What a powerful thought especially at a university devoted to faith and religion. Did this statement project and defend the espoused doctrine of the church? Of course not! It was intended to prompt the student to search and ponder. Are we so busy defending our perception of truth that we have laid aside that pure emotion that caused us to turn toward God in faith? Truth is the embodiment of individual elements of facts that emerge from our biases and perceptions. Is there more than one single version of truth?

Pilate was having a hard time figuring out exactly what was going on in Jerusalem.His working office as governor was not even in Judea; instead, it was located in the coastal town of Caesarea. He visited Jerusalem only during special days. Jerusalem was the center of the government, yet the operational function was quartered elsewhere. Disconnected from the day-to-day views of the community, Pilate was not sure exactly what to do with this Jesus figure. This conclusion is evident from the record set forth by John the Apostle.

Upon meeting Jesus, Pilate gets down to the base facts: "Are you the king of the Jews?" (John 18:33). Depending on how Jesus would answer this question would determine the actions Pilate would be compelled to take. Yet Jesus's answer stuns Pilate:

> Jesus answered him, "Are you speaking for yourself about this, or did others tell you this concerning Me?" Pilate answered, "Am I a Jew? Your own nation and the chief priests have delivered You to me. What have You done?" Jesus answered, "My kingdom is not of this world. If My kingdom were of this world, My servants would fight, so that I should not be delivered to the Jews; but now My kingdom is not from here." Pilate therefore said to Him, "Are You a king then?" (John 18:34–37)

Pilate's frustration was evident and part of John's story. Three times he attempts to secure a sensible reliable answer to his questions from Jesus. "Are you king of the Jews?" "What have you done?" "Are you a king then?" Jesus answers, "Did you arrive at this conclusion on your own, or did somebody influence you? My kingdom is not of this world!"

Remove yourself from the present and place yourself back in time in Pilate's shoes. Pilate was a visitor to Jerusalem. There were political considerations in any decision he would make. Jesus did not even claim to be a king in rebellion. Other "Messiahs," and there were quite a few who claimed the role of Messiah, were never shy to make messianic claims. Pilate was not even sure why Jesus was bound before him.

He at first thought that the clerical leadership of the Sanhedrin wanted to draw him into a religious squabble. And yet the best of the conversation was still to come.

> Jesus answered, "You say rightly that I am a king. For this cause I was born, and for this cause I have come into the world, that I should bear witness to the truth. Everyone who is of the truth hears My voice." Pilate said to Him, *"What is truth?"* And when he had said this, he went out again to the Jews, and said to them, "I find no fault in Him at all." (John 18:37)

Jesus notes that it was Pilate himself who identified him (Jesus) as a king. Jesus only asserted that he was born to bear witness to truth. Pilate, in the most honest moment of his political life, in desperate exasperation, exhales his infamous gasp, *"What is truth?"* For this reason, we spend some time analyzing the difference between facts and truth. Starting from this point is important. In the study of theology and religion, there has been an attempt to pass off facts as truth. Is there a difference between facts and truth?

We then must overcome some bias inherited from the arrogance of modernity. As moderns, we have a baked-in disdain for the past. For many, history has become the study of dead primitive people. Moderns enjoy the enlightened view of an educated future. We often claim that if we fail to study "the mistakes" of the past, we are doomed to repeat them. Notice that we do not say: "If we fail to study the success of the past, we will not enjoy their benefits." Our view of the past persuades us that the further back one looks we see a less than developed primitive humanity. In that view, we overlook the richness and value of oral tradition.

CHAPTER 2

ARE ALL BIBLICAL HEROES HEROIC?

Exploring the world and intellectual thought of ancient Mesopotamia is a critical first step. The Bible emerged in the political and social environment of Palestine during the first millennia BCE. This time period birthed very sophisticated governing and religious structures. These societal configurations existed thousands of years before a confederate Jewish government was ever imagined.

Religious developments within Palestine from 1,200 BCE to AD 100 formed as a subset by-product of the greater ancient Near East. Coming to terms with a religious-historical view of Palestine also requires an economic view of the land. So what exactly does that mean? Palestine then cannot be viewed as "an isolated island". It was not singularly oriented in its political structure. It was not uniform in its cultural structure. It definitely was not unbending in its religious structures. Yet many Old Testament Surveys begin with the unchallenged view that Judaism was a fully developed religious thought which differentiated Hebrews from all other nations. For example, the Hebrews were good and the Philistines were evil. This notion becomes challenged especially in the twentieth chapter of the book of Genesis. Surprisingly, it is also challenged in each of the various episodic stories surrounding the controversial figure of Abraham, a migrant just like the Philistines.

One must consider some potentially controversial views unearthed by recent archeological scholarship. Has our understanding of the past imposed bias that has influenced our reading of the messages within the

Bible? Religious and theological works have often been written within a context describing Israel as a single state actor. Can we challenge this premise while keeping true to our faith?

Gaining and establishing a perspective on reading the Bible is determined by many social and historical factors. Those facts interact with our present circumstances. When you begin reading the Bible with a compass tilted in a certain direction, it would be no surprise if one found the answer in that direction. Therefore, we will interact with some of those religious-based factors. The reader is challenged to read the messages in this context: If this story was told in a group setting, what resulting conversations would be generated?

The function of oral tradition lies not in the individual elements of the episode or story. Instead, oral tradition assumes a story line, and from that story line inspires discussions. From those discussions, values are communicated to the audience. The episodes in the Bible allowed the family opportunities to teach and pass down to the next generation values within the context of morals.

Already defined, the word *Torah* means "to teach." Either the Bible teaches us facts or it establishes a foundation under which teachings occur. If it teaches us facts, it is an instrument ill- suited for that purpose. As we read Part II, the various episodes will not be retranslated since the translation of the written text is not the 'point of consideration'. The issue is fundamentally different. Words and conversations need context to relate meaning. The context may be elusive in a written tradition. In the oral tradition, the words may take on a whole new meaning. The original meaning does not require a new translation. It requires one to fully appreciate and accept the social, political, and economic context of that day.

The stories intended to promote family-based discussions resulting in teaching(s). Family members discussed their own personal quest to figure out who they were in relation to their Creator. That is the origin of the oral tradition. The stories were only the beginning of the teaching. In the written tradition, the stories are the end of the teaching resulting in accepted orthodox forms.

What do we mean by that? An example based on visual-art communication in the television industry is proof. The TV crime drama

Murder She Wrote was aired from 1984 to 1996 and produced 264 episodes and an additional 4 television movies. The series, by any account, would tabulate at least 268 murders that occurred in the fictional setting of Cabot Cove, Maine. Cabot Cove was a sleepy distinctly American eastern coastal town of approximately 3,500 inhabitants. Tourism and fishing were major draws for the fictional setting. Over a twelve-year period, if we just list the facts, one in thirteen people were murdered there. Yet the show was never about the murder! The audience would turn the show on assuming there would be a murder. The name revealed that fact. The show captured our attention based on the cleverness used within the story line to teach a moral or value about ourselves.

Part of the process of opening the messages of the Bible involves teaching how to open them. The first eleven chapters of the Bible formed a dramatic response to the prevailing culture of that age. That culture was formed under the opinion that man was created by Marduk to serve the gods. The Hebrew response suggested something different. YHWH created man to thrive and prosper on the earth. The book of Genesis weighed in on a discussion that had been ongoing for thousands upon thousands of years. The first eleven chapters of Genesis likely represent a time period before 3,500 BCE. They are devoted to very specific stories that were codified in writing from the oral tradition at a minimum, at least 3,000 to 15,000 years after they had taken place. It includes episodic stories designed to spark timeless conversations challenging the status quo. The conversations included sensitive subjects. Those sensitive subjects looked at the nature of man, the nature of God, and the absurdity of a life ending in death.

Our adventure may end with a changed view of the biblical iconic figure of Abraham. Was he a heroic figure with such military strength that he could chase down the most powerful army of his day and rescue his nephew from certain slavery? Or was Abraham a cowering figure with no strength who surrendered his wife to other men to avoid being killed?

Abraham was introduced in the book of Genesis 11:29. His life is recorded as ending in Genesis 25:10. The Torah records at least twenty-one separate episodes involving Abraham. By linking those various stories consecutively, one improperly assumes a history is provided.

Nothing could be further from the truth. Those stories were randomly told at various gatherings. This fact then begs, or perhaps, answers the question: why in some stories is Abraham a protagonist and in others an antagonist? The answer might surprise you, and it is important to decide that question for yourself.

CHAPTER 3

FACTS AND THE THEOLOGICAL QUEST FOR TRUTH

Humans are unique among living things: we ponder our existence. Our most ancient writings reflect this tendency. Which came first, the chicken or the egg? We have puzzled over that inquiry for millennia. The Judeo-Christian tradition tells us that, but for the chicken, there could be no egg.

But how did the chicken get there?

Torah is the traditional Hebrew label for the Five Books of Moses. And *Torah* means "teach" —but teach what exactly? It's not a book of science, purporting to teach the laws of motion or physics. It is also not a text akin to the great works of history and philosophy such as Tolstoy's *War and Peace.*

The Christian community tends to dismiss, or at least to minimize, the Torah by calling it the Old Testament. If you label a bicycle "the old bicycle," it's likely because you have a newer one. In which case, the old one is merely taking up space. But the Torah is a vital component of the Word of God, and the Word of God is as relevant today as it ever was.

Here's a tantalizing question: could it be that how we understand the Five Books of Moses determines how we comprehend the whole Bible? And how we relate to the entirety of the Bible influences how we learn what it's attempting to teach. Once we've figured this out, the elemental puzzles of existence will open themselves before us. We are going to ask questions. Our first question is simple: would it change our view of God's Word if it was not a flawless road map? What if the

Bible was divinely inspired to urge each generation to ask themselves the most basic questions: who am I? Why am I on earth? How must I live among others equally created by God yet different in thought, temperament, and outlook?

Man is a storyteller. The Bible was born in the ancient, universal storytelling tradition. That process relied on oral (rather than written) transmission. We all love stories. We're addicted to television dramas and narrative films. We'll devour them even when we're reasonably sure how they'll end. We all have friends and family members who are especially precious to us because of their skill in telling a good story. In the ancient world, like today, songs told stories. Traveling thespians performed for audiences with thrilling tales of an era long ago. Those stories aided man's generational search for truth.

To begin our quest for truth, we compare facts to truth. Under that microscope, we then begin to ask: what role do facts play in aiding our understanding of the separate subjects of religion and orthodoxy. Then we have the ability to analyze if there is a disconnect between religion and faith in God.

Our quest for truth, unfortunately, has misdirected us to accept facts as truth. The famed historian Sir Edward Hallet Carr instructs us about facts: "A fact is like an empty sack; neither will stand on their own until you put something into them!"[2] In fact, Professor Carr takes his understanding of the craft of storytelling one step further by admonishing the student to "study the historian before you study the facts."[3] That is an exciting proposition when the enterprise and subject is something as settled as Napoleon's retreat from the invasion of Russia. Aren't the facts simply the facts? Do facts stand on the weight of their authority, or are they, as Professor Carr implies:

> History consists of a corpus of ascertained facts. The facts are available to the historian in documents, inscriptions and so on, like fish in the fishmonger's slab. The historian collects them, takes them home,

2. Edward Hallet Carr, *What Is History?* (New York: Random House, 1961), 25.
3. Ibid., 38.

> and cooks, and serves them in whatever style appeals to him.[4]

Oral tradition often informs us of history. But this is not a book about history. Perhaps it is not a book about theology either. It most definitely is not a book about facts. This is a book that allows us a moment to question how we know what we know about our faith. The ancients questioned their faith through the mode of storytelling. Elevating those stories to a written form was necessary. The desired end was to preserve the tale for future generations. In that preservation, the message of the stories was muddled in translation. Our blueprint examines just how that happened. The goal then is to introduce facts like fish on a fishmonger's slab, take them home, cook them, and serve them in whatever style that appeals to this point of view.

These questions must be considered in the context of this book: is the Bible a document from which statistical correlative data can be derived? In this present world is there only one point of view which is true? Is man compelled to search out that one view espoused and held by our Creator and squash all dissension from that truth?

Unanswerable questions arise out of facts. Pondering questions in the Torah are timeless and promote thoughtful reflection. Why are some born to a life doomed to die in miserable conditions while others seemingly enjoy pleasure? What are the intentions of my unknown Creator? Why are children born with muscular dystrophy and other maladies such as hypoplastic left heart syndrome? Why do the wicked and evil seem to prosper? Why has the only love of my life been reduced through disease to require 24-hour nursing care? Is the Creator of my soul also the judge of its eternity? We must ask in light of these questions: What does the Torah teach? Does the Torah teach facts? Or does the Bible guide us through a path of universal, seemingly recurring, questions over the course of human history?

The method of inquiry proposed in this book must first be established. No one could then claim that tricks were introduced to misrepresent the facts. The fact of the matter is that, facts do not speak for themselves. No one cares about all the previous crossings of the

---

4. Ibid., 6.

Delaware River before December 25, 1776. Those facts only apply when writing about those stories. For example, let's suppose that the fictional character Eddie Smith crossed the Delaware River on September 23, 1771. Is a question about Eddie Smith destined to be repeated in an American History class? No! Because those facts only support a story involving Eddie Smith. The only time that fact would be relevant is likely under the condition Eddie was late coming home and Mrs. Smith wanted an explanation!

There is a significant challenge for the reader. You must first consider whether the Bible teaches facts or provides an outline within which to relate to a knowable God. We will take facts and treat those facts in a manner that benefits our story. There is one not-so-subtle difference here. You should consider the questions posed in the Torah despite the facts. Morals and principles abound in the Bible. The modern Western tendency is to gloss over those relevant structures and elevate facts. The facts stand in the way of our view. In some cases, we will see how facts may prevent us from learning what the Bible really teaches.

What is our story? Did the title of the book catch your attention? *The Greatest Story Never Told!* Does our title imply that the story of creation has never been told? Of course, that is not a fact. Yet no one has told this story in this way. We will examine how the process of translated writings and developed religious doctrine has, in some instances, not captured the message of the Bible. Theology orders facts in a manner that benefits its preestablished story line. That would be just fine if we lived in a Garden of Eden. Since there are many theologies, many religions, and many facts, we must appreciate their contributions and failings. Our goal will be to engage in the noblest task of comparing creed and faith against the message that the Bible teaches.

What Does It Mean to Say That the Bible Is True?

When we think of the word *fact*, it is easy to misuse that word for *truth*. The most fundamental belief held among many is that the Bible is true. This notion is problematic. There is no specific delineation as to the definition of *true*. There is an old axiom: "The Bible said it! I believe it! That settles it!" There is no room to wiggle, or is there?

Something as true needs to be parsed either under equivocal terms or univocal terms. Equivocal language is common. Equivocal speech allows for several possible interpretations. One illustration of this is when a good chap tried to carve out some time from his wife to go bowling with his friends. However, the wife had other ideas for his time.

> CHAP: Dearest, I was thinking of spending the evening with my friends!
> WIFE: Beloved, let me know how that works out for you!

Classic univocal speech is always straightforward with no room for second-guessing.

> CHAP: Dearest, I was thinking of spending the evening with my friends!
> WIFE: Beloved, if you leave me with all this work, your marital bliss will end!

Our probe includes a discussion about the method of conveying messages. Does the Bible ever employ equivocal speech to send a message? In other words, what is the nature of our communication? Are biblical messages always univocal? Must truth only be univocal? Or can truth be communicated equivocally to send forth a more powerful message? Are emotions sometimes embedded in words, meaning their opposite definition? In other words,

Is the language used in the Bible only *literally true*?

Or does the language used in the Bible need only be *merely true*?

If the Bible were literally true, then it could only employ univocal messages where no meaning is veiled. Written texts and translations would be perfect instruments in that setting to communicate messages. The goal of the reader would then be to read and follow the directions, kind of like baking a cake for beginners. Illustrating equivocal language construction is instructive. Our good chap could venture to bowl a perfect 300 game and come home to harmoniously celebrate his achievement with his bride. Of course, we know that will not happen!

The ancient text reminds us: "He will cover you with his feathers, and under his wings, you will find refuge; his faithfulness will be your shield and rampart" (Ps. 91:4). The reader instantly knows that equivocal metaphorical language is employed. If the Bible were literally true, then what is conveyed to man is a graphic depiction of God as a giant winged chicken. That would be a fact. However, if one's reading of the Bible rests upon the standard that it need only be merely true, a much deeper meaning is gained. That would also be a fact.

Deciding that the Bible only needs to meet the standard of merely true allows an individual to reorient their approach in reading the Bible. The scriptures then provide a reasonable perspective from which to gain valuable spiritual insight. It prods the mind to do what God created it to do: think! That starting point is especially true in the broader double entendre writings contained in Hebrew poetry of the Song of Solomon chapter 8.

> Oh that you were like a brother to me
> who nursed at my mother's breasts!
> If I found you outside, I would kiss you,
> and none would despise me.
> I would lead you and bring you
> into the house of my mother—she who used to teach me.
> I would give you spiced wine to drink,
> the juice of my pomegranate.
> (Song of Sol. 8:1–2)

Many emotions flood my soul and consciousness when I read this scripture. As a father, after learning that verse, I have two options. I could meditate on the profound love of God for my soul or be thankful my daughter limited her displays of affection for her husband during the courting period. I very likely would have objected to either her boyfriend or fiancé's drinking of her "spiced wine" from the "juice of her pomegranate." As a counterargument from my daughter seeking to relax my parental grip, she could have appealed to scriptural authority.

A straightforward reading of translated written scripture as literal truth often obscures relevant cultural, historical settings. New problems emerge then to eliminate any possible moral lesson that scripture may teach. Reading the Bible in those instances as literally true, unrelated to the past, or the present, produces weakened teachings. Literal renderings have the potential to produce failed moral principles. The Bible is then reduced to a compromised historical fact pattern, stripping it of its profound message. Driving the Bible to such a position causes it to lose its authority to speak uniquely to all persons in all generations.

God created man with the ability to think and speak in both univocal and equivocal terms. Within that context, common, straightforward words can take on their absolute opposite meaning. That meaning is correctly understood then, but over time would lose its context. Translating sentences in a common language recorded over just several hundred years ago is difficult. To contextually translate idiomatic phrases and events from several millennia and from languages now dead is a much more difficult task.

Idiomatic phrases come and go in all cultures, both ancient and present. For example, the idiomatic phrase, "Go ahead, make my day," was taken from the 1983 movie *Sudden Impact*. In that scene, the protagonist of the film, Harry Callahan, interrupts a robbery to kill the bad guys. At the end of his retributive assault, one robber remained. That terrified robber attempted to flee and save his own life. He grabbed a waitress and threatened to shoot her in the head. The idiom now represents the injection of sarcasm into events of the absurd.

In univocal language construction, such a request by Dirty Harry would represent a simple, straightforward situation. This example further illustrates the role of that which is literally true from that which need only be merely true. If Harry Callahan literally meant for the robber to kill the waitress because it would make his day, then he would be in a confederate league of murder. Dirty Harry conveyed a more profound message: no matter which decision or action the bad guy took, he would not escape his brand of justice. A much different context and interpretation are at play. Harry wanted the bandit to think through his actions. Even his very name sends the message to the audience. His name was a part of the story!

The tension exhibited in the quest for facts and theological truth stands front and center. We want our religion to be reliable. We want our religion to be a fixed cemented stake in the ground upon which we can grab hold and find stability. Man seeks the one thing that will never be: permanence in an ever-changing world. Facts fail to live up to that permanence. Truth, an elusive mistress, fails to live up to that permanence. We seek permanence in a written text presuming it to be a written road map that sets forth specific lists of things to do, say, and believe. The Torah, however, is a much different book. Teaching dogmas or facts is not an objective of the Torah.

What Does Torah Teach?

The Torah was born in the ancient art of oral tradition. Engaging an audience around discussions served as a primary format to transmit values and morals. In ancient cultures, each age sought to provide the next generation with direction in answering basic questions about life. That next generation though sought those answers on their own terms, not the terms of the previous generation. The dialectical pattern of history has proven that when there are tensions in one generation, they will be worked out over time. The resolution, more often than not, is embodied in a form that rejects the previous set of assumptions.

In the Fertile Crescent, which included Canaan, after tens of thousands of years, the pursuit of meaning settled upon the grand conclusion that man was created to serve the gods. That conclusion made the most economic sense in light of the reality of daily toil, hardship, and man's limited life span.

The temple gained support over time because of its recognized connection with the gods and promotion of economic security. It emerged as an institution to buffer man from the harshness of government. Kings shared a certain amount of responsibility for the welfare of the citizens with the religious hierarchy. Societies encouraged the tension between the temple and government. The temple controlled markets, social norms, education, and worship. The king controlled armies, rules, regulations, and juridical matters.

In that environment, the practice of religion was centered in community welfare and justice. If one fast-forwards the clock from 3,500 BCE to AD 1,900, religion by then was not only separated from government, it promoted social stabilization functions as well. By ca. 450 BCE the Judeans were trickling back into Palestine from Mesopotamia. The written text attempted to establish a form of law and history. A branding iron of orthodoxy at least set the stage for a religion ordered and controlled by a priestly cast. Prior to this time being a Hebrew was not so good. Now it was the beginning of a nationalistic rallying cry.

Readers of the Bible in this day and age are often caught up in deciding what the Bible will mean to them. This requires a reader to respond to a written text. It focuses primarily on an existential application based upon the accumulation of our personal experiences. This book therefore proposes a return to the way of hearing the story preserved in the text. The book of Genesis should be told as separate episodes/stories that are not meant to be woven into a historical saga. Instead, these episodes were edited as a *Best Of* ancient stories preserved to teach. That is why the first five books in the Bible gained the moniker *Torah*. In short, one must imagine what the story would have sounded like. Probably the best analogy would mirror a theater play. In the theatrical production, showmanship would include actors stealing the scene with their oral skills.

Reading the text in its original oral tradition has allowed me to present to students a more consistent method for accessing a format to discuss values and morals. The Bible is not an academic text. It falls short as a history book. The Bible miserably fails as a book of creation science. However, when the Bible is approached as an accumulation of hundreds of different stories, each with their own special story line, those story lines teach morals, values, and principles. This in turn reveals the greatest story never told.

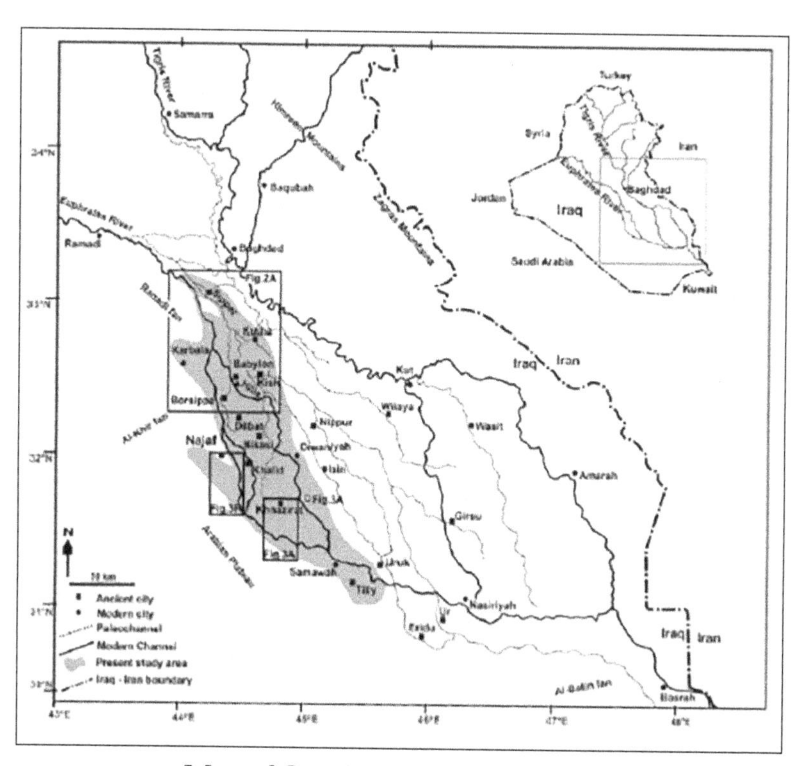

Map of Canals dug from Tigris and Euphrates in Mesopotamia region

CHAPTER 4

A SHORT PRIMER: THE DEVELOPMENT OF SOCIETIES IN THE ANCIENT NEAR EAST

Placing oral tradition in context, a knowledge of those societies is essential. Crucial to understanding how civilizations in antiquity were formed and existed was their economic origin. Ancient cultures produced an exceeding amount of vigor concerning civil, social, religious, and judicial systems. Those systems operated at full strength over five thousand years ago. In short, the Bible did not emerge from vacant lands. It appeared within a population already steeped in an active physical, emotional, civil, intellectual, and philosophical setting.

Ancient Ur was a thriving city-state by at least 3,000 BCE. Ur was a megacity of possibly 200,000 to 360,000 people. It existed upon the economic foundation of a focused irrigation-water-fed agricultural subsistence. It possessed huge constructed public and private buildings and homes. The city walls sported massive famed towers. A ziggurat (temple) presided dedicated to a special god historically associated with the city. In that society as well as others, ancient temples were woven into the warp and woof of the community. They served multiple functions. Temples were the economic center of a city and also dominated family life and the cultural religion.

Ur was founded as early as 6,000 BCE. Comparatively, it thrived for more than five thousand years before Moses led the Children of Israel out of Egypt. Cities then, as now, existed under rules of law. Ur's bicameral legislature was comprised of a house of Elders and a lower parliament of Men. Ur was located in the Fertile Crescent. This area is considered to be the birthplace of modern man.

Mesopotamia was suited for a specific agriculture only after the introduction of human-hewn modifications. It is generally recognized that rainfall agriculture requires at least 250 mm of rain per year. Mesopotamian rainfall did not rise to that level. Rainfall shortages and droughts would adversely impact larger settlement areas. In Sumer, a series of canals were dug into the ecosystem with human sweat and muscle. Irrigation-based agriculture thrived since it was the product of man's hand. The geography of the land encouraged this innovation. Those modifications were perhaps among Neolithic man's first great technological achievements. Channels allowed for the ingress of water into the area.

Small cities emerged after the canals were built. Soon after, more cities began to populate the landscape. Around the city, nomadic animal herders found easy markets for repetitive sales. Commercial trade routes also flourished in their infancy. At first, trade was conducted within the region. Later, business with other distant civilizations such as Egypt was initiated. Commerce and merchandising naturally promoted the influx of wealth.

Once the process of commerce began, disruptions to trade brought unintended consequences. For example, circa 2300 BCE, Sargon the Great conquered and consolidated his rule in Mesopotamia. Sargon's conquest of the Sumerian city-states introduced severe results. He gained fame as a military prize. However, history records the era as one of the first great ancient economic depressions. The consequences of his military prowess consumed him and his empire.

Sargon's downfall was related to his brutal nature. He was so cruel that the god Marduk was displeased with him. Some cuneiform writings suggest that the economic downturn in Sumer was an expression of the gods' disfavor. If the gods were pleased with man, then logically, appeasing the gods became man's higher purpose. Social norms were guided by aims and goals related to acquiring divine favor. Success, both economically and health wise, were linked as a representation of a person's standing with their god. The ancient book of Job candidly discussed that motif and theme under the Hebrew perspective. That perspective suggested Job's suffering was proof of his good standing with his Creator. At that time as well as today the book of Job remains a revolutionary statement contrasted with popular traditions theme.

Yet in that day, before Job, the growing distress would cause man to ask: what exactly was done that displeased the gods? A primary rule of commerce is as relevant today as it was in ancient times. Wealth is created when people expend energy. Economic models matriculated in ancient civilizations. Trade and commerce flowed from Sumer through Canaan into Egypt and back to Sumer. All civilizations are susceptible to disruption in economic cycles. Wars, floods, droughts, and governmental policies then, as now, played a role in economic cycles. Civilizations have consistently possessed economic versatility when left alone. Sargon considered political and military power as essential and failed to calculate how his conduct would disrupt the region. Therefore, the extent to which Marduk was either pleased or displeased with the actions of the community was often a conclusion based solely on present conditions.

Sumer grew into a collection of city-states in the Mesopotamian region. The growth of city-states became swelling points for population centers. Those population centers emerged as a product of early efforts at the task of creating water pathways for irrigation of the land. Man transitioned from a hunter-gatherer to an agricultural economy beginning circa 12,000 BCE. Overall, the transition began perhaps tens of thousands of years earlier. The topography and geology of the region facilitated that move. Water sources from the Tigris and Euphrates rivers ran on a parallel course toward the Persian Gulf. Ancient engineers devised a series of canals from those sources that benefited civilization. In time, a flourishing economy emerged. The bustling urban cultural population highlighted the need for cultural myths to connect with the past.

Canal Building

Canal building was an intensive, physically demanding activity. One can certainly appreciate the immense labor needed to connect cities and communities. That work required a year-round commitment. Districts survived when the canals were dug and maintained. Fields required attention! The pasturelands required fortifications. Meats had to be acquired. Administrations formed to divide responsibilities. Kings were perceived to derive their power from the gods. Temples were built to honor and sanctify a city's relationship with its god. The presence of the temple kept the power of the king in check.

Society compelled laborers. Men were needed to dig the ditches and to survey water pathways. Cooks were secured to feed the laborers. Engineers, masons, farmers, husbandmen, artisans, and specialty crafters created commercial traffic. Cities became recruiting hubs for labor. Building, repairing, and protecting the canals benefited the products derived from the land.

Life was tough. It began in the spring and involved a year-long struggle against a vicious geology that fought back. Man versus Mother Nature, the eternal battle continued generation after generation. Work was constant only to begin all over again. Year after year, decade after decade, century after century, millennia after millennia, the canals were the focus of life. After daily backbreaking work, short moments of relaxation occurred. Families enjoyed the pleasure of eating and telling stories. It seems improbable, but life was not much different from modernity. To be sure, modernity enjoys excellent dentistry and medical care, pensions, and retirement plans. But the daily issues that were addressed then have not changed much over the intervening 12,000 to 15,000 years. Then, as now, humankind possessed an internal urge to marry and begin to build a life. Establishing a presence requires work. People awoke in the morning, went to work, and then came home. Tomorrow was the same as yesterday. Routines developed over time.

Life introduced absurdity while man sought meaning. Man, the thinking creature, began to build a bridge over absurdity to promote a meaning. Storytelling and oral tradition were the primary tools in that effort. In some cases, oral tradition used both comedies and tragedies to move the story line. Allegorical stories and myths developed back at the cradle of civilization asked the most basic question: why is man here? Under what conditions is a person justified if another dies by his hand in self-defense? Will the gods punish righteous men along with the wicked?

After work, after dinner, in the comfort of his abode, with the wife of his dreams, with his children by his side, the stories born in oral tradition flowed. Those stories were spiced with tales of murder, intrigue, greed, hate, and love. They needed to capture your attention! The stories quenched the thirst of people pondering the purpose of humanity. The epic myths were legendary. They circulated for several thousand years and are even retold today. They most certainly had a ubiquitous following within the land of Palestine in the first millennium BCE.

Parables of destruction mirrored the condition of man. What never grew old was man's repeated generational quest for meaning. With each new age, the succeeding generation sought its identity on its own terms. The constant reformation of the canals and the land demanded an explanation. Whose idea was it that man should set forth each day as a virtual slave scouring the earth for his bread? Why are some people rich and others poor when we are all about the same basic objective? Why do some people seemingly rise above others when we support the same causes? Oral tradition thrived in addressing those inquiries. Legends arose couched in mythical stories of a time long, long ago. Those legends were formed within the crucible of promoting life, learning morals and messages.

Man sought answers based on forces that were believed to exist yet unseen. Fate was assigned as the favor or disfavor of the gods. In and of itself, life was a riddle and needed an explanation. Some suggested that life merely was! The young in time grew old. The old eventually died. The canals needed repair and contemporary state-of-the-art digs. As workers aged and could no longer manage the strain, fresh young men were brought in to take over. For thousands of years, tomorrow was the same as yesterday. There was no comfort in work. The reward for work was existence. You would do the same task tomorrow as was accomplished today. Man hopelessly set forth his mark to establish his presence. Like a spider sending forth its filament unable to attach, man observed that he was and then was no more.

Is this as good as it gets? That was a question to ponder! After dinner, that would make a great discussion cloaked in humor or intrigue to ensure its freshness. It would aid the mind to embrace the challenges ahead. The cultic practice of man coalesced around finding meaning within the existence of life. Oral tradition provided a format to communicate a message about relevant topics that were relatable and entertaining.

All of those questions and public discussions possessed the potential to produce a hard bitterness. Was not all of humanity in this endeavor together? Some people seemed lucky. Some seemed cursed. The enduring ancient myths began. Stories of the beginning of man attempted to account for the bitterness. These stories were contextualized to explain not the past, but rather the present. To illustrate the present day, it had to account for the past and create a myth. The *Enuma Elish* simply begins:

> When in the height heaven was not named,
> And the earth beneath did not yet bear a name,
> And the primeval Apsu, who begat them,
> And chaos, Tiamat, the mother of them both

Their waters were mingled together,
And no field was formed, no marsh was to be seen.[5]

In other words, before we began working this land, way back when, this is how it all started. That start would eventually go on to justify why tomorrow's work will be the same as today. Revealed was the extent of their existential orientation. Not much has changed over time. As they were, so are we.

Apsu and Tiamat lay inert and eventually mingled together. Of course, what else could have occurred? Salt water and fresh water lay side by side. Something was bound to happen. The mingling produced offspring. That offspring, over time, created top-tier gods, middle-tier gods, and demigods. As with human children, so much commotion occurred that Apsu (an original high-tier god) found it hard to secure his desired rest. Apsu devised an ingenious plan. He would kill all the offspring produced by his mingling to regain his ability to rest properly. He consorted with Tiamat to carry out this plan. Dad complaining was one thing, but Mom joining in the murder, well that was downright shocking and attention-grabbing.

Under Apsu's scheme, Enki (Ea), a middle-tier offspring, was to be killed. Ea characterized much more than the fresh water, which constituted his makeup. He represented a wise use of water, which corresponded to the use of irrigation techniques benefitting man. The story had a meaning. It was more than a murder mystery of intrigue. Modern irrigation was stronger than old established brute force (seas and oceans). One night, when all was calm, Ea conspired with all the offspring and moved forward to drown Apsu. It was either kill or be killed.

Mother Nature, in the dress of Tiamat, was soon reduced to widowhood with no effective control. Within her brutal heart, she sought to secure revenge. Tiamat married the ineffective and worthless Kingu and gave birth to eleven monsters to secure her revenge. Her goal was to kill all the other gods and demigods. The lines were set and established the war of ideas.

---

5. "Enuma Elish: The Epic of Creation, Tablet 1," in *The Seven Tablets of Creation*, trans. L. W. King, http://www.sacred-texts.com/ane/enuma.htm.

Alarm bells signaled the need for a defensive plan. The gods met in an emergency session to decide their course. They perceived that the only one who could save them was Marduk. Marduk was one of the first and original price negotiators. He had a steep price for his services. Dispensing his energy to protect the other gods would be hard work. He declared and negotiated his labor contract terms: he sought supreme authority!

Marduk prevailed in the war against Tiamat and Kingu and faced a new, unanticipated consequence of his effort: chaos. He set out to establish order on the earth and formed man to serve the gods.

CHAPTER 5

IS THE BOOK OF GENESIS A BOOK OF COSMOGONY?

Cosmogony is a word that refers and attempts the impossible, namely, explaining the origin of the universe. Some well-intentioned people claim to be able to do just that. Of course, having no original sources that documented the event, we are left to the musings of the myths. Do other Semitic allegorical myths use a creation-story backdrop to idealize and transmit messages? If so, we can accept as a premise that this format is consistent with the methods and manner of messaging during that age. We have already introduced *Enuma Elish*. We will also add the *Epic of Gilgamesh* into this topic. These were more than stories of drama and myth; they were used to explain and teach. The teachings from these stories were embedded and derived their authority from Sumerian and Mesopotamian oral tradition. The cultural reach of Mesopotamia influenced Canaan/Palestine as well. Famous legends flourished during the first millennium BCE. They espoused pervasive omnipresent story lines. This allegory of the *Enuma Elish* began by describing the commingling of two primeval waters, sweet (Apsu) and bitter (Tiamat), which were attributed as producing offspring (gods Anunnaki and Igigi). In the early versions, the Igigi were under the labor supervision of the The myth of the day was not only popular, it was society's accepted view.

Fast-forwarding in time to circa 1,000 BCE. The section of the Fertile Crescent known as Canaan (Palestine) experienced significant demographic changes. Occupation of Palestine then included such groups as Canaanites, Amorites, Hittites, Jebusites, and Hivites. The Habiru were among this melting pot of outcasts. Who were the Habiru? They were a ragtag collection of rebels living in remote highland enclaves. Little is known about this group except they appear as economically displaced factions. They presented security concerns to governmental authorities. The constant irritations between tax-collecting governmental agents and people living off the land created heightened security tensions. Locally, the sympathy of the escalated fights usually swayed in favor of those not associated with a governmental taxing authority.

All of those people lived in a vibrant social dynamic, not a vacuum. They struggled to gain an existence day to day off the land, married, transacted business, and died in Canaan. Their land bustled with the popular culture of the greater Semitic Near East. Its differentiated religions were similar variations with some unique cultural identifiers. For better or for worse, the highland Habiru stuck together when not fighting against each other for local dominance.

Against this backdrop, the Hebrew stories in the first eleven chapters of the book of Genesis emerged. It is fair to ask and even question what this book really is all about. Is the book of Genesis a story of creative formations? Did it intend to answer the "How" question of life? Why would someone in 450 BCE ask about a distant geological fact pattern? Is it possible the stories contained in the book of Genesis teach us something other than earth creation science?

I visited a congregation one particular day. During the morning service, we were treated from the pulpit with a sermon explaining why the earth is less than six thousand years old. The pastor traced back time from records in the Bible. He interpreted the Genesis story to be an actual written record of creation. Researching backward, to the creation of Adam on day six, time was set forth with the word translated as "day." Since the Hebrew word *yom* is translated faithfully as "day," the conclusion of this pastor was a biblically constructed timeline provided by God. With confidence, the genealogical record seemingly set forth an iron-clad position. The Bible was treated as a source document.

At lunch that day, the family conversation began. The sermon drew all of us together. My immediate family members, which held membership in the congregation, did not agree with the view as taught by the pastor. So I asked a tough question: what is the attraction of attending a church that espouses doctrine you consider to not be true? The reply was exactly what I expected. The family devoted themselves to similar social, political, and community values. In short, they did not attend this congregation to be overly influenced by all of the direct religious teachings. The elements of any friendship, social goals, and community involvement drew them together with like minded people.

What is the role of facts in the stories included in the book of Genesis? What part does the imagery contained in the Bible play in sending messages to its audience? What did the stories in Genesis mean to its intended audience? Should we look beyond the facts used in any of the episodes to cull out the story line? Or does the Bible teach direct religious teachings to which we must embrace? Do we, as created spiritual eunuchs, embrace facts because the facts will set us free?

The development of Hebrew culture and its cultic religious praxis existed as a subset of the more significant Mesopotamian tradition. The ancients who lived in Canaan would not have sought an explanation of how the world began. They were like you and me seeking common familial/community connections. They would not have attempted to record history or embrace a chronological order of time. They were interested in other more realistic and practical answers that promoted true principles to be embraced. The culture of the day declared that Marduk created man to serve the gods. That was a clear fact to be dealt with. The distinct Hebrew voice birthed in Genesis challenged that notion. YWHW created man to be fruitful and to multiply. It was then, and still today, remains a brave, bold declaration that allows us to focus on who we will be and how we will live in this world.

CHAPTER 6

EARLY SETTLEMENTS IN PALESTINE LATE BRONZE AGE/EARLY IRON AGE

We have learned from Mesopotamian cuneiform texts that the thoughts and concerns of people during those days were not much different from our own: taxes were high, work was unbearable, and the family offered its ability to domesticate civilizations and ease the burdens.

If we can draw an analogy from current times, we generally could agree that work is an essential element of our life. Yet when we get together as a family, we cherish those moments. As friends gather, we discuss our children's development, their success and struggles. We brag about how they are succeeding, or in some extreme cases, we have been known to stretch the truth to cover up uncomfortable facts. Fathers take pride in their sons and hope that matches for their daughters will be beneficial. Those circumstances concerning the inner yearnings of man have not much changed in its recorded history.

While the immediate political and economic circumstances have certainly changed over time, those standard components that make man human have not changed much at all. Stories in the Bible speak of jealousy, hatred, love, husbands not being faithful to their wives, mothers conspiring against their husbands, brothers rising against brothers, and men plotting evil. While nations have risen and fallen, the nature of man remains about the same.

Canaan served as an intersection between Mesopotamia and Egypt. It was a crossroads and backwater location. In a corollary of our recent

American nineteenth-century past, the infamous attempted to escape debt collection and law enforcement by crossing from a surrounding territory into the nation-state of Texas (before Texas was incorporated into the United States). They fled to escape the inevitable consequences of their obligations and left behind the moniker *GTT* carved for the debt collector to see. GTT stood for "Gone to Texas." As an independent state with no extradition, Texas provided an opportunity for people to start over. Canaan, as a remote location, offered a similar attraction to the Habiru. The wooded hills housed the unregulated uncontrollable country to which economic refugees could escape. Their presence created headaches and disrupted commerce.

The religion of Canaan circa 1,200 BCE corresponded to demographic structures in the late Bronze Age. Several major Mesopotamian cities were one hundred times the size of villages in Palestine. Israelite village settlements in Palestine rarely exceeded twenty-five acres.[6]

The size of our immediate community often influences the development of our core values and judgmental perceptions. Case in point, larger cities such as New York, Chicago, and Los Angeles often exhibit different values than smaller cities situated in states such as Iowa or Indiana. That is true today. It was also true thousands of years ago. Ideas, thoughts, values, and economic strength are more diverse in densely populated centers.

Some Mesopotamian settlements exceeded over one hundred thousand souls. Population density in early Iron Age of northern Canaan territory comprised two or three whistle-stops out of ten that would have exceeded one hundred souls.[7] Religious thought experienced by a young person growing up in that social framework would have been absolutely different than in Mesopotamia. The big-city Mesopotamian would have had more exposure to urban conditions and all those related trappings. Access to schools and social institutions thrived in major metropolitan areas during those days. Young boys and girls had access to more diverse relational partners. Work was specialized and

6. Karel van der Toorn, *Family Religion in Babylonia Syria and Israel* (Leiden, The Netherlands: Koninklijke Brill NV, 1996), 180.

7. Ibid.,189.

differentiated. Community social and economic life created wealth and opportunities.

Palestine/Israelite village settlements were self-subsistence communities. The norm for homes accommodated single families consisting of a father, a mother, and several children. The village clan existed under the umbrella of related families. A shared courtyard connected houses. The term representing the larger community clan in English correlates to the common word *family*. However, in Biblical Hebrew that word *family* was represented by several different words. Most commonly, *bet-ab* and *mishpacha* are used. *Bet-ab* is translated "house of the father" and is much different than a modern family since it would also include several generations, sons, daughters, their children, slaves, chattel, and, most importantly, all the financial resources to survive. The mishpacha included the broader group often led by the eldest uncle.

Israelite settlements differed significantly from their big-city counterparts. The custom of marriage within the colony was important since any other arrangement or allowance would have opened the potential for financial resources or property to slip out of the control of the bet-ab. The *mishpacha* is also roughly translated as "family" but then served another function altogether. Mishpacha should be understood as a familial function within a collection of related families, or perhaps, better understood as a clan. Among its many roles, it also served to protect community assets. Its women were an asset; and marriage within the community, the enclosure, the group, allowed the mishpacha to secure the corporate economic success of the clan. To think of marriage outside the mishpacha was a complicated concept. Its occurrence was not routine.

The word *mishpacha* occurs over three hundred times in the Hebrew text. Twelve occasions in Genesis the word is used.

- Genesis 8:19, "Every beast, every creeping thing, and every bird, everything that moves on the earth, went out by their *families* (mishpacha) from the ark."
- Genesis 10:5, "From these the coastlands of the nations were separated into their lands, every one according to his language, according to their *families* (mishpacha), into their nations."

- Genesis 10:18, "And the Arvadite and the Zemarite and the Hamathite; and afterward the *families* (mishpacha) of the Canaanite were spread abroad."
- Genesis 10:20, "These are the sons of Ham, according to their *families* (mishpacha), according to their languages, by their lands, by their nations."
- Genesis 10:31–32, "These are the sons of Shem, according to their *families* (mishpacha), according to their languages, by their lands, according to their nations. These are the *families* (mishpacha) of the sons of Noah, according to their genealogies, by their nations; and out of these the nations were separated on the earth after the flood."
- Genesis 12:3, "And I will bless those who bless you, And the one who curses you I will curse. And in you all the *families* (mishpacha) of the earth will be blessed."
- Genesis 24:38, "But you shall go to my father's house and to my *relatives* (mishpacha), and take a wife for my son."
- Genesis 24:40–41, "He said to me, 'The Lord, before whom I have walked, will send His angel with you to make your journey successful, and you will take a wife for my son from my *relatives* (mishpacha) and from my father's house; then you will be free from my oath, when you come to my *relatives* (mishpacha); and if they do not give her to you, you will be free from my oath.'"
- Genesis 28:14, "Your descendants will also be like the dust of the earth, and you will spread out to the west and to the east and to the north and to the south; and in you and in your descendants shall all the *families* (mishpacha) of the earth be blessed."
- Genesis 36:40, "Now these are the names of the chiefs descended from Esau, according to their *families* (mishpacha) and their localities, by their names: chief Timna, chief Alvah, chief Jetheth."

The word *mishpacha* is never used in Genesis to refer to a single family unit consisting of a father, mother, sister, and brother.

In Genesis 24:40, both the word *mishpacha* and the term *bet-ab* are used. Abraham's servant is instructed to go to the mishpacha and then further to clarify within that clan, proceed to the bet-ab, or more practically, to his father's house. Presumably from that point, he will have access to a marriage partner suitable for his son, Isaac.

The perspective of the mind of a young person growing up in that neighborhood is instructive. One simply did not betray the strength of the mishpacha by leaving the unit; in fact, one lived their life inside of it. Through the mishpacha, family strength was achieved. In the early Iron Age (circa 1,200–1,000 BCE), there was no concentrated domestic government. The family identity outweighed nationalistic connections. The mishpacha existed within isolated and rural confines. Clustered Israelite settlements had shared common walls. The eldest uncle was at the top of the social hierarchy. The unit created moments of festivity and community celebrations. These events likely included discussions about morals, values, and identity. Life was wrapped in a blanket around their family deity.

In 1 Samuel 20, we are invited into a picture of an early Iron Age mishpacha community. The occasion of a new moon signaled a time when the mishpacha gathered together as a single community to eat a meal. It is probable at these selected events that a joyous atmosphere included an abundance of enticements, rewards, and meat. We can notice this is the case because Saul was preparing to celebrate one such new moon cycle. In verse 5 of the chapter, Saul's mishpacha was getting ready for their monthly gathering occasioned by the new moon. It was a common event. The meal gathering was observed by Saul's family north of Judah and also by David's family south of Jerusalem. In David's instance, his mishpacha attached further meaning to this regular festival meal. They engaged in specific clan-community religiously significant activities.

> And David said to Jonathan, "Indeed tomorrow is the New Moon, and I should not fail to sit with the king to eat. (1 Sam. 20:5)

> David earnestly asked permission of me to go to Bethlehem. And he said, "Please let me go, for our family (mishpacha) has a sacrifice in the city, and my

> brother has commanded me to be there. And now, if I have found favor in your eyes, please let me get away and see my brothers. Therefore he has not come to the king's table." (1 Sam. 20:28–29)

The text informs us that David had a subservient obligation to his eldest brother.[8] There was a sacrificial event of importance to the family. This writing provides an example of how the bet-ab worked within the mishpacha clan structure.[9]

---

8. Karel van der Toorn, *Family Religion in Babylonia Syria and Israel* (Leiden, The Netherlands: Koninklijke Brill NV, 1996), 198.
9. The reader is encouraged to review *Family Religion in Babylonia, Syria and Israel* by Karel van der Toon for a fuller treatment of family social structures. The research finds the Akkadian word *habiru* eerily similar to the pronounced word *Hebrew*. The word conveys the definition of social and economic outcasts. The implication derived by Professor van der Toon suggests family structures in this segment of the world arose under severe economic conditions. Yet even in that severity, order existed.

CHAPTER 7

THE COMPOSITION OF ANCIENT SEMITIC RELIGIOUS PRACTICE

It is impossible to separate religious practices from the cultural past. Various civil and religious customs populate our postmodern society. Those practices and traditions vary slightly from household to household but, by and large, remain relatively fixed. For example, parades and football fill the American Thanksgiving tradition. Without even mentioning "turkey dinner" in the previous sentence, by merely saying "Thanksgiving," the implied tradition draws our thoughts there. Beyond the turkey, dressing and gravy is served, and, of course, cranberry sauce. We would find cranberries an unusual plated item at any family gathering outside of the Thanksgiving table. We can thank tradition for that!

Traditions come and go over time. They are derived from our hopes and aspirations as a people. We cannot divorce tradition from our local customs. To what extent do religious customs of the past differ from the present? Should religious customs and traditions differ from age to age? Or, since God is unchanging, must those traditions be fixed and permanent? The religion of the land of Palestine was a religion arising within the mishpacha family. Closely related clan defining traditions permeated the family structure. When the modern mind considers family, it is drawn to a nuclear family composition consisting of a father, mother, and dependent children. Early Israelite mishpacha units existed as independent financial units. They were the vehicle through which morals were handed down. The ancient Near East mishpacha was not a nuclear family. Like families today, it comprised an order designed to ensure emotional and financial stability.

Paying careful attention to the biblical record, we will find a significant relationship among all ancient Semitic practices, beliefs, and cultures. We have Abraham to thank for that. Akkadian and Sumerian cultures were devoted to family. Sumerian, Akkadian, and, later, the Hebrew cultures counted their family back three generations. The first book of the Torah, Genesis, established that practice to connect a dynamic relationship with the past.

The Bible confirms the focus of looking back three generations by the ancients. To the grandson of Abraham, Jacob, the declaration was given, "I am the Lord, the God of your father Abraham, and the God of Isaac" (Gen. 28:13a). Why three generations? It would be difficult for any age to look any further back beyond a father and a grandfather. These Semitic family traditions prevailed in Palestine. They originated in the greater Mesopotamian region. In Mesopotamia, the family household exerted claims for property rights. To further solidify the property rights, it was common for ancestral burials to occur under the dwelling of the existing family home or in close proximity. The deceased became "as gods" tied within the family social hierarchy. Drink and food oblations in recognition of the dead were offered. Familial religious customs were a significant element of Semitic identification.

The Babylonian version of the *Epic of Gilgamesh* introduces us to the hero Gilgamesh in the context of a family religious custom: digging wells:

> Surpassing all kings, powerful and tall beyond all others, violent, splendid, a wild bull of a man, unvanquished leader, hero in the front lines, beloved by his soldiers-fortress they called him, protector of the people, raging flood that destroys all defenses-two thirds divine and one third human, son of King Lugalbanda, who became a god, and of the goddess Ninsun, he opened the mountain passes, *dug wells on the slopes*, crossed the

> vast ocean, sailed to the rising sun, journeyed to the edge of the world, in search of eternal life...[10]

Gilgamesh sought eternal life. Enkidu, a mere mortal, walked with him as a brother. Protecting the family through oblations for the dead made sense to that culture.

> May Shamash grant you your heart's desire, may the path to the Cedar Forest be straight, may the nights be safe, with no danger lurking, may your father Lugalbanda protect you, may you conquer Humbaba, may the battle be quick, may you joyfully wash your feet in his river. *Dig a well when you stop for the night*, fill your waterskins with fresh water, each day make an offering to Shamash, and remember Lugalbanda your father, who journeyed to far off mountains himself.[11]

The preceding text described a common ritual. The whole point of the ritual was keenly focused on the living remaining connected with their family that had departed from this life. Lugalbanda was the father of Gilgamesh. Shamas was the god of the dead. The sprinkling of water served as a necessary oblation for the divine Lugalbanda, though dead. He benefited from the water poured to him. The obligations of the eldest son served as a cohesive glue. The family responsibilities recognized that the departed still retained acknowledgment and honor within the bet-ab.[12]

We can reasonably revisit a problematic account of Isaac in this culturally ingrained Semitic religious practice.

> Then Abimelek said to Isaac, "Move away from us; you have become too powerful for us." So Isaac moved away

---

10. Stephen Mitchell, *Gilgamesh: A New English Version* (New York: Free Press, 2004), 71.
11. Ibid., 105.
12. Karel van der Toorn, *Family Religion in Babylonia Syria and Israel* (Leiden, The Netherlands: Koninklijke Brill NV, 1996), 55.

> from there and encamped in the Valley of Gerar, where he settled. Isaac *reopened the wells that had been dug* in the time of his father Abraham, which the Philistines had stopped up after Abraham died, and he gave them the same names his father had given them. Isaac's servants dug in the valley and *discovered a well of fresh water* there. But the herders of Gerar quarreled with those of Isaac and said, "The water is ours!" So he *named the well* Esek because they disputed with him. Then they dug another well, but they quarreled over that one also; so he named it Sitnah. He moved on from there and *dug another well*, and no one quarreled over it. He named it Rehoboth, saying, "Now the Lord has given us room, and we will flourish in the land." (Gen. 26:16–22)

This is a very weird story. To the modern eye, the text appears to represent a land dispute. That basic conclusion though is deficient in context. To the ear of that day, the story would have represented so much more. The story line follows a simple chiastic outline, a literary technique in *telling* a story. Chiastic order follows a narrative structure that outlines the motif. The structure of the order is *A, B, B, A*. The A elements within the story are connected. Often the B elements provide supporting story line structure.

So let's break down what is really occurring in the story contained in Genesis chapter 26:

A1 (Genesis 26:1–6)

God issues to Isaac a command to stay in the land, and he will bless him. This was a promise initiated by God, an oath. This is where the story seems to take a turn. God wanted Isaac to be just like Abraham, his father.

B1 (Genesis 26:7–11)

Isaac appears to be just like his daddy. When he encounters a difficult setting in the story, he pleads to his wife Rebekah to tell anyone who asks about him that she was sister. This story line mirrors an encounter Abraham had with the Philistine king of the same name, Abimelech, in Genesis 20. In that episode Abraham passed off his wife as his sister.

B2 (Genesis 26:12–22)

Isaac moves away despite the command of God to stay in the land. Isaac was increasing with wealth as a bestowed benefit from God. Yet no matter where he tried to dig a well to honor his father, he was confronted by Philistines who wanted to hinder him.

A2 (Genesis 26:23–33)

The conclusion sets a perfect alignment with the storyline initiated in *A1*. God has blessed Isaac. Isaac's conduct was exactly like his fathers. An oath was eventually sworn between Isaac and Abimelech.

To the audience *who heard* the story, the conclusion would be much different than if it had been translated and read. The name of the town Beersheba consists of two words: (1) the word for *well* and (2) the word for *oath*.

For the young children in the audience, there is a wide range of questions they might ask. One set of questions might be like this: wait a minute, was the oath with God Himself? Or was it with another man? Why would those be the most logical questions? The name of the city was Beersheba. Of course, Isaac and Abimelech swore an oath to each other, but do not lose sight of why they swore that oath. The oath was initiated along ancestral patronage. That patronage was couched and promised under an oath initiated by God in A1 of the chiastic structure. This episode most certainly is packed with nuanced historical context long since lost to the modern ear. The name was actually part of the defined episode.

In this story, Isaac, like his father, lied to King Abimelech about the nature of his wife. But that distorted fact has no bearing or relevance in the story being told to its audience. That fact, dominant only in section B, was merely a supporting role. The illustrated motif was contained in sections *A1* and *A2*. The original audience would have *heard* and *focused* on the facts of well digging but in a different context of our age. The facts in written translations several thousand years later are excellent translations, but the original meaning of the story was lost in translation.

Repositioning our focus reminds us of the role of the Bible. Again, it is fair to ask, what does the Torah teach? And: who is teaching? The account of Isaac and Abimelech, despite its inaccurate and factually flawed history, teaches a powerful lesson. The lesson literally escapes the reader in the written translation. The moral teaching begins in the second verse of the chapter. The Lord appeared to Isaac and issued a command: "Do not go down to Egypt; dwell in the land which I will tell you!" (Gen. 26:2). That command was familiar to his father. So Isaac dwelt in Gerar, a Philistine stronghold. Eventually, Abimelech learned that Rebekah was, in fact, Isaac's wife and he ordered all men to keep their hands off her. The story was not about ensuring Rebekah's safety. Remember the command issued by God? "Stay in Canaan, and I (God) will multiply thy seed and give to you all these lands" (Gen. 26:3). That story grabbed the attention of its original audience in the oral tradition.

This episode can be compared and contrasted to the lessons in oral tradition from Abraham's misadventure in chapter 20. He passed off his wife as his sister. But the story in the oral tradition would have sparked family discussions around the central theme motif: will God slay a righteous nation if their hands are innocent of wrongdoing?

During the famine in Genesis 26, Isaac planted crops and his crops grew a hundredfold. His increase reached a point that the Philistines envied him and directed him to leave. So Isaac moved in direct contradiction to the command issued by God. The story comes to life in its oral tradition. Its emphasis made sense when one considers that it is God alone who can cause prosperity. That prosperity was occurring during the time of famine. Imagine hearing that story retold in 400 BCE? Your jaw would drop! Morals and meaning were taught as valuable lessons.

Our story line makes perfect sense in the context of the cultural practices. That this was a practice within the mishpacha is without question. That oblation tied the present with the past. Isaac practices that same pattern. He must go to the well of the oath since it was the connection with his father and the God of his father. The Philistines attempted to prevent such a link. If they could successfully prevent the relationship with the past, then the connection with the God of his father would have been broken. Isaac's men "contend," which is the meaning of the Hebrew word *esek*, and Isaac's men "strove," which is the meaning of the Hebrew word *sitnah*. The ultimate ending occurs when "the Lord hath made room for us" (Gen 26:22b). This conclusion draws on the resources of the beginning of the episode. The command was to stay in the land.

Why was it essential to include this strange account in our story? Connecting family patterns of oblation served as a cohesive bond for ancient Near Eastern Semitic cultures. The conclusion resulted in a feast. Most certainly, the source of water joined Isaac with his past. The way one connected with their present age was to be firmly rooted in the past.

CHAPTER 8

OUR METHODOLOGY STRIPPED OF ILLUSIONS

The methodology employed in this exercise takes data and facts and attempts to tell a story. In the first eleven chapters of Genesis, it is traditionally taught that the story communicates an account of creation. So we ask: is an episode about a murder on TV actually about a murder? Or something else altogether? Does that "something else" contain the most important elements of the episode?

We must come to understand and identify the nature of oral tradition. This is an easy point to ignore when discussing religion since orthodoxy and dogma seek their own preservation. But, the power of oral stories are the innovations provided by the person relating the story. Orthodoxy and dogma are entrenched and cannot easily be changed. Recognition and acclaim is offered to the most innovative storyteller. On the American Broadway play circuit, actors "steal" the scene through their dramatic innovations. Orthodoxy discourages innovations. Oral tradition encourages discussions that may result in different answers from time to time. This condition creates tension in an environment that rejects change. We like to think that God is unchanging, and his dictates to us must also be immutable. In that tension, we lose the vibrant living connection between the past and our present.

As an illustrative example, the seventeenth chapter of Genesis records Abraham's conversation with God. Several facts stand out. The name Isaac is a derivation of the verb "to laugh" or "jest playfully." The name Ishmael is a derivation of the verb "to hear." Specifically, the God named El has heard. With the proper twist of the tongue, the right cinching of the eyebrows, and the sophisticated emphasis of articulation, one easily imagines a hilarious story line. In verse 20, the biblical Hebrew could become downright laughable. "As for Ishmael, I have heard you." Lost in an English translation, the joke is neutered. The Biblical Hebrew only uses two words to nail the punch line. Both words are the same root derivation. Only the wittiest storyteller would know exactly how to spin that yarn. In that audience, with that special play right actor, the story comes alive. The children laugh. Preserving tradition comforts the parents and allows for familial bonding. Children then retransmit the story line to later generations. Perhaps a fact got lost. Perhaps even over time the facts were changed. Maybe even once in a while the unskilled tongue used seven words to respond. One key element always stood out. The disparate recognition of the names Ishmael and Isaac grated upon the ear. The story line was laughable.

Sometimes we want to listen to a comedy. Other times we want to listen to drama. There are moments when we are thrilled with that which is bawdy. And of course, sometimes a good old fashioned murder mystery will strike the right chord. Have you ever asked yourself which murder mysteries gain our attention? Which comedies rise to the top of general acclaim? Which sexually tensioned stories will we allow to play out? Which stories will we turn off?

The story of creation and other episodes in the Bible are powerful in their ability to engage universal messaging. They are stories that emerged out of a remarkable popular culture. They thrived because they asked the most important question: what is the meaning of life? The Hebrew solution to that question began to emerge after 1,000 BCE. However, that question had been asked and answered by societies for at least 10,000 to 12,000 years before the emergence of a Hebrew tradition.

The Hebrew tradition came to a fuller fruition after the Judean exile circa 450–400 BCE. That tradition questioned its political origin. That tradition questioned the viability of its faith in God. It had to account for a questionable past. It had to account for questionable forefathers. Abram, the Sumerian, met the qualifications of a strong candidate to serve as the founder of a nation. The Sumerians from the east were recognized as the first known culture. The Sumerian culture shared a linguistic origin with the Judeans. At the same time, episodes in Genesis allowed the people of the land to engage in realistic conversations. What is the origin of evil? Is earthly prosperity a demonstration of divine blessing? **Are poverty and poor health a reflection of God's displeasure? Who is man that God be mindful of him?**

Numerous cultures and civilizations arose and died before any Hebrew society formulated an answer to those timeless questions. The ancient allegorical myths promoted a common message: that man was created to serve the gods. Man's comfort or discomfort was of no significance. Man would die. The best he could hope for was to be remembered as a dead but great person of the past.

CHAPTER 9

THE BIBLE CONTAINS MULTIPLE DOUBLETS OF PREVIOUSLY RECORDED STORIES

There are over thirty doublets recorded in the ancient Hebrew text of the Bible. Doublets are duplicate stories constructed in chiastic thought bearing similar fact patterns. As we saw in the previous example of a classic doublet, Abraham and Isaac, in separate but eerily similar stories, tried to pass their wives off as their sister. But telling a lie about their marital status was not the point of the story. The facts opened the door for broader and different moral discussions.

Yet we only find doublets in Hebrew literature and nowhere else in any Semitic culture. Why? If doublets exist, would they not have precedence in other Semitic Sumerian or Akkadian writings? The answer might lie in the unique social political structures evident in Canaan during the first millennium BCE.

Ascribing single authorship to the Torah renders doublets as historical nonsense. However, doublets make historical sense if oral tradition dominated the transmission of religious tradition. It also explains why they appear as questionable inserts in the written format. Multiple editors took a similar story from different recitations and pulled those stories into a collection.

Israel and Judah were two separate countries with two independent monarchies that at various times promoted a state-based religion. Those different religions encouraged and enforced worship of gods other than El or the Lord God (YHWH). Professor Israel Finkelstein has completed some interesting initial research in his book *The Forgotten Kingdom: The Archeology and History of Northern Israel.*[13] The book is available from the Society of Biblical Literature, based in Atlanta, Georgia. It provides a more accurate picture by laying out-migration patterns and overlaying those patterns with local demographics. Finkelstein reveals a more fuller revelation of the two separate states. Information obtained from archeology since the 1990s should cause us to revisit not only the formation of confederate governments in both Israel and Judah but also their established religious structures.

Israel was a separate country from Judah. Even the Bible reveals high strains of political antagonism between Israel and Judah. They never trusted each other even when unified under the heroic figure of King David.[14]

In an oral tradition, even close family members would tell the story wrong, and someone would have to correct the record. Oral tradition in Canaan encouraged doublets. Oral traditions that emerged in antagonism occurred in Judah as a reaction to the horrendous version of a similar story existing in the north in Israel. Or perhaps the existing story served so well to encourage discussions that the meat of one story was borrowed for a different purpose.

Stories were told and eventually elaborated upon in an informal setting. I recall years ago how my younger sister and I related a story experienced in our family. Our father was a military officer who was a precision army marksman. He had a workroom in the basement with equipment sufficient to work on his guns and ammunition. He often took our family to Fort Knox, Kentucky, while he competed in shooting competitions with military men from around the country. The trip to Fort Knox each year was memorable. We stayed at the same motel in Elizabethtown, Kentucky, each year. This annual vacation was a grand

---

13. Israel Finkelstein, *The Forgotten Kingdom: The Archeology and History of Northern Israel* (Atlanta: The Society of Biblical Literature, 2013).
14. Scholarship must begin with the premise that King David had two armies, one to fight his wars, and another consisting of mighty men whose principle job was service to protect his own life. The 'הַגִּבֹּרִים' (ha-gabborim) would only be necessary in a political climate dominated by antagonism. Certainly Hebrew politics were only unified mythically under King David. See 2 Samuel 23.

time for our family because the motel had a pool. Having access to a hotel pool for one week, eating the sumptuous fare of the dining room, did not get any better than that for us in the early 1960s. Our father was an army marksman of significance. He often cleaned his guns on Sunday evening as the family sat down to watch such Sunday evening favorite shows like the Mutual of Omaha sponsored *Wild Kingdom*. My younger sister possessed a proud picture in her mind of her towering father who could shoot guns with few rivals.

In the 1960s the south end of Columbus, Ohio, was a close-knit Catholic community. St. Leo's parish was at the epicenter of traveling distance for young kids freely making their way to Schiller Park. At the corner of Mithoff and Jaeger Streets, a gas station stood that one summer sponsored a sale of baby chicks for five cents each (pay close attention because I do not remember the exact fact of the price). Anyone could walk home with a chick in their hand. The price was so low that a brother and a sister of fewer than seven years of age could afford to buy a few of them. In this instance, the fact of the price is immaterial to both the story line and the outcome. The chicks were an attractive nuisance to a six-year-old boy and a five-year-old girl. After completing the sale, my sister, Barbara, and I walked less than a block to our home at Gates and Jaeger Street. Mom and dad would surely love the chick just as we did. It was freshly hatched, cute, and adorable.

Eventually, the fate of the chick has been clouded by age, perception, and time. I was pretty sure that my dad walked two hundred steps with the hatchling in hand, through the alley connecting Mithoff and Jaeger streets to return the chick. There was no doubt my dad demanded the nickel back, possibly citing an Ohio law impairing minors from entering into a contract, and keeping the nickel as compensation for his intervention services. My sister had a different version of events. Convinced that our father took the chick into the backyard and shot it, our story line was never reunited. Our story consisted of an *A1, B1, B2,* and *A2*.

A1: Our Father was a man of strict precision and rules.

B1: Vincent and Barbara were intrigued by a normal nuisance to children.

B2: Vincent and Barbara bought a baby chick to share with the family.

A2: Our father was a strict disciplinarian looking out for the benefit of his children.

Dominating my sister's thoughts and recollection was her perception of who her father was. Her mind processed several facts. Our father liked to shoot. He was an active military disciplinarian. His displeasure of the chick was apparent. Those were all indisputable facts. However, he did not shoot the tiny hatchling.

Over forty to fifty years there existed within the family different oral traditions of days gone by. Now and then, as adults, we would talk and argue about the fate of the chick. Our children and cousins listened to both sides of the story. My children sided with my version with confidence in their father's memory. Aunt Barbara perhaps was not as reliable for their taste, but her daughter and grandchildren sided with her version. The important story line conclusion was this: it was much different back in the days when dads across America laid down the law. Even in that tradition, the story was not about the chick. Facts in this story step in to produce two different versions with the same conclusion.

Hebrew oral tradition follows that same microcosm trajectory. For example, if Genesis chapter six is read side by side with the seventh chapter, one easily notices a significant problem. Noah and the number of animals that joined him on the ark reveal differing accounts. As in all the episodes of Genesis, the facts serve to advance the story line. In that sense, both chapters tell a story to prove a point! God planned for man's redemption amid the evil of his own making. The Bible does not teach us math facts concerning occupancy rates on an old boat. It teaches us how to think about our relationship with God.

All ancient Semitic texts first began in oral tradition. The Torah compiles all the best of stories available in the fifth century BCE as a compendium manuscript. Perhaps that is a rather simplistic explanation. Based on the circumstances and the context, that conclusion, however, is much more plausible than suggesting somehow that the sixth and seventh chapter of Genesis represent a harmonic picture and an event that the author could not have witnessed.

Noah found a special place in God's heart because he offered comfort (ironically, *comfort* is a wordplay off his name when translated) against the coming devastation.

> But I will establish My covenant with you; and you shall go into the ark—you, your sons, your wife, and your sons' wives with you. And of every living thing of all flesh you shall bring two of every sort into the ark, to keep them alive with you; they shall be male and female. Of the birds after their kind, of animals after their kind, and of every creeping thing of the earth after its kind, two of every kind will come to you to keep them alive. And you shall take for yourself of all food that is eaten, and you shall gather it to yourself; and it shall be food for you and for them. (Gen. 6:18–21)

Chapter 6 records the same message we all learned in Sunday school. Noah was commanded to preserve two of every species. The next chapter records a similar yet different account.

> Then the Lord said to Noah, "Come into the ark, you and all your household, because I have seen that you are righteous before Me in this generation. You shall take with you seven each of every clean animal, a male and his female; two each of animals that are unclean, a male and his female; also seven each of birds of the air, male and female, to keep the species alive on the face of all the earth. For after seven more days I will cause it to rain on the earth forty days and forty nights, and I will destroy from the face of the earth all living things that I have made." And Noah did according to all that the Lord commanded him. Noah was six hundred years old when the floodwaters were on the earth. (Gen. 7:1–6)

In this separate account, the proverbial fish suddenly got bigger. There is a priestly distinction between clean animals and unclean animals. That priestly distinction would not have been plausible until at least circa 450 BCE or later. If an animal was clean, Noah was to take seven pairs, the male and his female. That equals fourteen clean animals. Two each of unclean animals were granted stowage, a total of four unclean. The intent of the story was not to record beasts; instead, the animals merely advance the discussions after the story had been told.

CHAPTER 10

THE CASE FOR J, E, P, D MULTIPLE AUTHORSHIP

Is the Torah a uniform work of a single author? Likely not. There are many circulating theories that focus on the seeming disconnections occurring in the Bible. Revisiting Exodus chapter 20, my favorite disconnect is recorded. When I read that pericope (Exod. 20:24–25), I often think of my kids on a certain January day. They wanted to play outside after a cold spell. My wife called out to them not to go outside in the snow without their boots. She set forth that commandment, then after a short pause, she proclaimed from a distant room in the house: "but if you do go outside without your boots, at least take your gloves." I laughed at the irony of the original commandment. Modifying the original command was tempered by the lack of deep snow. The adjustment of the motherly dictum set forth a conditional plea allowing for the modification of the old directive.

Palestine was a multicultural society with various traditions depending on where someone lived. It had rugged mountainous regions, desert like conditions, fertile plains, and coastal areas. Living conditions, customs, family experiences, and stories varied between areas.

> An altar of earth you shall make for Me, and you shall sacrifice on it your burnt offerings and your peace offerings, your sheep and your oxen. In every place where I record My name I will come to you, and I will bless you. And if you make Me an altar of stone, you

> shall not build it of hewn stone; for if you use your tool on it, you have profaned it. (Exod. 20:24–25).

We learn about the Ten Commandments. That is an easy, safe number. But the Bible records 613 commandments. In the version of commandments that we often teach our children we limit the dictums to ten easy to remember symbols located in Exodus 20:1–17.

The commandments that must be obeyed concludes with the seventeenth verse, which admonishes the faithful not to covet their neighbor's belongings.

Therefore, the appended casuistic commands which follows the apodictic commands demonstrates that a scribal editor is constructing a new argument piecemeal by adding something within the preserved text.

> An altar of earth you shall make for Me, and you shall sacrifice on it your burnt offerings and your peace offerings, your sheep and your oxen. In every place where I record My name I will come to you, and I will bless you. (Exod. 20:24)

The command directs individuals to make an altar of earth "in every place where I [God] record[ed] my [His] name…and upon it shall burnt offerings be conducted." In verse 25, however, a concession is granted that allows for the construction of a rock altar as long as no tools have touched and profaned the stone.

> And if you make Me an altar of stone, you shall not build it of hewn stone; for if you use your tool on it, you have profaned it. (Exod. 20:25)

Eventually in time, the Judeans found it both appropriate and necessary to construct a temple right in the city of Jerusalem. Solomon dedicated the first constructed temple in Jerusalem circa 900 BCE using hewn stone. Curiously, there was a complete disregard for the command limiting sacrifices to earthen altars, and failing that, only stones, not profaned by tools. But consider the entirety of the text, the initial apodictic commandment was so relaxed we now find that worship anywhere but Jerusalem is unacceptable.

> Since the day that I brought My people out of the land of Egypt, I have chosen no city from any tribe of Israel in which to build a house, that My name might be there, nor did I choose any man to be a ruler over My people Israel. Yet I have chosen Jerusalem, that My name may be there, and I have chosen David to be over My people Israel. (2 Chron. 6:5–6)

Can a case be made that the Hebrew religion was not universally held by all the people of the land? Absolutely yes. The text as written demonstrates this to be the case. Various editors compiled the Bible across an extensive period. Each inserted what they considered to be the word of God. The documentary hypothesis, at its most straightforward explanation, sets forth this theory. Editors spliced together multiple stories and traditions. It rationally explains why we have contradictory commandments side by side within the same written text, such as Exodus 20:24–25. The editors were mindful that the stories and legends in Israel were different from the stories in Judah. They were also different from the tales within oral tradition of the trans-Jordan region.

At its most complex, twentieth-century scholars such as Martin Noth have dissected the written text of the Bible searching for subtle language differences. That process considers such elements as dated language usage. Noted within the esoteric Semitic linguistic and social religious differences are their similarities. Noth built upon a theory advanced by the nineteenth-century German scholar Julius Wellhausen. Wellhausen was not the first to bring this idea into the marketplace of discussions, yet he certainly received the most notoriety for this proposition.

Illustrating this point, we need look no further than the first two chapters of the book of Genesis. The name of the Creator identified in the first chapter of Genesis is described using the Hebrew term *Elohim*. Elohim is not an actual proper name. *Elohim* is a term that is a plural form of the name El. The addition of the ending *El[o]him* (pronounced "heem") indicates it is a plural form of the word.

There is another name in the second chapter of Genesis. However, it is a name so sacred that the Hebrew tongue is not permitted to pronounce it. The English translation produces a form of that word with the name Yahweh, represented by the triad use of the distinct letters *YHW* (sic *YHWH*). In Hebrew, the holy tradition provides an injunction against pronouncing this name. That favor, or perhaps privilege, was reserved solely for the high priest in Jerusalem on the Day of Atonement within the chamber of the Holy of Holies.

Hebrew use of the tetragrammaton *YHWH* instead encourages the use of a title such as *haShem* (the Name) or *Adonai* (Lord). A discouraged version is least accepted by merely spelling out in Hebrew the name with each vowel Yod Hey Vav Hey. An orthodox convention was also adopted in theological writing to spell the name of YHWH in Hebrew with two simple *yods* (י י). The term *tetragrammaton* has been adopted to highlight the uniqueness of this name for the God of Israel. *Tetra* is a Latin word for "three." The Hebrew name for haShem only uses three letters.

In Genesis chapter 1, there are no references to the name YHWH (יְהוָה). That identification as a noun is found in chapter 2. Scholars such as Wellhausen and Noth see this as more than a distinction without a difference. To their point of view, this is a language construction, or a religious construction, that indicates the preservation of more than one separate tradition. There is some validity to that argument since the vowels comprising the tetragrammaton would not have been available before the mid eighth century BCE. A working theory then would suggest multiple authors and editors referred collectively as J, E, P, D:

> J—Jehova (the author who employs the use of the tetragrammaton)
> E—Elohim (the author who calls the God of Israel using merely the term *God*.
> P—Priestly (the author who is most concerned with promulgating the cultus of Jewish praxis)
> D—Deuteronomist (the author behind the cache of Torah scrolls that later became the book of Deuteronomy).

CHAPTER 11

TIMELINES MATTER

Beliefs often overcome facts when discussing such unknowable matters as the age of the earth, the dawn of man, the course of human history. Can the Bible be used as a scientific guide to aid our discussion of creation? Intersecting that discussion is an unintended consequence. There is a fear among some that if the Bible is not literally true, then perhaps it is not true at all. When beliefs are held for many generations, they are allowed to masquerade as facts. My dear sister never let go of the belief she held concerning the demise of the chick.

Creation theory in some cases attempts to prove the age of the earth, dating the earth at roughly 5,700 years old. It is not a complicated conclusion. A process is used that accepts biblical data along with extra-biblical texts. Adam, the first man, was created on day six by God. The biblical record incorporates into its text extra-biblical documents, which then become part of the official biblical history, to quasi-scientifically prove its point. Setting forth one such example of an extra-biblical text is found in the writing of the fifth chapter of Genesis.

> זֶה סֵפֶר, תּוֹלְדֹת אָדָם
> "This is the book," of the generations of Adam. (Gen. 5:1)

"This is the book" refers to a reference document being used by the author. It is a convenient historical record. The scribal editor looks back to another document to complete the picture he is painting for posterity. It is complete with names. The book records for us the age of people's fathers when they were born. The book tells us how old they were when they died. Recorded as such, the modern Western mind accepts it as true. Logic dictates the course of discussion: if you don't believe that book, then how could you trust anything the Bible says?

This important timeline fact is often introduced in any discussion about the age of the earth. It is merely a fact introduced in the story line. As a fact, it disrupts what we already do know and creates a steep chasm to cross. If we accept an age dating the earth at 5,700 years old, we admit the creation of man at a time that we know is inconsistent with available information. This presents a religious conundrum. By dating creation circa 3600–3700 BCE, we have to ignore all the abundant available extant cuneiform written records that demonstrate Mesopotamian city-states existed perhaps as far back as 4,000 to 6,000 BCE. The existence of those city-states did not populate overnight. They were built up over thousands upon ten thousands of years.

Paleolithic/Neolithic Sites Older Than 6,000 BCE

- GobekliTepe

GobekliTepe was first discovered in 1963 by an archeologist who initially identified the site as a Neolithic site intermixed with Byzantine and Islamic grave markers. The presence of Islamic grave markers in Turkey would not have been extraordinary. The initial analysis skewed the dating of the site by over nine thousand years. Timelines matter in this initial analysis. Those grave markers that were misidentified turned out to be critical astrological markers constructed circa 9,400 BCE aligned with the star Deneb in the Cygnus constellation.[15] The alignment is curious. The Deneb star represented the pole star for Paleolithic man. Two questions must now be asked. Why did the hunter-gatherer Paleolithic man deem it important to study the pole star? The second question for our story makes our case: how old is the age of man? The mere presence of such an engineering feat exhibited at GobekliTepe challenges and invalidates every previous conclusion regarding the engineering and construction ability of our hunter gatherer ancestors.

15. Andrew Collins, *GobekliTepe: Genesis of the Gods* (Rochester, Vt.: Bear and Company, 2014), 78.

Several facts must be known about GobekliTepe. There are five main oval enclosures: A, B, C, D, and E. Each of the ovals were constructed at different points in time and contained two central pillars with mean azimuths as follows:[16]

Site	*Azimuth*	*Date of Construction*
Enclosure B	337° / 157°	9400 BCE
Enclosure C	345° / 145°	9290 BCE
Enclosure D	353° / 173°	8980 BCE
Enclosure E	350° / 170°	8235 BCE

The discovery of the Neolithic GobekliTepe builders is an astonishing fact that compels one to reconsider all previous conclusions drawn about the existence of man. It certainly challenges the belief that the Earth is only 5,700 years old. GobekliTepe builders lived at the very least nine thousand years before the book of Generations could have been edited into the much later written book of Genesis in its extant Hebrew form. Most importantly, it causes one to reexamine the building capability of both Paleolithic and Neolithic man. We must ask not only how did these people build such advanced longstanding architecture, but also ask why did these people build such a center?

- The Ancient City of Jericho

A contemporary Pre-Pottery Neolithic site, the town of Jericho, emerged over eleven thousand years ago, which also demonstrated a building capacity. The Canaan city of Jericho enclosed a ten-acre settlement with a stone wall ten feet thick and thirteen feet high. The structure included a thirty-three-foot diameter tower that rose twenty-eight-feet tall. It also included a nine-foot ditch cut from bedrock extending a half-mile in length.[17] With no room for doubt, this city was intent on keeping something out. That something that was to be

16. Collins, 82.
17. Ibid., 218.

kept out was established nearly six thousand years before the Hebrew record of creation even allows for the existence of man.

The timelines are critical in understanding the context of the book of Genesis. The book of Genesis is not a history book with an appended chronology. To read Genesis, one must sit in the fifth-to-fourth century BCE; the reader must place themselves within the context of a world where *their* family migrated from Mesopotamia back to Canaan. The liberation of Judah by the Persians created a society seeking to connect with its past. A new culture and a new age emerged after the return from the Babylonian exile. The Judeans of the fifth century BCE did what all generations before them did and then stretched the line of inquiry a bit further. They asked a fundamental question: who is God, and does He care for me? That generation placed the question in an existential window that addressed them personally. If God was a God who really had my best interest, then man was born to be fruitful and multiply, not serve a pantheon of gods. It considered the meaning of life attributed by their forefathers. It was a generational quest to determine who they were!

The Assyrian exile of the northern nation of Israel in 722 BCE and the later Judean exile of 588 BCE seriously accelerated religious pondering in Palestine. The message of Genesis is pretty simple. It sought to explain the question, Who am I? not Who was Adam? Individuals seeking personal meaning compelled to ask that question for themselves.

Upon returning from the Babylonian exile circa 538 BCE, the Judeans awoke to a new existence disconnected from their past. The returning exilic community sought to connect with a past they never experienced. They had heard about Canaan from their parents in the oral tradition all of their life. They wanted deeply to connect with a land. They were neither Mesopotamian, nor were they citizens of Judah. They embraced their ancestry. For that reason, they left established urban living to create something new. In the post-exilic world of 450 BCE, a Hebrew faith began to emerge. It found solidarity by binding the various antagonistic traditions of northern Israel and southern Judah. One of those traditions included legends that their God created them to be fruitful and multiply. All that was needed was a story to communicate the message.

That was an easy way to begin because it reflected exactly what they were doing, beginning all over. If one starts with creation, then they indeed began with the beginning (Beresheit). A contrast of opposing views aided that end goal. A difference between the old popular culture and the new story served that purpose. The Judean children were well versed in popular culture. In fact, they were brought up in it since they lived in Mesopotamia. The popular culture recognized the famed and compelling story of the *Enuma Elish.* Marduk created man. But that story would not serve any good in the new world the Judeans wanted to create.

The sixth tablet of the *Enuma Elish* described the popular story most certainly circulating among Mesopotamia and Palestine during that time in a written form:

> When Marduk heard the word of the gods,
> His heart prompted him and he devised a cunning plan.
> He opened his mouth and unto Ea he spake
> That which he had conceived in his heart he imparted unto him:
> "My blood will I take and bone will I fashion
> I will make man, that man may
> I will create man who shall inhabit the earth,
> That the service of the gods may be established, and that their shrines may be built."[18]

If the Hebrew religion was going to compete against popular culture, it had to explain why man was on Earth. It had to address several questions: Who was (El) God? Who was YHWH? What is the origin and role of evil? Why did God create man? Which came first, the chicken or the egg?

The problem in Palestine was complicated. Not everybody was signing up to go back to Judea. Life was not that bad in Mesopotamia.

18. "Enuma Elish, Tablet 6" in *Sacred Texts*, trans, L. W. King, http://www.sacred-texts.com/ane/enuma.htm.

Families were already settled, children were born, young boys courted girls, and matches were made for future generations. If God had wanted the Judeans to be in Judea, why did he not prevent their deportation in the first place? Life was better under the Persians. Deported families in Mesopotamia often recounted the constant fear of corrupt Judean taxation and controls. Anger and fire burned through Grandpa's nose as he cursed Jehoiakim's puppet government, first siding with Babylon, then secretly negotiating conspiracies with Egypt.

Who needed that way of life!

PART II

He, however, who begins with Metaphysics, will not only become confused in matters of religion, but will fall into complete infidelity

Moses ben Maimon

CHAPTER 1

IN THE BEGINNING: A NORTHERN EXPOSURE OF TRADITION

As we move forward in our discussion, it will not be immediately clear why this chapter is titled "In the Beginning: A Northern Exposure of Tradition." For now, we will assume that the first chapter of Genesis was given birth in the northern region of Israel apart from the southern state of Judah. In later chapters, we will be able to more fully appreciate the genesis of this book (yes, pun intended).

"In the beginning" is one of those phrases that has reached a particular prominence in usage. It is a phrase that most people have heard within the popular view of creation. The editors of The Scofield Study Bible spent considerable effort to highlight this concept of beginning by noting, "The Bible begins with God, not with philosophical arguments for His existence, beginning."[19] However, that comment seems misplaced for two reasons. The Hebrew word *beresheit*, the first word in the Bible, is composed of two elements. The first is a preposition underscored by the presence of the letter בְּ. This letter is reasonably translated as "in." The second element of the word is dominated by the three Hebrew letters רֵאשׁ. This combination evokes a strong association with a specific impression. *Beginning*, *first*, *chief*, or *head* occurs 593 times in the Hebrew scriptures as a standard word denoting events or people as either the first things, firstborn, or the head of activity or clan of people.

---

19. C. I. Scofield, *The Scofield Reference Bible: The Holy Bible* (New York: Oxford University Press, 1989), 2.

It appears that our translators, even before they begin their work of translating, have already colored our theological thought process. The Scofield scholars do not provide support for their proposed argument. That "The Bible begins with God..." is a coloring of the proposition and one of faith, not fact. How could one take exception to an edited note in the Bible? Especially if that note carries the weight of spiritually thinking about God?

The translation of *beresheit* as a single word is not part of a statement about God. It is contextually best interpreted as a reference to other popular myths. It is an antagonistic statement to contradict the popular culture of the day. The Scofield editors have ignored the most important element of Hebrew grammar. The word as constructed contains no definite article. A definite article would be needed in order to arrive at a translation "In *the* beginning." The Hebrew *bet* is supported with a *sheva*. The most supportable translation would be "In *a* beginning," which means something else entirely.

We are now drawn to a definitive point of the book of Genesis:

בָּרָא אֱלֹהִים, אֵת הַשָּׁמַיִם, וְאֵת הָאָרֶץ

The translation is not difficult: "God (Elohim) created the heavens and the earth."

There is no confusion. A careful translation focuses on the subject and verb to produce reflective writing. "Elohim created." One might even reasonably conjecture that a possible variant would read, "Elohim is creating." When the author first penned the phrase, "God created the heavens and the earth," it was indeed a shocking statement that demanded an explanation. It was a bold stand and declaration all in one phrase. That Elohim created the heavens and the earth defied several thousand years of factual religious and cultural indoctrination. The simplicity of six Hebrew words drew the attention of empires, kings, and peoples.

Famous related legends and myths such as *The Epic of Creation* abounded throughout the ancient Near East. We can approximate the epic's composition to the first millennium BCE based on the analysis of the remaining fragments of the text. The story line intended to help man contemplate the purpose of humanity. In that exercise, it was essential to initially broach the sensitive subject of just how the world came about being in the first place. Man existing here on earth was problematic; expanding the dialogue of the sensitive topic was important. If the world exists (in a purely rational manner, of course), then why is man here? And if man is indeed here, is there a purpose to life? Man is not immortal! Man's days are limited. Almost all the ancient literature that has survived from the ancient Near East sought to describe that experience within the viewing lens of the single most meditative question: which came first, the chicken or the egg? All Semitic literature that sought to answer that question contained similar story line structures. They involved adventurous heroes and man's quest for all that he can achieve: fame. Man would die; immortality was out of his reach. Fame was the best he could hope for.

The mythical epics of creation sided in the camp of "the egg." The oral tradition of Mesopotamian myths predate the Hebrew book of Genesis by as much as four thousand years. The written tradition predates the Hebrew declaration by at least between one thousand to three thousand years. When factoring in the oral tradition for those mythical stories, we understand just how ingrained it was in popular thought:

> When the skies above were not yet named
> Nor earth below pronounced by name,
> Apsu, the first one, their begetter
> And maker Tiamat, who bore them all,
> Had mixed their waters together...[20]

Ancient societies were well ordered, not primitive. The facts of existence were widely promulgated by the time the Hebrew scribes began their activity. Palestine was a backwater country dominated politically by empires to which they were subservient. Semitic language construction and culture eventually gave birth to Hebrew and Aramaic strains. Connections between the Hebrews and Habiru back to their Sumerian roots are widely accepted. The ancestry of its Semitic-based

---

20. Stephanie Dalley, *The Epic of Creation in Myths from Mesopotamia: Creation, The Flood. Gilgamesh, and Others* (New York: Oxford University Press), 233.

language and cognate words were derived from both their Akkadian and Sumerian origins.

The Epic of Creation borrowed heavily from the older Akkadian epic, *Enuma Elish*:

> When in the height heaven was not named,
> And the earth beneath did not yet bear a name,
> And the primeval Apsu, who begat them,
> And chaos, Tiamut, the mother of them both
> Their waters were mingled together,
> And no field was formed, no marsh was to be seen;
> When of the gods none had been called into being,
> And none bore a name, and no destinies were ordained;
> Then were created the gods in the midst of heaven.[21]

In both myths, there are commonalities. The ancient Near Eastern mind focused on its existential destiny, not the fate of past generations. Corresponding to that focus was an acceptance of a water-based origin of first things. The term *first things* recognizes that the water-based system was a popular starting point to review one's mortality and one's purpose.

The premise of that perspective was that life began under a water-based system. Genesis borrowed that thought as well. Two primeval waters mixing and swirling together was a comfortable metaphorical manner to describe sexual tension. One stream is bitter; one pool is sweet…and what happens next? Tiamat's womb now contains deities that emerge on the scene. Beginning is the framework of the writing. Understanding the sense of beginning, we now can proceed.

The Heavens: Lost in Translation, Elegant in Oral Tradition

Creation captures your attention. The act of creation is quirky. It is mystical. Ascribing the action to Elohim was groundbreaking in and of itself. As a name, Elohim was not recognized in any of the more ancient

---

21. L.W. King, "Enuma Elish, Tablet 1" Sacred Texts, http://www.sacred-texts.com/ane/enuma.htm.

previous pantheons of deities, Near Eastern or Egyptian. The dynamics of the language now took hold of the psyche. Order is important. Elohim first created the heavens. In the frail English translation, the postmodern Western mind is redirected from grasping the most crucial concept expressed.

The structure of Semitic biblical Hebrew rests on a foundation of triconsonantal roots. In plain English, that means most words consist of three consonants. Oral traditions predated written traditions. Myths were transmitted orally, then later reduced to a written form. The Bible followed that model. Before us now are the two words translated into English as *heavens* and *water.*

The Hebrew consonants *Mem*, *Yod*, *Mem* form the foundation for both words. The word *heaven(s)* is a plural beginning with the consonant *Shin*, which adds a fourth consonant to a word in a language constructed with three consonants.

English Word	*Hebrew Word*	*Pronunciation*
water	מַיִם	mayim (three-consonant word)
heavens	שָׁמַיִם	sh'mayim (four-consonant word)

The Hebrew letter *Shin* ש is pronounced as "Sh."

Literal English translations lose that key marker. That marker, however, was not lost on the ear of its intended audience.

The oral tradition reminds us of the reality that the transmission occurred primarily in a family setting. Stories were told in part to provide relaxing comfort. They were also preserved and retold to explain just why man existed. Possessing the gift of storytelling was an acquired skill. It requires a bit of savoir-faire. Talkative uncles told the best stories. They possessed a talent to imply double entendre meanings.

Transmission of the tale involving the heavens and water would have been illuminated by the most special raconteur. It required a particular emphasis on the distinct "sh" sound produced by the consonant *shin.* In this setting, a very lively and production of the word for water was produced after the exaggerated lisping "Shhhhhhhhhhhhhhmayim."

The Torah is given to man by God as teaching. It is a light for decent living. The episodes in the Torah have both allegorical and symbolic meanings. Practical laws are established and principles are encouraged. Unraveling the teaching in the Torah has proven to be problematic in its written form. It is not a straightforward process for the language constraints of translations. Mythical teaching also includes some facts. The Western mind often bites too quickly at those facts (Remember our admonition: don't bite at the first apple!).

> In a [the] beginning Elohim [God] created the heavens and the earth. The earth was without form and void; and darkness was on the face of the deep. And the Spirit of God was hovering over the face of the waters. (Gen. 1:1–2)

The author suddenly takes a detour.

> Then God said, "Let there be light"; and there was light. And God saw the light, that it was good; and God divided the light from darkness. God called the light Day, and the darkness He called night. So the evening and the morning were the first day. (Gen. 1:3–5)

The detour was important because it focuses our attention back to the subject of beginnings. As compared to previous religious thought, the status quo was accepted and never questioned. Elevated for our view is the connection of creation, especially the creation of the heavens and water. It was not until day two that God returned to the primeval waters occupying the expanse.

> Then God said let there be a firmament in the midst of the waters, and let it divide the waters from the waters. (Gen. 1:6)

The waters identified in this particular verse are not the oceans, or lakes, or seas that now constitute the waters of the planet Earth. These were the primordial waters that form the heavens. Order is important. God first created the heavens (ha-'sh'mayim'). Our reading of this verse in a translation deprives us of the viewpoint of the original intent. We are blinded to the original purpose of the 'heavens' since we now look up to 'the heavens.' Yet the oral tradition implicit in its employment of the double entendre created a totally different point of view. Is the meaning forever lost in a written translation? At its most logical, it challenges the deities in existence during the fifth century BCE.

One must reorient their position to understand the reference point fully. Close your eyes and feel the nothingness of the atmosphere around you. This area from the base of the planet up throughout the vastness of outer space, this space is "the heavens" considered by the author, as he is describing the creative act of Elohim. What we refer to as air and outer space, the author of the first chapter of Genesis refers to as the heavens. Its existence then as primeval waters was an accepted fact of the popular culture at that period. However, what garnered the attention of the audience was its unprecedented assignment as something created. That should also gather our attention in this age.

Consider this point: the creation of the heavens occurred when no planetary bodies existed. The planet Earth, *ha'eretz*, as well as other planets and stars, were created after the heavens *(sh'mayim)*. The creation of Earth was an isolated act. The sequence must be appreciated and not misunderstood. Absent the existence of the heavens, the earth could not have been created. Before something (the planet) was created, there needed to be a space (ha'sh'mayim) for it to exist.

Verse 6 of the first chapter of Genesis at first glance, appears to be speaking about the waters upon the earth. However, the reality is much different.

> And God said, Let there be a firmament in the midst of the waters, and let it divide the waters from the waters. (Gen. 1:6)

The firmament indeed divided the waters from the waters. In this instance, the referent waters were what we know of now as the combined air we breathe and outer space.

The earth could not sustain life within the context of the original primordial water state. This is where oral tradition almost certainly bound families together. It supplied a Hebrew tradition to draw pride into its culture. Our ancient ancestors viewed the sky as solid above them. The author wrote with an understanding that life must be sustained. God placed between outer space and our atmosphere a "firmament" (*rakiya*). The translation of the language obscures the point. God placed a rakiya in the sky. This Hebrew word has a contextual meaning associated with a beaten metal plate. So of course, in the oral tradition, the objective was to make the story much livelier. The one who told the story would have pretended to beat a piece of copper or iron as a divider between the water above the rakiya and the water below the rakiya.

Try to imagine what it must have been like to be a young adolescent youth living in Palestine around 450 BCE. The northern country of Israel had been devastated by the Assyrian tyrant Sargon II hundreds of years before. Your family was now living in the arid Judean Negev desert away from the plush Sharon Plain. Mountainous cliffs and deserts replace the once flowing rivers and green hills of the Mesopotamian plain into which you were born. Grandpa told tales about Judea. He reminisced about the way it was way back when. You sought to make sense of your status in life. Evening conversations focused on stories of a God who transformed a creation.

The chaos would be relatable. Life was chaotic. The absurdity of metal plates existing as a dome over the earth separating man from God had a ring to its foundation of hope. In reality Elohim was the Creator. Separation from Elohim was also a reality. The metal plate brought that point home. The Assyrian and Babylonian exiles proved nothing on earth could be counted upon. The story attempted to allow its audience to connect with their experiences and their physical existence. The separation was part of the episodic story line.

That story line of Genesis was much different from *The Epic of Creation*, or the *Enuma Elish*. It was intended to not tell a story as much as it was intended to generate conversations after the story was told. In the Mesopotamian stories, man was created to serve the gods. In Genesis, the earth was created for man. It was different and produced hope. It was not history. It was, despite the theological ponderings of the Scofield redactors, not even an epic about God.

The *Enuma Elish* attempted to address the circumstances as proposed by the ancients of Sumer and Akkad. It is not always comfortable to compare Hebrew religious thought to its prevailing religious thought of the ancient Near East. However, ignoring that process does a disservice to our comprehension and understanding of the context. All religious thought attempted to make sense of life and provide a focus on the meaning of life. By comparing the Hebrew attempt at this activity, one observes the superiority of the system and model.

The firmament separated the water under the sky from the water above the firmament. It was easy to understand. Between man and God, a metal plate was erected. The sub-story within the plot concludes rather succinctly. God called the water (*mayim*) located above the rakiya sh'mayim, which was easy to do by simply adding the "sh" sound to an existing word[22].

In Genesis 1:8, the plotline gains an intriguing thickness. Evening and morning now constitute a second day. The Hebrew word *yom* appears for the second time. For the six days of creation, the conclusion of each activity is recorded with a simplistic tone. "Evening and morning was the day_____."

Day 1: "And there was evening, and there was morning, day one"
Day 2: "And there was evening, and there was morning, day two."
Day 3: "And there was evening, and there was morning, day three."
Day 4: "And there was evening, and there was morning, day four."
Day 5: "And there was evening, and there was morning, day five."
Day 6: "And there was evening, and there was morning, day six"

Arguments and debates spring up about facts attempting to resolve a most obtuse question: was the world created within six twenty-four-hour periods? How one answers that question is often driven more by their end game. That end game seeks to protect an established

22. Sh'mayim is likely derived from the root Shin Mem Heh, yet that is an unused root in the text. The scribal editor created a link supported in the oral tradition. It was a great addition to a very nice story.

framework rather than encourage discussions. Religion in that context then is not about exploring, it is about compliance. That type of model fails to establish a framework to understand what is really going on in the written text. That methodology promotes an inaccurate, restrictive, limited model.

For example, in the year(s) 2018/2019, the Hebrew record of the age of the earth is 5,779 years old. This identification requires acceptance of unprovable data, namely, the identification of the point in time of the creation of Adam, the first man. The establishment of the creation of the heavens and earth, and the creation of Adam, are traced in this scenario from various genealogical records adopted and preserved in the Torah. One merely engages a belief that those records are historical documents purporting to identify chronology. Again, to bolster this argument, circular logic is employed. The beginning point of the discussion accepts the Bible as the Word of God. Since God cannot lie, one must accept this conclusion as both evidence and proof. It is a circular argument to be sure and persuasive, when understood as a tenant of belief, but not necessarily reliable.

We have highlighted this argument about day two for a specific reason. The situation is highlighted partly to illustrate the illogical path necessary to accept that point in particular and partially to accommodate the separation of the primordial mess that governed the day-one landscape illustrated by the Genesis scribe. For now, let us go back to day one. The Spirit of God hovered over the face of the waters. This hovering occurred over the pre conditions. There was no differentiation in writing between our current atmosphere and with what we know of as outer space. That premise was accepted. At the beginning, all inner space and outer space were all one. This was not a scientific explanation. It was a recognition of the accepted beliefs at that time. On this day, God said,

> "Let there be light! And there was light and God saw that it was good and God divided the light from darkness. (Gen. 1:4)

Something specific is going on here. It chiefly informs us that day one does not suggest a twenty-four-hour time block. This is concluded with a high degree of certainty. Speaking light into existence and dividing the light from the darkness, we are left to wonder in amazement and curiosity precisely what just happened. Light was created on day one. Three days later, we are entreated to a distinctly different creative action. On day four:

> And God said: "Let there be lights in the firmament of the heaven to divide the day from the night; and let them be for signs, and for seasons, and for days and years." (Gen. 1:14)

Lights in the sky, above the rakiya, served a purpose. On the fourth day, however, the explanation is much different and much fuller. These lights identified on day four, in the firmament, specifically gave light upon the earth.

That begs the question, What purpose did the light on day one serve? Providing sunlight was not its purpose at all. The two great lights, the sun and moon, were not created until day four. Absent a sun around which the earth must engage an orbit, a year could not pass. Perhaps one might suggest that a rotation of the planet could abstractly and theoretically spin on its own. That again requires circular logic. It would prove a point not needing to be confirmed, unless one was protecting another position altogether. Moving to the end, the concept of seasons, days, and years takes form. Years originated on yom areva day four.

The design intended in the oral tradition regarding the view of *yom* as a period of time seems at best nonsensical—that is, unless you create an entirely new interpretation for it. To rigidly hold to a view that yom could only mean a twenty-four hour period completely ignores the first three days of creation where it could not have meant that at all. We also introduce into our analysis an unhealthy model where context is whatever any future society deems the context to be.

The fact that these stories were introduced and communicated orally strongly supports the notion that they intended to create a model from which one must understand why God created the world and all the things therein. That must be the working premise. The Western mind, however, fixates not on the why; but instead, it focuses on the how. It leads the reader to miss the point of the story. Understanding the contrast of Genesis against the prevailing popular thought of the day was the message. That earlier popular convention prevailed by suggesting man was created to serve the gods.

Exploring the message of Genesis by comparing it against ancient myths and stories involving the *idea of beginnings* must be engaged. The investment should consider a model in which the spoken word often means the exact opposite or something else entirely. Sure enough, the translation and interpretation of the word *yom* is "day." That is a necessary translation since our language is finite. However, words often mean their exact opposite within context. For example, our previous related story of the man going out for the evening, let us revisit that conversation:

> CHAP: Dearest, I was thinking of spending the evening with my friends!
> WIFE: Beloved, let me know how that works out for you!

What is the best translation for this communication exchange? Is it accurate to univocally translate this conversation within a literal context? Did the wife solicit from her husband knowledge of how his evening will work out for him? In this contextual situation, the words mean something different than the translation. That is the power of words and communicative language. That is also why the ancients needed a referent that made sense with their world. Our ancestors were not asking how, they were asking why!

In the Genesis episode day three brings the formative creative process down to earth. The text suggests the planet existed in its original water (*mayin*) form without landmass. This verse reminds us that our translation should not be literal. The literal translation of verse 9 reads as follows:

> Let the waters under the heaven be gathered together unto one place, and let the dry land appear. (Gen. 1:9)

All of the oceans and seas had not gathered into a single location. Yet the literal translation suggests just that. The context within the oral tradition was a fixed point that the Creator separated the water mass for dry land to appear. Plants would soon emerge to support animal and human life.

Day three introduces a point of translation revelation. Whereas in verse 2, the Spirit of God hovered over the mayim. We now are introduced to another wordplay on the oral tradition structure of Hebrew. God called the separated waters yamim.

English Word	*Hebrew Word*	*Pronunciation*
water	מַיִם	mayim
seas	יַמִּים	yamim

The story was rich and delightful to hear. This was an incredible oral conclusion that resonated with its audience over the years. An easy to tell, easy to remember, fun story line. Something that would surely pass from generation to generation with limited ability to allow for deviations, thereby ensuring its enduring legacy.

On day one, God created the heavens and the earth. We especially learn that God said, "Let there be light." God does not explicitly say, "Let there be darkness." Man's imagination is left to speculate. On day two, God made the firmament. On day three, the incredible happens.

> And God said: "Let the earth put forth grass, herb yielding seed, and fruit-tree bearing fruit after its kind, wherein is the seed thereof, upon the earth." And it was so. (Gen. 1:11)

The ancients were ascribing the creative acts of nature, year after year after year. In their ecology, the earth itself brought forth grass and herb yielding seeds and fruit trees.

God allows for creative acts within a system of nature. These creative acts appear to take their course under God's divine will. The earth need not be only 5,779 years old. The sequence of time required for the ground to bring forth grass, the herb-yielding seed, and trees bearing fruit could be a process of billions of years. The how was not the subject of the activity! The sun, the moon, the stars had yet to be created. The creation of the sun occurred on day four. Without the sun, we know the grasses and trees could not grow. In the oral tradition, the story built up to the why climax. As on the two previous days, God saw all that had been done and considered it "good."

The story of creation in Genesis stands in comparison to *Enuma Elish*. Drawing similarities can be helpful in understanding its message. The heavens above did not exist, and the earth had not come into being.

In the text of the *Enuma Elish* in Tablet 1, the earth had not coalesced. Before meadowlands had coalesced, reed beds were found. Comparing the Hebrew account allows clarity. It parallels the much earlier written tradition of *Enuma Elish*. From here, one must pause because there are remaining similarities and many differences. The starkest difference illustrated the purpose for which man resides on the earth.

Context is established within the story line. In the *Enuma Elish*, Tablet VI, Marduk decides to create man to toil for the gods so that the gods would enjoy some rest. But that is a much later point in the story. The more immediate problem for Apsu and Tiamat is their disgust for the created order, viz the established demigods. Those demigods created way too much noise. Apsu was not getting his sleep. Complicating the situation even more was the apparent strength and growth being acquired by the demigods. A course of action had to be taken.

> Thus were established and were…the great gods.
> But Tiamat and Apsu were still in confusion…
> They were troubled and…
> In disorder…
> Apsu was not diminished in might…
> And Tiamat roared…
> She smote, and their deeds…
> Their way was evil…
> Then Apsu, the begetter of the great gods,

> Cried unto Mummu, his minister, and said unto him:
> "O Mummu, thou minister that rejoicest my spirit,
> Come, unto Tiamut let us go!
> So they went and before Tiamat they lay down,
> They consulted on a plan with regard to the gods, their sons.
> Apsu opened his mouth and spake,
> And unto Tiamut, the glistening one, he addressed the word:
> ...their way...
> By day I can not rest, by night I can not lie down in peace.
> But I will destroy their way, I will...
> Let there be lamentation, and let us lie down again in peace.[23]

Even Tiamat was displeased with the demigods and only at first objected to Apsu's plan to kill and eliminate them. Tiamat eventually acquiesced to Apsu's design.

There is a parallel that can be observed between the episode in Genesis and the *Enuma Elish.* That parallel is in contrast. Elohim saw his creation and immediately recorded a positive note. He saw that it was good. Apsu and Tiamat, on the other hand, were begetting demigods who in turn were generating other demigods of increasing strength and stature. Both Apsu and Tiamat were displeased with the outcome of the world they had caused to come into existence.

It is premature to rush to judgment at this point because the story has not fully unfolded. Of course, in Genesis, we eventually learn that YHWH had himself become displeased with the wickedness of the heart of man and plots a similar course previously pursued by Apsu and Tiamat. But that point will be fully scrutinized in due time. A baker need not take his bread out of the oven until it is fully ready. Our progress within the story is not yet prepared to address man's sinfulness

23. "Enuma Elish, Tablet 1" in *Sacred Texts*, trans. L. W. King, http://www.sacred-texts.com/ane/enuma.htm.

in contradistinction to man's purpose (the why of the episode) on the earth.

In asking why, a premise must first be laid out to substantiate any difference(s) in the episodes. Our authors do just that. The episode in the story related in Genesis confounds the mind on day four. Creating the stars in the heavens, including the sun and moon, brought more than light upon the earth, it also brought rule (*meshel*).[24] That rule brought order. Establishment of order was the context. Someone or something with power over another body or object rules that person or object. The Hebrew account included meshel. This oral imagery evoked the perception of dominion with the translation of rule.

Once the principle of meshel had been established, a mystery unfolded. Light was divided from the darkness. Though we have not accounted for the creation of darkness as the Western mindset wants to do, we have defined the creation of dominion, which the ancient Near Eastern mind intended. Elohim saw on day four that his created order was good.

The principle of dominion is evidenced in the creative selection of words employed by the text. At the close of day four, dominion and meshel emerged. Dominion is commanded by Elohim on day six as well. That dominion was over the fish of the sea, birds of the air, and animals of the land. However, a contrasting different Hebrew word has been employed, not *meshel*, instead, the word *radah*.

> And God blessed them; and God said unto them: 'Be fruitful, and multiply, and replenish the earth, and subdue it; and have *dominion*[25] over the fish of the sea, and over the fowl of the air, and over every living thing that creepeth upon the earth. (Gen. 1:28)

---

24. מְשֹׁל, pronounced "meshel," translated as "rule."

25. Radah, "raw-daw," a primitive root; to tread down, i.e., subjugate; to crumble off (come to, make to) have dominion, prevail against, reign (bear, make to rule, (r, over), take. *Strong's Hebrew Lexicon* compares *radah* against *meshel* [sic] as a similar root meaning a primitive root; to rule: (have, make to have) dominion, governor, ...indeed reign, (bear, cause to have) rule(ing, -r) have power. See *Strong's Hebrew Lexicon*, accessed July 26, 2019, http://www.eliyah.com/cgi-bin/strongs.cgi?file=hebrewlexicon&isindex=dominion.

Hebrew Word	*Pronunciation*	*Translation*
רָדָה	radah	dominion
מְשֹׁל	meshel	rule

This word has a different context than *dominion*, even though most English translations continue to employ the translated word *dominion*. Employment of the word *radah* is found in Ezekiel 29:15. It was a dominion, however, the context is a rule-based on militaristic dominance. In Leviticus 25:43 the word *radah* is employed within the context of a slave relationship. It is easy then to understand the involvement of a dominion operating under meshel. Dominion referred to a strict strength of force. The latter employs fear. That context of dominion is elucidated in man's relationship with the animals. It reflected a degree of anxiety.

Now the ancient Near Eastern mind has been prepped to more fully ask questions in the family setting. We are ready for the why. The fact of darkness was a present circumstance and condition of the created order of Apsu and Tiamat. It was also a created condition of Elohim. Day one, in contrast with day four in Genesis, allows one to consider the inherent sinfulness and the presence of evil in the created order. Was it darkness?

In the *Enuma Elish*, man was created solely to work for the gods. In that model, man was not sinful. Man needed to consider life within a construct of fate. Man had no control over his own destiny. Fate dictated outcomes based on the pleasure of the gods. In Genesis, meshel interacted to control darkness. That darkness identified in Genesis perhaps can be equated with the destiny of fate under the whimsical folly of the demigods. It is not a stretch of the reading to conclude thus. Because the outcomes are opposite, they stand in stark comparison. Under Elohim, order in nature rules man. Under Apsu and Tiamat, the folly of the demigods enslaves man. What remains in Genesis for days five and six is the integration of animal life and man within creation.

Man is unique in that creation. Meshel was introduced on day four. Meshel was associated within the separation of darkness. One would therefore not find it out of context for the word to next emerge in the

Torah in Genesis 3:16 after Adam and Eve disobeyed the command of God.

> Unto the woman he said: "I will greatly multiply thy pain and thy travail; in pain thou shalt bring forth children; and thy desire shall be to thy husband, and he shall *rule*[26] over thee." (Gen. 3:16)

Dominion is again introduced as a story line to facilitate conversations. The sinfulness of man was that single issue that provided a distinct stamp. It characterized the difference between God's relationship with man and his relationship with all other parts of creation. It is true that at some point in the story, the serpent is characterized as cursed. The connection of meshel to darkness points directly to man's predicament and the role of the serpent in that cursing.

A giant skyscraper cannot simply stand on a concrete structure. That internal structure requires a reinforced rebar grid to strengthen the concrete against the onslaught of the winds. Nor can proper context be applied without all the background. It is vital that the foundation of the creation story used in the Torah be carefully considered. On day five, the monstrous sea creatures populating the waters began teeming with life. The birds of the air were created along with all the tremendous winged creatures. This day is different. In the *Enuma Elish*, Apsu and Tiamat could not stand the commotion of the demigods. Creation is teeming with animals causing commotion.

In comparison, the creation by Elohim was accompanied with a command to teem with life, be fruitful, and multiply. After that command Elohim looked upon the situation and saw that it was good. No more magnificent statement could have been made in Palestine to counteract the hopeless philosophy espoused by the popular culture than those two simple words: *fruitful* and *multiply*. Those two words did not appear in days one through four. They appear on days five and six.

---

26. אֶל-הָאִשָּׁה אָמַר, הַרְבָּה אַרְבֶּה עִצְּבוֹנֵךְ וְהֵרֹנֵךְ--בְּעֶצֶב, תֵּלְדִי בָנִים; וְאֶל-אִישֵׁךְ, תְּשׁוּקָתֵךְ, וְהוּא, יִמְשָׁל-בָּךְ *meshel.* Translation: "To the woman He [God] said: 'I will greatly multiply thy pain and thy travail; in pain thou shalt bring forth children; and thy desire shall be to thy husband, and he shall rule over thee.'"

On day six, God commanded the earth to bring forth the living creatures, cattle, and creeping things alike. Broaching the summit and looking directly at the apex of the story, the author of this episode in Genesis has now reached the peak of the mountain of his story line.

> And God said: "Let us make man in our image, after our likeness; and let them have dominion over the fish of the sea, and over the fowl of the air, and over the cattle, and over all the earth, and over every creeping thing that creepeth upon the earth." (Gen. 1:26)

Elohim created the heavens and the earth in verse 1. That creation was recorded in the singular third-person point of view. An outsider observing an action either past or present is a third-person account. In verse 26, the pronoun *us* is employed. One must concede that it was written as a direct quote by a third person to represent a plural form. There was no mistake of the intention of the author since it is followed in the correct grammatical form consistently in verse 26.

Missing no beat in the music, the author in the very next verse returns to a standard third-person singular account.

> And God created man in His own image, in the image of God created He him; male and female created He them. (Gen. 1:27)

The distinction between days one through four as compared to days five and six are again explicit. Be fruitful and multiply. The story line is almost finished for the night as the favorite uncle winds down this heartwarming tale. God saw that all of his creation was good. And there was evening, and there was morning on day six. Unlike all previous days, the author concludes with an astounding principle: God saw that all He made on all previous days was very good.

The words of the Torah stand in contrast to the predominant philosophy of its day. It stands against the philosophy of all ages, even the postmodern search for social collectivism. Man must singularly be fruitful and multiply. It is an ageless message of hope. Only when we compare the Torah to the *Enuma Elish* do we benefit from the instructive value God intended in nurturing our soul.

CHAPTER 2

GENESIS 2: A SOUTHERN ALTERNATIVE VIEW OF CREATION

> These are the generations of the heaven and of the earth when they were created, in the day that the LORD God made earth and heaven. (Gen. 2:4)

As in chapter 1, it will become evident later why the genesis of this episode is identified with the southern Judah traditions. Provenance and dating a writing aid in our contextual analysis. Therefore, we will need to become familiar with two words that will enhance our reading of the story once told. Both words are translated at times using the same English word. One might argue that it is a reasonable translation, yet it fails to convey the correct meaning. The English word is *generations*. The two separate Hebrew words *towlĕdah* and *dor* both loosely mean "generations."

In the first eleven chapters of the Bible, the word *generations* is used seven times in the form of the noun *towlĕdah*. The Hebrew word *dor* is employed three times. Since they are different words and have distinct pronunciations, it is important to list their usage within the context of the audience hearing the story where the word is being used. The usage of both words would have raised different questions by the audience when the story was concluded.

תּוֹלְדָה :

Genesis 2:4, "These are the generations of the heaven and earth."
Genesis 5:1, "This is the book of the generations of Adam."
Genesis 6:9, "These are the generations of Noah."
Genesis 10:1, "Now these are the generations of the sons of Noah."
Genesis 10:32, "These are the families of the sons of Noah after their generations."
Genesis 11:10, "These are the generations of Shem."
Genesis 11:27, "These are the generations of Terah."

The word *towlĕdah* has relative etymology with the word יָלַד, (*yalad*), which is normally linked in a context that demonstrates child-bearing lineage. The word *dor* however refers to a generational dwelling place or even class of people such as the eldest uncle.[27]

דּוֹר (dor):

Genesis 6:9, "These *are* the generations (*toledot*, pl.) of Noah: Noah was a just man *and* perfect in his *generations* (*dor*)."
Genesis 7:1, "And the LORD said unto Noah, Come thou and all thy house into the ark; for thee have I seen righteous before me in this *generation* (*dor*)."
Genesis 9:12, "And God said, This *is* the token of the covenant which I make between me and you and every living creature that is with you, for perpetual *generations* (*dor*)."

The reader is introduced to different opposing thoughts: *toledot* (generations) and *ba'yom* (in the day Genesis 2:4). When the word *toledot* is used, it is often referring to generations of descendants with

27. See *Strong's Concordance* with Hebrew and Greek Lexicon; "H1755," accessed July 29, 2019, https://www.blueletterbible.org/lang/Lexicon/Lexicon.cfm?strongs=H1755&t=KJV.

an accompanying list of individuals who were married and gave birth to others. It is a word that spans a segment of time, not a single day.

The Bible relates a story that is based on the creation of the heavens and the earth. That space of time involved an undetermined period of time, perhaps many untold generations. We have no point of reference to assigning any specific number to toledot. It is a plural form meaning at least more than one.

"Many generations" is the premise that makes sense when reading Genesis chapter 2. If it were merely one day, then the word *generations* is nonsensical. If it were the case that the heavens and earth were created and the formations that occurred on the planet occurred over many generations, then the referent "in the day" makes sense. It makes no sense the other way around though. Compare how the redacting translators of the New King James version bend the story to appear to create a factual history:

> This is the history of the heavens and the earth in that day when they were created, in the day that the Lord God made the earth and the heavens, before any plant of the field was in the earth and before any herb of the field had grown. For the Lord God had not caused it to rain on the earth and there was no man to till the ground; but a mist went up from the earth and watered the whole face of the ground (Gen. 2:4–6 NKJV).[28]

> These are the generations of the heaven and of the earth when they were created, in the day that the LORD God made earth and heaven. No shrub was on the earth; there was no field. The Lord God had not caused any cycle of rain, nor was there yet a need for rainfall since there was not any man to labor over the field. A mist went up from the earth to water the face of the ground. (Gen. 2:4–6)[29]

---

28. C. I. Scofield, *The Scofield Reference Bible: The Holy Bible* (New York: Oxford University Press, 1989), 5–6.

29. https://www.mechon-mamre.org/p/pt/pt0102.htm

Two different translations appear to say similar things and still say something slightly different. These translations fail when they miss the point of the story. For example, the NKJV specifies creation included the earth and the heavens (plural). The Jewish Publication Society translation relates creation in the day God made earth and heaven (singular). Both are adequate translations if the word needed no oral context.

But the story line is not about creation as an act. This unique account tells us about man's position in relation to creation. The first chapter of Genesis records that on day six God created cattle, creeping things of the earth, beasts in the field, and ultimately man. The author wanted us to know that man was special. Creation of man in his eye reflected the image of God. In the second chapter of Genesis, the author has a different account that builds and expands upon an existing oral tradition.

> And God said: "Let the earth bring forth the living creature after its kind, cattle, and creeping thing, and beast of the earth after its kind." And it was so. (Gen. 1:24)

While it does not explicitly include man within that specific sentence, it does not exclude man from that creation process. Instead, the Elohistic author of the northern tradition takes care to point out that man was created in the "image" and "likeness" of God. As we progress in our reading, the Yahwistic author of chapter 2 looks to the earlier oral tradition and affirms the Semitic tradition that emerged from Sumer. From the dirt of the earth, man was created.

This is a direct reference to the existing oral tradition carried down from the north and borrowed from Mesopotamia. That tradition was derived from the common shared cultural traditions. That culture was evident throughout the Near East. Those traditions associated a creation of man by Ninhursag, goddess of the earth.

> Let him be formed out of clay [sic. earth/dirt], be animated with blood.[30]

The Yahwistic author had to contend with popular myth(s) on the one hand and the antagonism between the two Hebrew states, northern Israel and southern Judah. The Yahwistic author also injected into the prose an element not included by the Elohist. God breathed into man the breath of life. This breathing illustrated the difference between the animals of creation and man. Man stood alone with the breath of God within his soul and body. Man became a living soul. God placed man in the Garden of Eden and put him in a unique position among those creatures also formed from the earth. The southern author improved and updated the facts of the story while retaining the story line.

The Drama of Oral Messaging

There are two thoughts contained in three verses that are important to recognize within a coherent thought. Yet these three verses are not consecutive. One would not expect these verses to be consecutive. Chiastic Hebrew poetry formations need not accept such a premise.

> And out of the ground made the LORD God to grow every tree that is pleasant to the sight, and good for food; the tree of life also in the midst of the garden, and the tree of the knowledge of good and evil. (Gen. 2:9)
>
> And the LORD God commanded the man, saying: "Of every tree of the garden thou mayest freely eat." (Gen. 2:16)
>
> But of the tree of the knowledge of good and evil, thou shalt not eat of it; for in the day that thou eatest thereof thou shalt surely die. (Gen. 2:17)

---

30. Barbara C. Sproul, *Primal Myths: Creation Myths Around the World* (New York: Harper Collins Publisher, 1979), 114.

In this episode, two trees are identified. Of all the trees man could eat, from one alone, he was restricted. The restriction applied to the tree of knowledge of good and evil. Man was not prohibited from eating of the tree of life. The story builds to its climax in chapter 3. Man was exiled from the Garden of Eden specifically to restrict his access to the very tree that previously contained no restrictions.

> And the LORD God said: "Behold, the man is become as one of us, to know good and evil; and now, lest he put forth his hand, and take also of the tree of life, and eat, and live for ever." Therefore the LORD God sent him forth from the garden of Eden, to till the ground from whence he was taken. (Gen. 3:22–23)

The drama within the oral form of messaging transports the family to a discussion point. In a shocking turn of events, man now serves the ground from whence he was brought forth. The English written translation is somewhat impaired. The English translation evokes a metaphor. It should in its elementary inaccuracy cause one to raise their brow. When one tills the ground, one plants and harvests. So in a real sense, perhaps there is nothing to be puzzled over. The Hebrew word employed contains a preposition and a verb *l'a'vad* (to serve). It is also the Hebrew root from which the word *slave* is derived.

With no real differentiation in English, the Hebrew mindset has employed an explanation that correlates with the popular myths of that day. Of course, the Hebrew worked and toiled and made their way in the world from the ground in which he was taken. In popular culture, the gods and fate compelled man's destiny. Work benefitted the gods. Now man was introduced to the first curse of God, the ground from which he was extracted. The elements and origin of evil is expanded upon in this twist:

> Thorns also and thistles shall it bring forth to thee; and thou shalt eat the herb of the field. In the sweat of thy face shalt thou eat bread, till thou return unto the

> ground; for out of it wast thou taken; for dust thou art, and unto dust shalt thou return. (Gen. 3:18–19)

In the oral tradition a natural pause occurred to allow for discussions that would have taken place at this juncture. Written texts do not allow for that dynamic interchange between people. That bar of interaction hampers one's ability to personally resolve their own unique questions. Without a back and forth discussion, pro and con, the intent is somewhat degraded. We now are presented with a thought that requires contemplation. Of all the trees that God could have protected man from, why did he place a guard next to the tree of life?

> So He [God] drove out the man; and He placed at the east of the garden of Eden the cherubim, and the flaming sword which turned every way, to keep the way to the tree of life. (Gen. 3:24)

In very humanistic terms, the most logical guard post would have witnessed a setting with angelic cherubim sporting a flaming sword. The mission under those terms would have guarded the tree of knowledge of good and evil. Just the opposite occurred. God commissioned a guard at the tree of life, leaving unguarded the tree of knowledge of good and evil.

I have three children. In my logic, if I would have built for them an area to reside in, the riskiest area within which they would play or operate would have built in protections. For example, I once had a small tree house erected for them built by my friend Ed. It was a room built off the ground, in a tree, with sufficient steps to climb to protect against falling. Carpet was laid for a degree of comfort. To accurately view the children, windows were installed. It sported a shingled roof. The steps leading up to the house had dual easy-to-grip handrails. It had many layers of protection against worst-case calamities. In the Garden of Eden, no such risk measures were employed, merely a command.

What is the value of an imperative command? Paul the Apostle, of Hebrew Semitic stock, wrestled with this question. He sat in Greece pondering the "sinfulness" of the conduct he observed. The existence and presence of his own inherent sinful inclinations at times overpowered him.

> I found that the very commandment that was intended to bring life actually brought death. For sin, seizing the opportunity afforded by the commandment, deceived me, and through the commandment put me to death. (Rom. 7:10–11)

Paul's observation of life during the first century AD had some similar observations of man in 450 BCE. This likely was not an original observation. It was a part of the conversation within his community. Paul wrote this in his epistle to the Romans. It was written within the social religious existence of his environment. He was in the decadent metropolis of Corinth. The Corinthian community was renowned for its lax moral codes. That laxness was also evident in the church community. Paul borrowed from his past traditions to regulate logic. The current situation served for him as an open catalyst to examine his own sense of righteousness.

Warring factions fight for our attention. The command was issued that man must confront. Do not eat! If it had been me, I would have said to my kids, "Now, you see that angel with a sword over in front of that tree! He will remind you not to eat from the tree. If you try to eat from it, his sword will cobobalte you." Of course, this is slight satire and jesting. The point, however, is made. God created the antagonizing warring factions and subsequently issued a command He knew to be unavoidable by the nature of the command. Think not? Why did man not eat from the tree of life when he had full access to it? The parallel between the ancient myth of the *Enuma Elish* and the biblical account of creation is evident and instructive.

The Original State of the Created Order

In the written translation, a theological statement about God seems to arise but quickly dissipates under inspection. That would be a reasonable venture if God was writing a book about himself. In other words, we must return to our original premise. Many questions would have naturally arisen during a family discussion such as: what does Torah teach? More specifically, what does Torah teach regarding the introduction of evil and man's original state? Did man "fall" after eating the fruit of the Garden of Eden? Was man's fate inevitable? Was man created as fallen impaired creature from the start? The audience must first have considered the nature of facts.

Does the Torah teach facts? Or does the Torah provide a framework within each generation to ask age-old existential questions? I submit the latter is the case, and as a proof, we need merely look at the original Hebrew text. Reminding ourselves that the story in Genesis originated in an oral tradition, the fate of man now unfolds.

> And they were both (עֲרוּמִּים pronounced "arum*im*") naked,[31] the man and his wife, and were not ashamed. Now the serpent was more cunning (עָרוּם pronounced "arum")[32] than any beast of the field which the Lord God had made. (Gen. 2:25–3:1).

aromim: plural form—they were both (plural) naked
arum: singular form—the snake was cunning

Hebrew Word	*Pronunciation*	*Traditional Translation*
עֲרוּמִּים	arum*im*	naked
עָרוּם	arum	cunning

31. עָרוֹם ârôwm, "aw-rome" or עָרֹם'ârôm; from "H6191" (in its original sense); nude, either partially or totally:—naked. See *Strong's Concordance* with Hebrew and Greek Lexicon; "H1755," accessed July 29, 2019, https://www.blueletterbible.org/lang/lexicon/lexicon.cfm?Strongs=H6174&t=NKJV.
32. עָרוּם ârûwm, "aw-room"; passive participle of "H6191;" cunning (usually in a bad sense):—crafty, prudent, subtil. See *Strong's Concordance* with Hebrew and Greek Lexicon H6174, https://www.blueletterbible.org/lang/lexicon/lexicon.cfm?Strongs=H6174&t=NKJV.

These two verses run consecutively in the Bible, only separated by a sixteenth-century printer's desire to produce a written text that was readable. To the native ear, a message was being transmitted. That message in the oral tradition was not that Adam and Eve were naked and the snake was cunning.

The translation of these verses has become the machination of tinkering, forever rendering the story impotent concerning what it should cause us to consider. It should cause us to question how we stand as sinful beings before a holy Creator! Families would have discussed the nature of being righteous. In its present written translation form, it fails to accomplish that intent. It does accomplish that purpose in the original oral tradition. The written translation, however, squelches its true meaning. The mistranslation is lost in the words *naked* and *cunning*. The implications wrapped inside the Hebrew word arum were not lost in oral transmission, yet makes no sense in a written translation. The root was similar and a twist of the tongue highlighted the meaning. The written translations depict Adam as a frail victim. That is the wrong context of the word to describe Adam and Eve and the snake. All three were in the same condition. Man's eternal condition was the topic of discussion. Was man a fallen creature after he ate the fruit of the tree, or was man a fallen creature by design?

In the oral tradition, it was understood the man and woman were *arumim* and the snake was *arum*. The audience would not have differentiated between the conditions. The much later translations of *naked* and *cunning* mean two different things. The original audience would have understood both the state of the man and the woman and the snake as a similar condition. That would have led to a much different discussion among the family. Ascribing one status to one set of actors and another status to the other actor would not have occurred to the ancients. Despite that actor being the snake, all three were similar.

The story completely misses the point unless the same original condition is applied to all sets of actors (Adam, Eve and the snake). Let us conduct an experiment and use that same condition for both parties in the oral tradition with a proper retranslation.

> And they (Adam and Eve) were both cunning (in a bad sense), the man and his wife, and were not ashamed. Now the serpent was more cunning (in a bad sense) than any beast of the field which the Lord God had made. (Gen. 2:25–3:1)

We now have a real story line to talk about after dinner! Which is worse, the people or the snake? Does this translation test out? What was the reaction of Adam to the Lord God? His reaction was a crafty, cunning (in a bad sense) dismissal of his actions by blaming the woman. What was the response of Eve to the Lord God? Her reaction was a crafty, cunning (in a bad sense) dismissal of her actions by blaming the snake. The original oral tradition does explicitly what the translation fails to do: identify the true condition of man.

To blame the fall on a single act of Adam and Eve ignores the message. Adam and Eve were created in the condition of arumim. That condition certainly had to be compared to several data points. The author was comparing their state to popular culture resulting in a contrast. It also had to be compared to the reality of why this world was not a Garden of Eden. This episode injected an entirely new premise into the discourse. It rejected popular thought for a new Hebrew tradition.

The redactor was transmitting the origin of evil as man's original condition. That was part of the story. It was communicated and passed down. The difference between the man and woman and the snake was illustrated. Before they ate the fruit of the tree of knowledge of good and evil, they were not בּוֹשׁ (*buwsh*), or more correctly, יִ תְ בֹּ שָׁ שׁו. They were not shaming themselves. In this conversation, the subject matter is highlighted. If Adam and Eve did not shame themselves in arum, then why do we? Paul the Apostle had to accept his own sinfulness and still live with himself. It created an opportunity for him to accept that his Creator would also be his Redeemer.

Characterizing man's original condition by a degree of craftiness in a bad sense was consistent with every story line regarding Jacob, the son of Isaac, coincidently the namesake of Israel.

The word יעקב [33] Jacob in Hebrew, carries the element of a crafty (not in a good sense) oral tradition wordplay from the word עקב. Jacob was crafty in his own right from his mother's womb. He attempted to circumvent the natural order. In short, he was a good old-fashioned red-blooded well-adjusted man.

Hebrew Word	*Pronunciation*	*Usage*
יעקב	Ya'ăqôb (Jacob)	name
עקב	aqab	to supplant, circumvent, take by the heel, follow at the heel, assail insidiously, overreach

This is in complete agreement with Paul's view as he considered his own experience in life. He attempted to account for the law, the command, and the disposition of man. He considered himself a representative "reasonable man." He found himself in the same predicament as Adam:

> What shall we say, then? Is the law sinful? Certainly not! Nevertheless, I would not have known what sin was had it not been for the law. For I would not have known what coveting really was if the law had not said, "You shall not covet." But sin, seizing the opportunity afforded by the commandment, produced in me every kind of coveting. For apart from the law, sin was dead. Once I was alive apart from the law; but when the commandment came, sin sprang to life and I died. I found that the very commandment that was intended to bring life actually brought death. For sin, seizing the opportunity afforded by the commandment, deceived me, and through the commandment put me to death.

---

33. Both the words עקב and יעקב are derived from the same root. See Strong's Concordance with Hebrew and Greek Lexicon "6117," https://www.blueletterbible.org/ lang/lexicon/lexicon.cfm?strongs=H6117&t=NKJV.

> So then, the law is holy, and the commandment is holy, righteous and good. (Rom. 7:7–12)

Man in all his craftiness was no match for the snake. Following it through its logical conclusion, man was also no match for himself! He couldn't control himself at times. Paul's conclusion that the law and commandment was holy further illustrated the original condition of both Adam and Paul.

Instructional allegories are contained in the story of the tree of knowledge of good and evil and the separate tree of life. Because they are myths, does that make their guidance less instructive?[34] Mankind now has a framework in the eternal search for meaning. Two options are presented:

Option 1: If one needs to hold firm that the Bible must be literally true, then two trees still must exist in the Garden of Eden. Eating from one of the trees is impossible. It is guarded by cherubim with a flaming sword. The downside to holding fast to this opinion is the corollary that when one physically eats from the other tree, the tree of knowledge of good and evil, then one's eyes are opened to nakedness and evil. We would try not to account for any of the messy logistical problems burdening this view. For example, the tree of life, since it is a gateway to life, must have existed for thousands upon thousands of years with the same green leaves. By its nature it could not have experienced any decay. Another logistical problem is obvious: do we need to eat the natural fruit of the tree of knowledge of good and evil? We seem to already be pretty evil symbolically and mythically without actually eating from that tree.

Option 2: If one holds that the Bible need not be literally true, then a broader meaning of the tree of life can be applied. The power of an allegory can purge our thought process of rubbish and allow us to consider the elements that influence our everyday decisions in life.

---

[34] It is no small reference here to allow the distinguished Wheaton College Professor of Old Testament's voice to be heard in this matter. The conservative John Walton introduces this idea of mythology in several writings: See Walton, John C. *Genesis: The NIV Application Commentary* (Grand Rapids: Zondervan, 2001); and Walton, John C. *The Lost World of Genesis One: Ancient Cosmology and the Origins Debate* (Downers Gove, IL: Intervarsity Press, 2009).

The essential questions from the second chapter of Genesis are now before us and ready for discussion: Is it possible for man to never have access to the tree of life? Am I condemned only to experience death after one man ate from the tree of knowledge of good and evil? What is man's existential purpose? What is our fate?

Man became domesticated. Myths and archetypes emerged in the ancient world to address man's domestication. His past was one of a hunter gatherer. He moved into urban domestic living. The woman led the way.

CHAPTER 3

THE *EPIC OF GILGAMESH* AS A MYTHICAL ACCOUNT OF CREATION

The *Epic of Gilgamesh* proposed a mythical account of creation. Man was created from clay (dirt of the earth). Stephen Mitchell captures this essence in his commentary and translation of the epic:

> Now go and create a double for Gilgamesh, his second self, a man who equals his strength and courage... When Aruru heard this she closed her eyes, and what Anu commanded she formed in her mind, she pinched off some clay, she threw it into the wilderness, kneaded it, shaped it to her idea, and fashioned a man, a warrior, a hero...[35]

Man was full of virtue. Engaging in war was ironically a significant virtue he possessed. This contrast in the oral tradition was filled with absurd humor. In the *Epic of Gilgamesh*, there is an erotic element also found in the Hebrew record of creation. In the epic, the exotic, primitive Enkidu roamed in the fields, thwarting the plans of an individual wild-game trapper. It occurred to the trapper that the only way to domesticate this wild being was to introduce him to a woman.

> There he [Enkidu] is. Now, woman, make your breasts bare, have no shame, do not delay but welcome his

35. Mitchell, *Gilgamesh*, Book 1, 74.

> love. Let him see you naked, let him possess your body. When he comes near uncover yourself and lie with him; teach him, the savage man, your woman's art, for when he murmurs love to you the wild beasts that shared his life in the hills will reject him.[36]

Enkidu welcomed his introduction to the temple prostitute. In ancient societies, temple prostitutes served as supports to ensure fertility. The trapper found a perfect remedy to Enkidu's spoiling of his traps. However, the trapper quickly leaves the story because Enkidu was no mere accident. Enkidu was created to counter the powerful demigod Gilgamesh. Gilgamesh would leave no virgin for her lover. He spoiled the path with the degradation of other's wives as he saw fit. A significant problem embroiled the city of Uruk. Enkidu, the man, was the answer. The gods created him. Gilgamesh was on a trajectory to meet his match.

> She [Temple prostitute] was not ashamed to take him [Enkidu], she made herself naked and welcomed his eagerness; as he lay on her murmuring love she taught him the woman's art. For six days and seven nights they lay together, for Enkidu had forgotten his home in the hills; but when he was satisfied he went back to the wild beasts. Then, when the gazelle saw him, they bolted away; when the wild creatures saw him they fled. Enkidu would have followed, but his body was bound as though with a cord, his knees gave way when he started to run, his swiftness was gone. And now the wild creatures had all fled away; Enkidu was grown weak, for wisdom was in him, and the thoughts of a man were in his heart. So he returned and sat down at the woman's feet, and listened intently to what she said. "*You are wise, Enkidu, and now you have become like a god.* Why do you want to run wild with the beasts in the hills? Come with me. I will take you to strong-walled

---

36. *The Epic of Gilgamesh*, trans. N. K. Sanders (Assyrian International News Agency Books Online), http://www.aina.org/books/eog/eog.pdf, 5.

> Uruk, to the blessed temple of Ishtar and of Anu, of love and of heaven there Gilgamesh lives, who is very strong, and like a wild bull he lords it over men."[37]

The parallels between the Hebrew record of creation and the dawn of man as outlined in the *Epic of Gilgamesh* are astounding. "You are wise, Enkidu, and now you have become like a god." These words force their way into the mind-clearing path to define man's purpose in life. Why is man here on earth? What is man's purpose? The ancient epic sets forth a myth proposing that answer:

> When she had spoken Enkidu was pleased; he longed for a comrade, for one who would understand his heart. "Come, woman, and take me to that holy temple, to the house of Anu and of Ishtar, and to the place where Gilgamesh lords it over the people. I will challenge him boldly, I will cry out aloud in Uruk, 'I am the strongest here, I have come to change the old order, I am he who was born in the hills, I am he who is strongest of all.'"[38]

Enkidu's purpose was to challenge Gilgamesh. He proposed it based on his strength. From that moment, a myth defined man's purpose. Is that the climax? Of course, man is strong, yet man dies. The *Epic of Gilgamesh* explains the frailty of humanity along with its imposing strength. That strength even at its apex had a limited life. Enkidu must die for his exploits with Gilgamesh. Enkidu curses the trapper for introducing him to the temple prostitute and curses the temple prostitute for his seduction and eventual taming. Man is born, steadily grows, then fails, and ultimately dies. It is the way of all flesh.

The Hebrew record poses a similar story line. Identifying the story as a myth does not mean that it does not possess a truth. It is true. The Hebrew root word for knowledge is (יָדַע) *yada*.[39] The ancient author

---

37. Ibid., 5.
38. Ibid., 5.
39. The similarities between the acquisition of knowledge by both Enkidu and Adam support the contention that in oral tradition these story lines were

made no distinguishing comment regarding knowledge and sexual encounters. Enkidu's knowledge and wisdom came after his encounter with the temple prostitute. In the Hebrew account, Adam is naked with the woman and both are oblivious to their nakedness. They had no real concerns, unlike Enkidu. They did not roam the wilds. They were content in a garden, yet naked, until that fateful day.

In the third chapter of Genesis, the verb *yada* appears. Twice it occurs in the fifth verse.[40] Gaining knowledge of something is key to understanding the context of the story line. It is clear that the first usage of the word, "For God doth *know*...," indicates it is a cognitive assent. But the second usage of the word *yada* is less clear. It is obvious there is a metaphorical euphemism being enlisted.

> For God doth *know* that in the day ye eat thereof, then your eyes shall be opened, and ye shall be as God, *knowing* good and evil. (Gen. 3:5)

This episode is a timeless story. The rehearsed tone allows each generation to do what it has done since the dawn of man. It enabled each generation to question the purpose of their own humanity. Central to the purpose is the reality of life and death. The origin of life was consigned to myth. Death did not need a myth; it was a reality. Each generation in antiquity as well as today search for meaning. Who am I? Who is God? Has my Creator forsaken me? The psalmist asked that very question in his day: "What is man that thou art mindful of him? And the son of man that thou visitest him" (Ps. 8:4).

The adversary appears in this story to dissuade. The snake reminds Eve that God knows that if you (Eve) eat from the tree of knowledge (yada), you will be like him. This parallels the temple prostitute's observation of Enkidu after just having experienced his first sexual

---

exploited. See *Strong's Concordance* with Hebrew and Greek Lexicon "H3045," accessed July 29, 2019, https://www.blueletterbible.org/nkjv/gen/4/1/p0/t_conc_4001.

40. כִּי־יֹדֵעַאֱלֹהִים כִּי בְּיוֹם אֲכָלְכֶם מִמֶּנּוּ וְנִפְקְחוּ עֵינֵיכֶם וִהְיִיתֶם כֵּאלֹהִים־יֹדְעֵיטוֹב וָרָע Translation: "For God doth know that in the day ye eat thereof, then your eyes shall be opened, and ye shall be as God, knowing good and evil."

activity. In Genesis 3:7, after Adam and Eve ate of the fruit, they knew (yada) they were naked. The Hebrew record is now contextualized:

> And the LORD God said: "Behold, the man is become as one of us, to know good and evil." (Gen. 3:22a)

It would be foolish to ignore the earlier myth of the *Epic a Gilgamesh* and suggest there is not an analogy between the two stories. Gilgamesh was a demigod, seeking eternal life. When he found a plant that would help him secure that eternal life, the snake stole the plant from him.

Is there any doubt that more happened at the tree than mere eating of prohibited fruit? The Genesis author introduces us in chapter 4 to a whole lot of knowledge. Adam knew (yada) his wife in verse 1, and she conceived and bore a child. He obviously knew (*yada*) her a second time and a second child was born. Cain knew (*yada*) his wife and a child was born (verse 7). In verse 25, Adam knew (*yada*) his wife again and another child was born. It is a safe proposition at this point to account for all thirteen pregnancies in the fourth chapter of Genesis as the direct result of someone knowing (*yada*) someone. The Hebrew record uses no other term at this point to communicate conjugal relations. Yet the word means much more than its written translation. It goes beyond cognitive facts and sexual relations to address the very existence of the family and relationships within the family as well as relationships with God. It was much more than sex. It was a reality imposed upon the search for meaning.

Correctly identifying these relations is essential in the story line. Man either merely "is" and then will die or has a purpose. The humanistic answer of the ancient world is laid out in the *Epic of Gilgamesh*. Man will die. That is unavoidable. Even the demigod Gilgamesh fails in the end to secure eternal life. The journey for Gilgamesh is to discover the secret of eternal life. He meets someone not different from him, Utnapishtim. Utnapishtim built a boat to survive a flood instigated by the god Ea. The boat secured a safe passage and harbor for his family and animals of the earth. Utnapishtim was granted eternal life for his obedience. Gilgamesh could not fulfill the task set forth by Utnapishtim to secure that which he feverishly sought: eternal life. He was banished from the shore and forced to return home. The wife of Utnapishtim then revealed a secret. If Gilgamesh were to journey to the bottom of a water bed, he would find a prickly plant, that if he possessed it, he would secure the eternal life he sought. Gilgamesh then devised a plan to tie stones to his feet to carry him down to the bottom of the water, find the plant, and return to his boat.

Eternal life, however, is whisked from Gilgamesh's hand when the snake entered the scene. The snake stole the plant and left Gilgamesh to his destiny, death, and the futility of fame. It was not merely life that Gilgamesh left behind, so the story had a humanistic twist as much as possible. Generations to come would hail the glory of Gilgamesh. Fame would be the extent of his legacy.

> The destiny was fulfilled which the father of the gods, Enlil of the mountain, had decreed for Gilgamesh: "In nether-earth the darkness will show him a light: of mankind, all that are known, none will leave a monument for generations to come to compare with his. The heroes, the wise men, like the new moon have their waxing and waning. Men will say, 'Who has ever ruled with might and with power like him?' As in the dark month, the month of shadows, so without him there is no light. O Gilgamesh, this was the meaning of your dream. You were given the kingship, such was your destiny, everlasting life was not your destiny."[41]

This story had a moral. Gilgamesh was instructed not to be saddened by this conclusion; instead, he was beseeched to take advantage of it. In his death, there was a particular element needed by man to obtain hope in living a just life in this present world. In short, make the best of your time here.

In the Hebrew account, man met a similar fate. The ancient Hebrew account could not have ended any other way. Man dies. The difference between the two accounts resides in applying the concept that the

41. *The Epic of Gilgamesh*, trans. N. K. Sanders (Assyrian International News Agency Books Online), http://www.aina.org/books/eog/eog.pdf, 24.

chicken came before the egg. The element of rule meshel introduced on day four of creation is reintroduced in chapter 3 verse16. There is an absurdity introduced in scripture that was openly present and part of the oral tradition.

> To the woman he said, "I will greatly increase your pains in childbearing; with pain, you will give birth to children, your desire will be for your husband, and he will *rule* over you." (Gen. 3:16)

Written translations often take out of context and ignore the entirety of the episode of the story line. It is akin to taking a snippet of a broader meaning and making the smaller part a representation of the whole. The translation is deemed accurate, but the opposite message gets communicated. God next turns to Adam. All who listened to this story in ancient days would have understood that the husband listened to his wife. It would have been impossible then, as now, for a husband to live happily as a supreme ruling lord never challenged by the counsel of his wife. The idea that man cruelly and tyrannically subjected his wife to an inferior cultural position is itself a modern myth created by reading the text. To the ancient then, as now, it was absurdly funny. The oral tradition presented a meaning exactly opposite from the written text.

Written traditions could take the past out of focus and out of its proper setting. This misappropriation in part created a negative myth of male paternalism in the Bible. It is an accurate literal translation simply imposed on an inaccurate context.

> And unto Adam He said: "Because thou hast hearkened unto the voice of thy wife, and hast eaten of the tree, of which I commanded thee, saying: Thou shalt not eat of it; cursed is the ground for thy sake; in toil shalt thou eat of it all the days of thy life." (Gen. 3:17)

Short Tutorial on Family Dynamics within an Ancient Near East Mishpacha

Available to us today are well-documented realities of family relations in ancient Palestine. Chapter 31 of the book of Genesis provides a glimpse into family life of that time period. A short recap points back to our conclusion about Adam and Eve's own dynamic within the family. Families lived in close-knit communities side by side to protect and preserve the assets and land as an inheritance within the clan (*mishpacha*).Villages in Palestine formed from the mishpacha existed with perhaps a hundred souls and were closely related. In such an environment, it would be unthinkable or at least difficult for the woman not to have a powerful voice. Women produced the next generation. Women were equally concerned about preserving and increasing the inheritance, not only for the present but also for the future. Contrary to ill-informed popular beliefs about the historical subjugation of females, the Bible suggests women knew their value and performed their role in the mishpacha.

Jacob was living in Padan Aram, in Mesopotamia. Jacob's name told us everything we would need to know about him. Jacob was a cunning man, and not in a good way. He devised a plan to do the unthinkable and immoral! We would naturally expect that based on his name. He wanted to break away from the mishpacha and go back to Canaan. That mishpacha was under the leadership of the eldest uncle, Laban. It was Laban who took the young lad, his nephew, into his clan twenty years earlier. The story comes alive when told from the perspective of the ancient ear! The action proposed by Jacob was profoundly aggressive. If every young man merely came, benefitted, and then moved away (in that economic environment), wealth and assets would continually be impoverished.

That pericope today is clouded in a commercial environment where young men can and are encouraged to do just that since operating businesses provide those incentives. In the ancient world, however, a young man's perspective would have been to benefit the mishpacha. Jacob's very name likely made him an antihero in a story line about morals. A young man sought the protection and benefit of a mishpacha.

Laban's generosity provided incentives and protections. How much more could Laban have incentivized the labor agreement? He offered him two of his daughters, along with their maids. That common offering ensured the next generation would survive. Understanding that fact is the key to unlocking these concerns. Rachel and Leah had to address Jacob's insane plan to leave. They also had an economic interest at stake and saw their interest vanishing before their eyes.

> Is there yet any portion or inheritance for us in our father's house? Are we not accounted by him strangers? for he hath sold us, and hath also quite devoured our price. For all the riches which God hath taken away from our father, that is ours and our children's. Now then, whatsoever God hath said unto thee, do. (Gen. 31:14–16)

Those two women controlled their position within the mishpacha. Their voice gave Jacob permission to do that which Elohim spoke in his heart. The text is clear that their primary objective was the preservation of assets to be passed down. It was under such a cloud that Rachel not only gave the consenting permission; she was also the one who stole the family idols. The idols were sacred in ancient cultures because they protected the value and work of the mishpacha. Not only did Rachel agree, give consent, and approve of this unthinkable plan, she initiated the actions necessary to transfer godly blessings to their future endeavors by retaining Laban's idols.

Absurdity of life and the search for meaning introduced in the story line emboldened the story. At the same time, the absurdity elevates the story and makes it a timeless classic.

> To the man He [God] said "Because you listened to your wife…" (Gen. 3:17a)

In oral tradition, the audience would have thrown up their arms in severe exasperation! What else could Adam have done? Of course, the women sitting in the family circle during this rendition would have gotten their jabs in. The woman was created from a man just a short while earlier to "help" him.

The story does not relate historical facts standing pure and unvarnished from any interpretation. It is not a fact for the sake of a fact. Instead, the story is still focused on initiating discussions to pondering questions: Why is man here on earth? Who is man? Who is God?

The culture of that day had an idea that was popular, and the Hebrews of the fifth century BCE had a different response to that popular culture within which they were living. Separating their voice from all previously circulating myths was challenging. It was magnificent in its approach to embellish and reinterpret existing cultural story lines.

Ethnicity charged the story line. It created a philosophical division between the Habiru's (Hebrews) and all other Semitic-based language people. The snake stole Gilgamesh's plant. The snake in Genesis was more subtle than any beast of the field. So subtle that it deceived Eve and Adam. Voluntarily man surrendered his divine protections. Enmity existed between the snake and the woman. Hearing the story created eye rolls. Absurdity already was present in the story line. Otherwise, the snake would have prevented the woman from eating the fruit of the tree of knowledge of good and evil.

Recognizing the equivocal messaging in an episode helps us understand its message. Relating facts was not the objective of the writer. If that were the case, then the story would be doomed to a single generational understanding. Some stories are like that. They only make sense in the present circumstance because they explain that circumstance. They, in short, are one-hit wonders! However, stories that live on beyond multiple generations address the continuing existential saga of the human experience.

Gilgamesh's epic seeks to explain humanity's frailty. The inevitable fate of Enkidu and Gilgamesh was also a condition not unfamiliar to Adam. But wait, there is more! Not only was the outcome of death decreed for all three, but an explanation of life was also introduced. Enkidu became like a god when he encountered the temple prostitute within a sexual experience. He then became a strong man and was able to challenge Gilgamesh.

Adam also became like a god after his sexual encounter with Eve.

> And the Lord God said, "The man has now become like one of us, knowing good and evil." (Gen. 3:22)

This is not a history lesson to be memorized and recited in Sunday school devoid of values. The biblical record is timeless in its ability to place us in confrontation with our reality. Is fate and fame in this life our destiny? Man can freely eat of the tree of knowledge of good and evil, or he can abstain. There are no guarantees except the tree of life is under armed guard. This instructive story line guides the actions of all who hear this story. How shall we live in this present world? Why, of all the trees, is the only one that can produce life hidden from man? Why of all the trees is the only one that can produce death freely available to man? It is time for that discussion.

CHAPTER 4

NOAH: A CHALLENGING ACCOUNT OF RE-CREATION

The story of Noah is often compared to the *Epic of Gilgamesh*. Both include a hero, a boat, and a quest. But that comparison is often initiated for the wrong reason. One of the major reasons for the comparison is an attempt to verify Noah's great flood. When that comparison occurs it seeks to prove the Noahic events as actual history. It is a stretch to say that because both the Epic of Gilgamesh and Noah's great flood include water and boats, we now have proof that the story of Noah was an actual event. Ironically, those who assert the veracity of Noah's flood just as quickly dismiss Gilgamesh as being a fabricated myth. It uses flawed logic with the enlistment of unverified facts.

Getting to the heart of the Noahic episodes recorded in the Bible is not very difficult and requires a little background setup. Perhaps the story of Noah existed in an oral tradition before 750 BCE. That is very likely. There is no doubt that a pure 'Hebrew' text could not have existed before the 8th century BCE. What is very sure, however, is the established oral and written traditions of the fabled Gilgamesh. Those traditions manifestly predate Abraham circa 1,800 BCE. Since Abraham was the legendary patriarch of the Jewish nation, it would unmistakably be no small conclusion that the context and setting of the Noahic episodes arose well before 1,800 BCE. At issue then would be, where did the events take place and when? These two questions drive the entire analysis of the written text subverting it's story line.

The challenge however for us is to ask the straightforward question: should we rely upon a fable such as the *Epic of Gilgamesh* to prove the actual existence of an ancient flood. Does such a methodology then, in turn, confirm the real life of Noah? When the intent of a modern reader seeks to prove a fact based on a myth, it is important to ask why. The answer may not be so obvious. The story, as told in the ancient setting, was never about the flood. It was about the questions that would have arisen within the mishpacha setting.

So we come to the same familiar crossroad. Does the Torah teach? And what does the Torah teach? Can we learn any lesson(s) from the story(ies) embedded in the episodes of the heroic Noah? First, we must put aside any preconceived bias to defend the historicity of Noah over and above understanding the story line. The sixth chapter of Genesis allows us to observe an established pattern unlike any other construct in antiquity. We are confronted with a most evil race. We are not even sure if this race is wholly human, the Nephilim.

> And it came to pass, when men began to multiply on the face of the earth, and daughters were born unto them, that the sons of God saw the daughters of men that they were fair; and they took them wives, whomsoever they chose...The Nephilim were in the earth in those days, and also after that, when the sons of God came in unto the daughters of men, and they bore children to them; the same were the mighty men that were of old, the men of renown. And the Lord saw that the wickedness of man was great in the earth, and that every imagination of the thoughts of his heart was only evil continually. And it repented the Lord that He had made man on the earth, and it grieved Him at His heart. And the Lord said: "I will blot out man whom I have created from the face of the earth; both man, and beast, and creeping thing, and fowl of the air; for it repenteth Me that I have made them." (Gen. 6:1–7)

The account in Genesis is a most confusing story unless it is not a story unto itself but rather merely an introduction to Noah. Ironically, this is not the first time in Semitic thought that a deity designed a plan to wipe out its creation. First, a rubric outline must be implemented. The biblical Hebrew identifies the presence of a race of giants and possibly another race as *beni-ha Elohim*, or "the sons of the gods." The textual reconstruction of this text addresses it from a two-tiered approach. One must either treat the text apologetically with a firm reliance on the translation or one must follow the story as originally told.

On the one hand, the written text suggests that the translation should not be translated literally. For example, while the text literally says the "sons of the-gods," the ancient Hebrew includes the definite article *hey* (the). One then reads into the text an explanation not present in the written account itself. That explanation identifies the *beni-ha'Elohim* as fallen angels. Verse 4 allows for an articulation of that reason. The Nephilim are introduced. The Nephilim derive their name from the root letters *Nun-Pei-Lamad*. These three letters when translated as a verb means "to fall." Hence, some expositors deduce the Nephilim are "fallen." If there are fallen "sons of the-gods," then in turn an assignment of the Nephilim are fallen angels. We now are confronted with an excellent translation but a flawed story because Noah's righteousness no longer is the subject of the story. The story line is lost in translation.

The redacting theologians who wrote the story as a translation in both the King James Version of the Bible and the New King James Version of the Bible try to ignore this difficulty and bypass a proper written translation altogether. No mention of the Nephilim occurs in those written translations.

> And it came to pass, when men began to multiply on the face of the earth, and daughters were born unto them, That the sons of God saw the daughters of men that they were fair; and they took them wives of all which they chose. And the Lord said, My spirit shall not always strive with man, for that he also is flesh: yet his days shall be an hundred and twenty years. There were giants

> in the earth in those days; and also after that, when the sons of God came in unto the daughters of men, and they bare children to them, the same became mighty men which were of old, men of renown. (Gen. 6:2–4)

We now have a mystery. The mystery remains unsolved in the King James Version of the Bible as written. Over time, the flawed written tradition completely ignored the story as originally told. The story line then changed: "The giants were fallen angels with superhuman strength. God needed to destroy all of humanity just to get rid of this evil race." You have got to hand it to the ingenuity of the human mind, a new story emerged. But does the Torah teach that lesson or another lesson altogether different from that?

Can we get to the original story as told? Let us debunk the flawed new story one step at a time. Could these giants actually have been fallen angels? Well, of course! But the author specifically did not use the traditional word to describe an angel of God. That Hebrew word is *mal'ak* (מַלְאָךְ). Since that word for *angels* was never used, it is problematic to read into our conclusion that these beings are fallen angels. Yet a person reading the King James Version and countless other versions of the text would never know that.

Question 2: can we identify with certainty the *beni-ha'Elohim*? Yes! The biblical Hebrew text explicitly identifies the giants as the Nephilim. The Nephilim were not strangers to mythology prevalent in Canaan. The ancient epics such as the *Epic of Gilgamesh* remind us, the Nephilim were heroes of long ago. They were examples of the best that man could achieve: fame. To see them present in Semitic oral tradition was not unusual at all.

In this oral tradition setting, the best that man could achieve is represented in negative terms. That contrast is highlighted in the heroic Noah. The author insists on the reliance of an oral tradition as the basis of the story line. It is a subtle reliance that exposes the explosion of the facts needed to understand the story. These Nephilim, in verse 4b, were "the mighty men that were of old, the men of renown (Gen. 6:4b)." The "renown" element of this story as written was part of the oral tradition. Later, a redacting author assumed you had heard of these people before.

"Remember them?" the author chides. These were the men of *Olam* long ago, men of *ha'shem* or rather, men of "the-name." More literally, these were the men of "the great name." The story line drips with the ripened fruit in its cultural setting. Those who heard the story in its original setting focused on how similar the man Noah was to Enkidu. They would not have fixated on the demigod Gilgamesh. This background was the context for Noah, like Enkidu, merely a man.

Life in the ancient Near East culturally integrated the popular stories of the greater Mesopotamian Fertile Crescent. Hebrews living in the ancient world were part of that greater society. Their ancestors migrated from Mesopotamia. Abraham was from Ur of the Chaldees. He was a big city Akkadian of Sumerian extraction. He migrated from a wondrous metropolis with several hundred thousand people. He left a dynamic bustling economy to live in an agrarian cattle herding outback. Palestine was a land dotted with small villages comprising no more than a hundred to a few hundred souls. There were limited settlements. In postmodern terms, he moved from a thriving community such as Boston to a rural village in a swampy desert remote location. Most certainly, when he arrived in Palestine, at least one person said, "You're not from around here, are you?"

The written text confronts us with only a few possible paths forward. But only one pathway makes sense. The written tradition forces us to explain the presence and existence of the Nephilim. But the oral tradition only uses that element of the story to highlight the righteousness of Noah as a modern Enkidu. It updated the story to relate to an audience in Canaan. Literal written translations of the oral tradition do indeed perform a role of preserving. Yet in that preservation, a corruption of the text occurs. The main point of the episode risks being lost. In this instance, it is fair to ask what the text is emphasizing? Does it compare and contrast Noah as a righteous man different from all others before him? Or is this a history of a giant race? A literal interpretation of the written text creates some intrigue and also too much baggage. A blind eye to the ancient past then constructs a methodology under which the oral context has no relevance. It created a new framework foreign to its original audience and understandably mangled it beyond recognition for the present.

In the oral tradition alone, we are introduced to the Nephilim for one purpose: enter Noah, a true son of God. In reality, the writer relied on oral tradition embedded in the familiar ancient Near East myths and allegorical sagas as articulated and retold. The story included the usual referents about the ancient traditions of creation. For example, in the *Enuma Elish*, the Annunaki were a race from whom their offspring, the Nephilim, emerged. Marduk created man from the clay of the earth. He assigned the Annunaki to their role after the creation of the world from the primordial waters.

Later historical books, such as the *Book of Enoch*, give some context for a cadre of associative intriguing beings and events. The Hebrew written text also provides a second reference identifying the Nephilim as the sons of Anak, or the Anunaki. The explicitness of scripture reminds us of the gigantic appearance of this race:

> We seemed like grasshoppers in our own eyes and we looked the same to them. (Num. 13:33)

One point is clear and without question. The relating account of the Nephilim is not disconnected from the story of Noah. Their insertion supports and is an integral part of this Noah episode. Otherwise, the normal chiastic structure in Hebrew tradition makes no sense at all.

> But Noah found grace in the eyes of the LORD. (Gen. 6:8)

Genesis 6:9 begins a toledot: "These are the Generations of Noah." However, we already know that the story of Noah does not start in verse 9 with the toledot. Arguably, the story line of Noah cannot begin in Genesis 6:8 when we first meet Noah. The story of Noah begins in the oral context of the existing Mesopotamian cultural traditions. The Nephilim were the counter-Noah. They set the stage to introduce us to the new kind of hero. The Nephilim were the great men of old of which everyone was familiar. Those men settled on fame as their fate. They were men of great fame. They were evil. The oral tradition begins with those men of old. That is the introduction to Noah, a contrast. Noah found favor, or grace, in the eyes of God. He was much different than all those who came before him and others around him.

The story line of the various episodes of Noah are significant within the book of Genesis. Each episode segues into a different story. They end when Abraham and his descendants are introduced. The account of Abraham begins in chapter 11 verse 26. By all accounts the first eleven chapters of Genesis tell a much different story from the rest of the book. The book of Genesis establishes at least two covenants in these early chapters. A covenant with Adam and a covenant with Noah are established. That covenant story line begins at Genesis 5:32.

> And Noah was five hundred years old; and Noah begot Shem, Ham, and Japheth.

In the eleventh chapter of Genesis, the Noahic covenant concludes. An affluent Sumerian migrant enters the written text. That migrant and his family shunned the wealth of the Akkadian Empire and rejected its range of gods and demigods. As a young man, Abram would not have had any specific interest in El, the deity associated with northern Palestine and the Phoenician coastal area. In this regard, chapters 1–11 of the Torah is also a story introducing Elohim (plural of El).

The accounting of Noah constitutes almost half of the story line of the first eleven chapters of Genesis. In this sense, in the written text, there is a time before Noah and a time after Noah. Establishing the Noahic covenant with all of humanity is a major task of the Torah. This covenant is illustrated by the very first societal problem before we meet Noah: two deaths. The oral tradition emphasized this element of the teaching. Why is this an important teaching? It is important because man is not eternal. Enkidu died; man dies; it is a fact. At question though is how death comes about. Since there is no moral dilemma in a natural death under natural causes, the Bible need not address it. But what about a death that occurred at the hands of another man?

The killing of Cain and the self-defense killing by Lamech of the young man who assaulted him are in center focus in Genesis 4. In the instance of Cain, a murderer, God's response was to send him on his way. In the self-defense claim of Lamech, what could anyone do?

Was he not justified in protecting his interests? The contrast of these deaths produced discussions late at night around the family meal. Those discussions taught values. Those stories therefore are part and parcel of the Noahic episodes. This is revealed by the first statement from God after Noah and his family emerge from the ark. It tells us all we need to know:

> Whoso sheddeth man's blood, by man shall his blood be shed; for in the image of God made He man. (Gen. 9:6)

This statement by itself is at best weird, unless the entirety of the oral tradition and subsequent written context is considered. That context resides in distinct discussions about murder versus justified homicide. The saga of Cain and Lamech.

Why was God's first statement after the flood in the context of one person taking another person's life? In the flood episode, God was acting on par with Tiamat and Apsu. That in itself should send us a chilling message. Noah's flood was not a staged event to destroy all of life and start all over again. That ending would never have occurred to an audience listening to the story. Instead, the oral tradition reminded us that Noah was not a man searching for fame, he was a true son of Elohim.

If God caused a great flood to kill all evil men, only to save one righteous man, Noah, surely God knew that was an exercise in futility! In the oral tradition, the fact that Noah's father, Lamech, had shed blood would have interested the audience. It would have caused extended sessions of questions and answers over the value of life. Is there a difference between murder and self-defense? Both actions resulted in the death of someone! It took the most heinous of crimes, fratricide, and compared it with the most reasonable moments of personal self-defense. That was a necessary comparison to introduce Noah since man is arum.

In the written tradition, Torah first establishes the value of man's life. If this is not established at the outset, then the Bible would have no relevance for any future generation. The value of the Genesis accounts of Noah are apparent for several reasons: (1) Man need not pursue evil! (2) Despite man's condition as עֲרוּמִּים, pronounced arum*im*, man can be righteous like Noah! (3) We can be righteous before God in our frailty and humanity. (4) Created in God's image, we must righteously treat others.

Is there a meaningful lesson behind the variant accounts of Noah recorded in the book of Genesis? God commanded Noah to build an ark. Was the purpose to save humanity and remake the world the right way? Of course not. That would simply be the most far-fetched conclusion to the story in the oral tradition. It would produce no teaching about God or man. Let's face it, very limited instructions are supplied to Noah regarding the construction of an ark. With less than one hundred words included in the architectural design, we know it must be at least three floors to house every known animal, male and female.

How Competing Antagonistic Doublets Elevate the Torah

The presence of doublets in the Torah resulted from a fractured population that lived under tolerant antagonism. The edited written version poured together various stories in circulation. The written text then created an illusion that the separate stories are a single contiguous historical account. This is what we see then as we unfold the narrative of Noah. Like most murder mysteries, the story is never about the murder. It is about how the murder is solved and the cleverness used in the process. Therefore, it is reasonable to suggest that the murder of Abel by Cain was not a murder mystery at all. It was a setup for the story line in the oral tradition. Also, the eating of the fruit from the tree of knowledge of good and evil was not about apples at all, it was a setup for the story line the Bible intended in the oral tradition, the condition of man. Enter the hero of the creation story, Noah. His name properly translated means 'comfort'

To what extent can we consider the story line of Noah as a story arising in the context of a creation account? Two sections in the story of creation begin with similar introductions. In Genesis:

> These are the generations of the heaven and of the earth when they were created, in the day that the LORD God made earth and heaven. (Gen. 2:4)

The author wants us to know he is recording the generations (toledot) of a specific activity: the heaven and the earth. As we progress further in Genesis, we arrive mid scene in the fifth chapter wherein the generations of Adam are recorded. So why are we being reintroduced to material we should already know? Yet this written account reveals an unusual twist. The author does not hesitate to explicitly relate in this accounting that the name Adam represents a third person plural form, not a single man with the name Adam.

> He created them male and female, and blessed them, and called their name Adam, in the day when they were created. (Gen. 5:2)

The New King James Version of the text imposes a more spellbinding twist: that translation states that God called them mankind and ignores the traditional translation altogether.

> This is the book of the genealogy of Adam. In the day that God created man, He made him in the likeness of God. He created them male and female, and blessed them and called them Mankind in the day they were created. (Gen. 5:1–2 NKJV)

All of the "them" that were created were generally called Adam (sic. mankind, NKJV). The word *adam* has a reference to the clay color and occurs ten times in the Hebrew scriptures as a reference to that color. The word *Adam*[42] also occurs an additional 553 times in its root form in the Hebrew scriptures.

One must now interpret not a word but a context. In Genesis chapter 5, does the first verse use the word *them* as a reference to both Adam and Eve? Or does the text use the word *them* as a reference to the broad creation of men? The next verse seems to clarify that point explicitly. Context helps us here.

---

42. Larry Mitchell, *A Students Vocabulary for Biblical Hebrew and Aramaic* (Grand Rapids, Michigan: Zondervan), 67.

> This *is* the *history*[43] *(toledot)* of the heavens and the earth when they were created, in the day that the Lord God made the earth and the heavens, before any plant of the field was in the earth and before any herb of the field had grown. (Gen. 2:4–5a)

> This is the book of the genealogy *(toledot)* of Adam. In the day that God created man, He made him in the likeness of God. (Gen. 5:1)

The editing author intended to allow the separate toledots (generations) to offset each other within the constituted framework. The framework compared the creation of the heavens and the earth with an independent comparison of the origins of man. That lines up with chiastic Semitic writing style. It makes much more sense as a flowing story line and appears that it was the intent. In short, the original editors of the written text intended these two stories to sit side by side but not as a history lesson. It was to retain the oral tradition prompting moral discussions. The editors planned to teach something altogether different.

A compelling discussion engaged by man since the dawn of time has focused on the question of the introduction of evil. My eldest brother was born with muscular dystrophy. He was born with a visible sentence of a cursed life. He lived each day knowing that his muscular system would decline. At the end of his life, the muscle of his heart would cease to pulse blood through him. The presence of evil escapes no family and demands a discussion by comparing both toledots. Presented now is a comprehensive account of the introduction of evil. God cursed the ground in the first toledot.

> And unto Adam He said: "Because thou hast hearkened unto the voice of thy wife, and hast eaten of the tree, of which I commanded thee, saying: Thou shalt not eat of

---

43. The New King James Version completely mistranslates the word *toledot* in favor of *history*. See NKJV, accessed July 30, 2019, https://www.biblegateway.com/passage/?search=Genesis+2&version=NKJV.

> it; cursed is the ground for thy sake; in toil shalt thou eat of it all the days of thy life." (Gen. 3:17)

The second chapter of Genesis concludes with the familiar verse:

> And they were both naked, the man and his wife, and were not ashamed. (Gen. 2:25)

This toledot, however, does not conclude with the ending of the second chapter. In fact, the story line spills over into chapter 3. That simplistic nakedness is continued in the narrative and enumerated in the curse.

And unto Adam He said: "Because thou hast hearkened unto the voice of thy wife, and hast eaten of the tree, of which I commanded thee, saying: Thou shalt not eat of it; cursed is the ground for thy sake; in toil shalt thou eat of it all the days of thy life." (Gen. 3:17)

The connecting thread between both toledots (Genesis 2:4–3:19 and Genesis 5:1–6:7) is the cursed condition.

> And he called his name Noah, saying: "This same shall comfort us in our work and in the toil of our hands, which cometh from the ground which the LORD hath cursed." (Gen. 5:29)

> And the LORD saw that the wickedness of man was great in the earth, and that every imagination of the thoughts of his heart was only evil continually. (Gen. 6:5)

The story of creation was an account written thousands of years after the event. The purpose of the writing was to preserve and maintain an oral tradition. That activity caused man to consider and debate his value and role. The story line had to account for a significant problem then and now. If God created man, how do we account for the origin of evil? Did God create evil? And for what purpose did God create evil? Like their ancestors in Sumer, the Hebrews worked the land year after year. Yesterday was the same as tomorrow.

The toledots contextually connect the two stories but do not fully explain why Noah would "comfort" us.

> And he called his name Noah, saying: "This same shall comfort us in our work and in the toil of our hands, which cometh from the ground which the LORD hath cursed." (Gen. 5:29)

Noah's comfort of man would have been achieved only if evil was entirely eradicated. One presumes the flood intended to rid the earth of such types as the Nephilim. Yet the Nephilim persist way beyond the days of Noah at least until the end of the Bronze Age (circa 1,200 BCE) according to later accounts in the Torah. When the Hebrews left Egypt and scouted out the land of Canaan, the record indicates the Nephilim were living in Canaan.

> We saw the Nephilim there (the descendants of Anak come from the Nephilim). We seemed like grasshoppers in our own eyes, and we looked the same to them. (Num. 13:33)

Eradication of the evil man was never Noah's mission nor was it God's purpose. That conclusion is obvious. Noah sailed on a boat with his family and a select group of animals. After Noah gets off the ship, there is a fourth connecting toledot.

> Now these are the generations of the sons of Noah: Shem, Ham, and Japheth; and unto them were sons born after the flood. (Gen. 10:1)

Noah did not provide eradication. Noah did not even provide an answer. Noah merely was one who trusted God. Righteousness was his moniker. Despite all events occurring around Noah, he singularly kept his vision toward the voice of the Creator.

The story(ies) about Noah in Genesis were not intended to be consistent as a single story. They were edited to best represent the meaning in the oral tradition.

> And God said unto Noah:[44] "The end of all flesh is come before Me; for the earth is filled with violence through them; and, behold, I will destroy them with the earth." (Gen. 6:13)

The northern name of God is invoked in this version of Noah's ark. "And Elohim said unto Noah!" His directions of what he was to do were pretty clear in the northern version of the oral tradition:

> And of every living thing of all flesh, two of every sort shalt thou bring into the ark, to keep them alive with thee; they shall be male and female. (Gen. 6:19)

As the reader moves into Genesis chapter 7, the southern Judean name for God, YHWH,[45] is employed. This name transition reflected a merging southern influence. Indeed this confluence marks a distinct antagonism in the Torah. This antagonism must be accepted since the Bible teaches us of the inherent hostility existing in relations not only with God but also with man. Those relations were evident with the first man born on Earth, the murderous Cain. These conditions were also prevalent after the flood. In Genesis chapter 7, the editor of the story found it necessary to insert the story as retold from the Judean perspective.

> Of every clean beast thou shalt take to thee seven and seven, each with his mate; and of the beasts that are not clean two [and two], each with his mate. (Gen. 7:1)

The redacting scribes of Genesis were aware of the northern and southern traditional versions of Noah. In one version, Noah was commanded to bring to the ark seven each of the clean beasts (fourteen in total per clean animal) and two of the unclean animals (four in total). This version of events understood the imperfect version as told by refugee

44. וַיֹּאמֶר אֱלֹהִים לְנֹחַ Translation: And Elohim said to Noah… (Gen. 6:13a).
45. וַיֹּאמֶר יְהוָה לְנֹחַ Translation: 'And YHWH said…" (Gen. 7:1a).

northerners from Israel. Centuries before, those Hebrews considered themselves much better than their inferior southern counterpart.

Our analysis of Genesis should not focus upon a discussion of exactly who redacted and wrote each chapter. That pursuit would miss the entire point of the story line.

These stories originated out of a long-embedded oral tradition. Reading Genesis chapter 8 as a translation from Hebrew would make very little sense! That it was meant to be told is clear by the word games the orator would engage with his audience.

Hebrew Word	*Gen.1 Translation*	*Pronunciation*	*Gen. 8 Translation*
רוּחַ	Spirit of God	ruakh	wind
תֹהוּ	unformed	tohuw	
תְהוֹם	deep	tehowm	deep

> Now the earth was *unformed* and void, and darkness was upon the face of the *deep*; and the *Spirit of God* hovered over the face of the waters. (Gen. 1:2)

> And God remembered Noah, and every living thing, and all the cattle that were with him in the ark; and God made a *wind* to pass over the earth, and the waters assuaged; the fountains also of the ***deep*** and the windows of heaven were stopped, and the rain from heaven was restrained. (Gen. 8:1–2)

God told Noah to get in the ark. Beginning in chapter 8, God causes a ruakh to pass over the water. In Genesis 1:2, God also caused a *ruakh* to pass over the waters. In Genesis 1 and Genesis 8, there is a clear connection in the words told in the story. Using the word *ruakh* allows the orator to employ double entendre meanings. It could apply to both the Spirit of God and wind. Also in both instances, the similar sounding Hebrew words *tohuw* and *tehowm* are used. *Tohuw* is translated as a "formless void' in its usage in Genesis chapter 1.

Tehowm also appears in both renderings. No storyteller worth their salt in grabbing people's attention would have overlooked such a golden nugget. In both story lines the message is communicated through the words *tehowm* and *ru'akh*.

The whole purpose of the Noah episode requires a reevaluation.

> And the Lord saw that the wickedness of man was great in the earth and that every imagination of the thoughts of his heart was only evil continually. (Gen. 6:5)

But for the wickedness of the heart of man, the earth would have been a Garden of Eden. Consider this setup as the audience would have listened to their favorite uncle spinning a yarn.

Genesis chapter 8 as a written text is an extremely confusing chapter. It does not make full sense in its out-of-context present form. There are two separate traditions embedded in this text. Both were once a part of two separate oral traditions.

In oral tradition, the imagery used by the skilled teller of tales would have reminded his audience of creation. Man was created in God's image. The earth was without tohuw, and the ru'akh of God hovered over the face of the deep. Contemplate that imagery in light of all previous very popular myths of creation. Tiamat and Apsu commingled their formless watery void. It is not hard to imagine where this story is heading. God was going to wipe out everything except the single righteous Noah. The irony, absurdity, and imagery are on full display.

The irony first! Listen to the mindset of God as man exits the boat and offers a sacrifice for his safe passage after the recent events:

> And the Lord smelled the sweet savour; and the Lord said in His heart: "I will not again curse the ground any more for man's sake; for the imagination of man's heart is evil from his youth; neither will I again smite any more every thing living, as I have done." (Gen. 8:21)

The very first thing God Himself points out after the flood is important to observe. Every imagination of the heart of man is continually evil. This begs the question, "Okay, then why the flood?" God surely possessed foreknowledge as to how this story would end. The power of relating the story orally facilitated the subcontext messaging.

The story line could not climax in the receding of the waters. The climax to the story was the response of God after it was all said and done. How do we know that the peak of the story was God's response? For that, we move from the irony of the conclusion to the absurdity in the story imagery.

The name for Noah we are told in the written tradition means rest/comfort.

Hebrew	*Pronunciation*	*English*
נֹחַ	nō'·akh	Noah
נָחַם	nacham	to be sorry/comfort/regret/ compassion
רִיחַ	ruakh	smelled (Gen. 8:1 translated *wind*)
נִיחֹחַ	nichowach	soothing

Noah's name is the key to the puzzle. It is derived from the Hebrew root *nôwach*,[46] consisting of the Hebrew letters *Nun*, *Vav*, and *Chet*. Noah built an altar to God and immediately offered a burnt offering. That sacrifice included one of at least one of every clean animal. At this point we see why Noah needed at least more than one set of animals in the story.

The imagery in the conclusion is vividly retold. All listeners are waiting for the story line to be nailed perfectly. The nuwach (Noah) and ruakh (wind) have been restated for drama. It is now a *nichowach*,[47] knitting together a tale for the evening. In short, it is humorously translated as a "sweet savor" (the odor of the burnt offering). Of course,

46. See *Strong's Concordance* with Hebrew and Greek Lexicon "H5117," accessed July 15, 2019, https://www.blueletterbible.org/lang/lexicon/lexicon.cfm?strongs=H5117&t=KJV.

47. וַיָּרַח יְהוָה, אֶת-רֵיחַ הַנִּיחֹחַ, וַיֹּאמֶר יְהוָה אֶל-לִבּוֹ לֹא-אֹסִף לְקַלֵּל עוֹד אֶת-הָאֲדָמָה בַּעֲבוּר הָאָדָם Translation: "And YHWH smelled the sweet savor." In this oral account, the derivation is a play on the words *wind* (twice) and *comfort* (nowach).

in Hebrew, the one who told the story created a drop the microphone moment. *Nichowach* comes from the very same root word as *Noah.*

There is now a sufficient story line created for the postmodern to consider the account of Noah as perhaps a competing creation account, or even a re-creation account. Genesis chapter 1 has particular commands within precise wording:

> And God said: "Let the waters swarm with swarms of living creatures, and let fowl fly above the earth in the open firmament of heaven." And God created the great sea-monsters, and every living creature that creepeth, wherewith the waters swarmed, after its kind, and every winged fowl after its kind; and God saw that it was good. And God blessed them, saying: "Be fruitful, and multiply, and fill the waters in the seas, and let fowl multiply in the earth." (Gen. 1:20–22)

Three Hebrew words are signal towers within the earlier Genesis passage: *sharats* (teem), *parah* (fruitful), and *rabah* (multiply). The context is an accounting of man. It is an explanation of why man is here. It answers the mail with respect to the questions that would have been asked. It created a moment wherein one could engage in purposeful pondering: why am I here on earth? The answer was to teem, be fruitful, and multiply. Generation upon generation added a variant twist to the same story. Brothers and sisters may have argued as to the proper ending of the story. That's how all family related traditions emerge. In a session one day, an innovator was likely questioned. "If we are created in God's image, why is it that my thoughts are not always pure? If I am an honest broker in this discussion, why is it that all my thoughts are continually impure?" This type of back and forth possibly required an alteration to the creation account. The same elements of Genesis 1 are contained in Genesis 8, with one slight twist in verse 8:21b. In this story, God promises never to smite any more "every" living thing. Yet in the oral tradition, the obvious is left unsaid: from time to time the presence of evil clearly smites segments of the creation.

Hebrew Word	*Pronunciation*	*English Word*
רֶמֶשׂ	reh'mes	creepeth
שָׁרַץ	shä'rats	swarm
פָּרָה	para	fruitful
רָבָה	rabah	multiply abundantly

> And God said, "Let the waters *swarm* (shä'rats) with swarms of living creatures. (Gen. 1:20a)

> And God blessed them, saying: "Be *fruitful* (para), and *multiply* (rabah), and fill the waters in the seas, and let fowl multiply in the earth. (Gen. 1:22)

> Bring forth with thee every living thing that is with thee of all flesh, both fowl, and cattle, and every *creeping* (rehmes) thing that creepeth upon the earth; that they may *swarm* (sha'rats) in the earth, and be *fruitful* (para), and *multiply* (rabah) upon the earth. (Gen. 8:17)

The story lines in Genesis 1 and 8 are identical. They connected with the resident population of Palestine in the fifth century BCE. There should be no doubt the relationship between Noah and the original Hebrew account of creation. Any child hearing the story would have related the connections. That is what makes this a part of the greatest story never told.

CHAPTER 5

AN ANALYSIS OF THE CHRONOLOGIES (TOLEDOT) IN THE BOOK OF GENESIS

It has happened over and over time and time again! What is that? A person in good faith makes the decision to read the Bible from the beginning to the end only to get mired down in the sections of chronologies. The chronologies are the seemingly benign records of individuals who were born, lived, begat children on their own, and then died. As we read them, it is common to experience a high degree of boredom. Looming over us like a shadow hangs guilt because we tell ourselves that we should enjoy reading the Bible no matter what section or chapter it is.

I have found the chronologies to be interesting. So it is necessary to come to terms with the role of *toledots* in the Bible. Revealing the value of toledots allows a clear window into their overall purpose in the oral tradition. Toledots had several functions. The Toledots served as an introduction to either the main story of the teaching or another story line altogether. The key to reading a chronology in the Bible is to focus on the story line, not the genealogy. That is very easy to do when you reorient your thought as to the purpose of a chronology. The word *toledot* is derived from the verb *ya'lad (to give birth)*. Let's face it, do we really care if Shem begat Arphaxad. Neither of those two figures stood out as men either of admiration or scorn. We look to the Bible for spiritual guidance. In that quest for guidance, the chronologies have something to offer!

The toledots are listings of chronologies and at face value appear to play a secondary role of identifying names. Our task is to cull moral lessons from the Bible. The chronologies assist in identifying and fulfilling that intent. There are ten lists of chronologies in the book of Genesis. Each of them serves to support a story line.

Bible Verse	Subject	Story Line
Genesis 2:4	History of the heavens and earth	The text does not provide a history; it serves as an introduction to another story, the creation story of man.
Genesis 5:1	Book of the generations of Adam	It provides an emphasis on the story line reminding the reader that God created man in his own *likeness*, and man thereafter begat men after his own likeness.,דְּמוּת pronounced "dem·ûth," translated as "likeness." The culmination of the toledot ends with the birth of Noah and his sons.
Genesis 6:9	These are the generations of Noah	A very short toledot that records Noah as the father of three sons. The context of this *towlĕdah* was that the earth had become corrupted.
Genesis 10:1	These are the generations of the sons of Noah	A divided earth

Genesis 11:10: Genesis 11:27:	These are the generations of Shem These are the generations of Terah	Precursor story(ies) mirroring the elevation of the mishpacha over the state. Beginning with Shem, the eldest son of Noah, they find their fulfillment in the conclusion of the Sumerian founder (Abram) of the faith of the nation of Israel.
Genesis 25:12: Genesis 25:19	These are the generations of Ishmael These are the generations of Isaac	Emergence of Isaac as the claimant heir of Abraham
Genesis 36:1	These are the generations of Esau	Polemic against nations understood to have a
Genesis 37:2	These are the generations of Jacob	An introduction to Jacob's son Joseph

Towlĕdah of Genesis 2:4

> This is a history of the heavens and the earth when they were created, in the day that the Lord God made the earth and the heavens. (Gen. 2:4)

There is an unusualness about this Bible passage. As we remind ourselves that the word *towlĕdah* is rooted in the verb *ya'lad* (to give birth), we immediately take note that no births or generations are listed. Usage of this word first occurs outside that context in the oral tradition. In short, the word *towlĕdah* is translated as the word "history" in both the King James and New King James translation. In neither case does the word mean history at all. If the word was intended by the author to mean history, one would rightly expect a history of the earth and also a history of the heavens. That element is absent.

What is present? What can aid our understanding of this passage? The next verse provides guidance. There was no man to provide labor on the earth. That was the context of Genesis chapter 2 verses 5, 6, and 7. The *towlĕdah* did not serve as either a chronology or history, but rather an introduction to the creation story of man. This was not a history of the heavens and earth. This was an introduction to another story line altogether. God formed man. God provided the very breath of life. He then placed him eastward in a garden. That garden was the cradle of civilization, Shinar (Sumer).

***Towlĕdah* of Genesis 5:1**

Advancing forward in our reading, we next come to the *towlĕdah* of Adam. This *towlĕdah* has a specific ending: the birth of Noah. Focus in very practical terms what this would have sounded like if you were thirteen years old and listening to the story at a mishpacha/family festive dinner. What would this chronology have sounded like? Would a child listening to the tradition remember over the course of their life that Jared had a son named Enoch at the age of sixty-two? Likely not!

This is the book of the generations of Adam. (Gen. 5:1)

The *towlĕdah* provides the form of a chronology, but at this point, any similarities cease. The emphasis of the story line sets the course of the tradition. Adam was created in the דְּמוּת *dem*·üth' likeness of God, and accordingly, Adam begat sons in his likeness.

Hebrew Word	*Pronunciation*	*Translation*
דְּמוּת	dem·üth'	likeness

The author in the story was explicit in his intention to supplement his thoughts with the impartial inclusion of all mankind in the creation of man. This creation was formed in the likeness of God.

> In the day that God created man, he made him in the likeness of God (דְּמוּת dem·üth'). He created them male and female, and blessed them and called them Mankind in the day they were created. And Adam lived one hundred and thirty years, and begat a son in his own likeness (דְּמוּת dem·üth'), after his image and named him Seth. (Gen. 5:1b–3)

Seth, in this instance, was more than just a name for a boy. *Seth* is derived from the Hebrew root word with a specific definition to appoint, fix, constitute, or make something like something else. It has many similar meanings, but in the oral tradition, the most obvious meaning would have combined two separate words within the story to define the story line.

Hebrew Word	*Pronunciation*	*Translation*
דְּמוּת	dem·üth'	likeness.
שֵׁית	shēth	Seth (contextually meant make something like something else)

Knowing this now it is easy to imagine the resulting line of inquiry after this story was unveiled. The author could not have intended a chronology or genealogy unless of course, the intention was with an informed comedic purpose. Very likely the adults hearing the story would have groaned with a short belly laugh at the name of Seth combined in usage with *dem·üth'*.

This *towlĕdah* begins with Adam and ends with the name of a man who will provide comfort: Noah. Comfort was the purpose assigned by God to Noah's life. Through the hand of a special man, reconciliation and comfort would be achieved. Yet in Noah's eventual story line, that specific comfort one could argue was never experienced. Instead, a radical destruction of the earth took place. One is left to ponder "comfort" in their own experience with their Creator.

Obviously the *towlĕdah* was neither a chronology nor a history. The *towlĕdah* of Genesis 5:1 reminded us that Adam, the son he made in his likeness, along with all of mankind, contained a likeness of their Creator.

Towlĕdah of Genesis 6:9

> These are the generations of Noah: Noah was a just man and perfect in his generations, and Noah walked with God. (Gen. 6:9)

It is important to review the events prior to and immediately after this *towlĕdah.* God decided that he had enough of the wickedness of man. Determined to obliterate not only man but also all the cattle and beasts of the field from the face of the earth, a veiled story line emerges. Yet this story line was explicitly part of all ancient Semitic cultures. This was a serious state of affairs. In such a climate, it would make absolutely no sense to record a chronology of any man, let alone the only one who would survive the oncoming flood.

So how do we make this an entertaining story suitable for after-dinner enjoyment? Our experience in life allows us to enjoy moments that include dark tales. The genre of dark tales has its own unique counterculture appeal. In this environment, the *towlĕdah* exposes such a climate. We will focus not on the three sons of Noah: Shem, Ham, and Japeth. Instead, we venture into a crawl space filled with destruction, ruin, and decay.

Hebrew Word	*Pronunciation*	*Translated*
שָׁחַת	shä·khath'	destroy/cause ruin/ decay

Immediately after the identification of Noah's three sons, the intent of the *towlĕdah* is illuminated:

> The earth also was *corrupt* (שָׁחַתshä·khath') before God, and the earth was filled with violence. And God looked upon the earth, and, behold, it was *corrupt* (שָׁחַת

> shä·khath'); for all flesh had *corrupted* (שָׁחַת shä·khath') his way upon the earth. (Gen. 6:11–12)

The predicament of the earth and all men uniquely identified the condition of *שָׁחַת shä·khath.'* If the earth was *שָׁחַת shä·khath'*, and man, in general, was also was *שָׁחַת shä·khath'*, then it was only logical within the oral tradition that God must perform an action involving *שָׁחַת shä·khath'* (destruction).

The great flood was a ruinous onslaught of rain. It was the first record of rain in the Bible. Therefore, it has led some to conclude it was the first in history. Is the rain the point of the story? Or perhaps is the flood an incidental secondary point of the Great Flood of the Bible? I would suggest that the Bible really teaches us that the flood was not the point at all. The flood became the focal point in the written tradition. In the oral tradition, *שָׁחַת shä·khath* was the focal point. The flood was merely the instrument.

Men scour ancient archeological records in vain seeking confirmation of a flood. In that quest, they attempt to demonstrate a proof of the text and in so doing fail to ask the most logical questions arising under the story in the oral tradition. You can almost see the stunned expressions as family members carefully recline in their chairs in an ancient setting. The moral of the story has been uncovered. God does nothing more to us than we do to ourselves!

We ascribe natural disasters as a result of *force majeure. Force majeure* is a phrase that points to a "superior" force and is often used within the story line of a natural disaster coined as an "act of God." Naturally occurring events are as God intended. Force majeure events are unavoidable. This message within oral tradition was obvious. The flood was nothing more than a continuation of an existing condition.

> And God said unto Noah, The end of all flesh is come before me; for the earth is filled with violence through them; and, behold, I will *destroy* (שָׁחַת shä·khath') them with the earth. (Gen. 6:13)

Firestorm conversations were ignited among families. The justice of God was examined under the microscope of life. Actions of God (*force majeure*) were identified as unavoidable and were defined as שָׁחַת shä·khath'. Irony in this dilemma was resolved since the ultimate action equaled the offense, which was also equal to the weight of the remedy. Concluding with our third *towlĕdah*, it is more than clear that the story had nothing to do with either chronology or the relation of a historical event. It taught a moral lesson both about the nature of man, the actions of man, the nature of God, and those force majeure actions of God.

Towlĕdah of Genesis 10:1–32

This *towlĕdah* is often referred to as the Table of Nations. The list is deceptive because it records seventy nations. These nations presumably are the descendants of Noah after the flood. The corollary between Adam and Noah and other sections of the Torah are astounding. Both Adam and Noah have three sons. Seventy Israelites migrated from Canaan into Egypt at the conclusion of the book of Genesis. Seventy leaders of the Israelites ascend Mt. Sinai with Moses at an important point in the formation of God's covenant revelation. Ironically, tradition also ascribed that the infamous goddess Ashera was the mother of seventy demigods. That was an important point in refocusing the Israelite nation toward monotheism.

Exploring the unique stories in the towlĕdah is an easier process when broken down one by one. The Torah teaches. Again we ask: what moral lessons does the Torah teach? Answering that question begins after discovering the clues embedded into the story line.

> Now these are the generations of the sons of Noah, Shem, Ham, and Japheth: and unto them were sons born after the flood…These are the families of the sons of Noah, after their generations, in their nations: and by these were the nations divided in the earth after the flood. (Gen. 10:1 and 10:32)

Our modern society is not much different from the past. There is a yearning expectation in our present society that contradicts the sum of human history. To what extent does man live in perfect harmony among his own nation? To what extent do countries live in harmony as neighbors? Is it an artificial expectation that society should live in harmony? Or does the Torah teach us that a fractured society is a reality from which we operate? In the current American political/social divide, the common stated objective seeks to restore fractures between relationships. Our question for discussion therefore is: what is the most logical way to address a political environment where everybody is divided one against another? That was the problem that the author of Genesis chapter 10 had to address. By viewing the text as a comment, instead of history, we perceive different starting points and different outcomes. It is easy to surmise that the current theme in our political life is completely rooted in the realities of the past.

Nimrod, the great powerful Sumerian king, was a man of great fame. It is speculated that perhaps he was the great Sargon. Others have concluded that Nimrod was a composite description of the demigod Ninurta. What is the exact point of this chronology? The intent could only have been to separately locate great civilizations within nations of the past and tie them together with the present. This was an embracement of the cultural past with their forefathers.

> And the beginning of his [Nimrod's] kingdom was Babel, and Erech, and Accad, and Calneh, in the land of Shinar [Sumer], [and] out of that land went forth Asshur, and builded Nineveh, and the city Rehoboth, and Calah. (Gen. 10:10)

The author was careful and targeted the distant Mesopotamian past from Shinar. But for the next-door neighbor, Egypt, the text and story become less entangled. The reason for these lesser entanglements is clear, and one needs no elaborate explanation to that which was already known. The Egyptian and Philistine people were already known to the local audience.

> And Mizraim [Mizraim was the formal name for Egypt] begat Ludim, and Anamim, and Lehabim, and Naphtuhim,And Pathrusim, and Casluhim, (out of whom came Philistim,) and Caphtorim. (Gen. 10:13–14)

The Torah leads us into a strong, robust discussion. There are some mysteries that need to be discussed. The chronologies and stories left the audience with many unanswered questions. For example, in the previous chapter of Genesis 9, the hero of the flood becomes very unheroic.

> And Noah the husbandman began, and planted a vineyard. And he drank of the wine, and was drunken; and he was uncovered within his tent. And Ham, the father of Canaan, saw the nakedness of his father, and told his two brethren without. And Shem and Japheth took a garment, and laid it upon both their shoulders, and went backward, and covered the nakedness of their father; and their faces were backward, and they saw not their father's nakedness. And Noah awoke from his wine, and knew what his youngest son had done unto him. And he said: Cursed be Canaan; a servant of servants shall he be unto his brethren. And he said: Blessed be the LORD, the God of Shem; and let Canaan be their servant. (Gen. 9:20–26)

Both the placement location and the content of a *towlĕdah* was intentional. The editors wanted to solicit questions as if the conversations would take place. Questions such as, Why did Grandpa Noah curse Canaan for the actions that his father Ham engaged in? The point of oral tradition was to promote discussions, not provide doctrine. Ham noticed that dad was lying drunk naked in the tent. He suggested that his two older brothers cover him up. We are not exactly certain why this action taken by his son irritated Noah. One could plausibly argue dad would have thanked his son's for their discretion. However, the teaching point of the special directed curse is never discussed. It is assumed, and that assumption is not evident today. Nonetheless, a curse was given. Should the reader be bothered by this? If the curse was even justified, why was the curse leveled against his grandson? Why Canaan, instead of the interloping son, Ham?

The condition becomes all the more apparent when we learn about exactly who the sons of Canaan were.

> And Canaan begat Sidon his first born, and Heth, and the Jebusite, and the Amorite, and the Girgasite, and the Hivite, and the Arkite, and the Sinite, and the Arvadite, and the Zemarite, and the Hamathite: and afterward were the families of the Canaanites spread abroad. And the border of the Canaanites was from Sidon, as thou comest to Gerar, unto Gaza; as thou goest, unto Sodom, and Gomorrah, and Admah, and Zeboim, even unto Lasha. (Gen. 10:15–19)

The chronology relates the fact that the Canaanites controlled Palestine. Extended control encompassed the land from Gerar unto Gaza on the southwestern coast unto Sodom and Gomorrah in the southeast. Beginning with Sidon in the north, the control dominated the land unto the Negev desert and Egypt in the south. The *towlĕdah*, viz chronology, located nations within the proximate geographic point. This point is definitely reinforced by the specific marker location of the Philistine strongholds of Gerar and Gaza. The point of the chronology was not to communicate history or bloodlines. Instead, the message was communicated that the earth possessed a divided population both before and after the great flood event.

Towlĕdah (s) of Genesis 11:10–32

The towlĕdah (s) preserved in this tradition technically comprises two traditions that segue and complement each other. Beginning with Shem, the eldest son of Noah, they find their fulfillment in the conclusion of the Sumerian founder of faith, Abram. The eleventh chapter of Genesis is perhaps one of the most confusing in the Torah since the oral tradition absolutely relies upon the prevailing cultural story line.

The *towlĕdah* ends with Terah leaving Ur with his two sons Abram and Nahor and his grandson Lot. They were migrating to Haran in modern-day Turkey. He originally purposed to relocate to Canaan. The Torah never explains why such a move perhaps was necessitated. The Torah never fully explains why after setting out for Canaan, Terah abandons that move in favor of relocating in Haran. The Torah provides vague obscure references that are more evident when the intent within the oral tradition is engaged rather than an analysis of the evolved textual tradition.

The precursor story identified in the chronologies listed in the *towlĕdah* of the eleventh chapter of Genesis indeed answers those questions. The Tower of Babel story introduces the heroic figure of Abram. But why?

The ancient text "Enmerkar and the Lord of Aratta" preserves for our generation a tale known throughout the ancient Near East in the fifth century BCE. The story outlined the drumbeat of war between Enmekar king of Uruk (Uruk is the city of the heroic Gilgamesh, located in modern-day Iraq) and the king of Arrata (likely modern-day Iran).

Enmerkar sought to build a majestic temple to the god Enki (Ea) through tribute (tax revenue) acquired by force if necessary from the land of Aratta.

> Let the people of Arrata bring down from the mountain stones from their mountain, build the great shrine for me, erect the great abode for me, make the great abode, the abode of the gods, famous for me, make me prosper in Kulaba [Erech/city of Sumeria], make the abzu [the fresh groundwater aquifer under the city was known for sexual fertilizing power] grow for me like a holy mountain, make Eridug gleam for me like a mountain range, cause the abzu shrine to shine forth for me like the silver in the lode.[48]

48. "Enmerkar and the Lord of Aratta," accessed September 5, 2019, http://etcsl.orinst.ox.ac.uk/section1/tr1823.htm.

The king of Arrata obviously objected to a condition placing him in subservience to another king. It is likely that the feeling of an eventual war dominated the social economic, political, and military climate for at least a decade or more. Messengers and ambassadors representing both cities were sent back and forth negotiating for the kings. They would relate how their position would benefit the gods. Of most interest in this related epic are two tandem historical markers: common speech and the introduction of clay tablet (cuneiform) writings.

The entire purpose of the epic is thus related:

> At such a time, may the lands of Cubur and Hamazi, the many tongued, and Sumer, the great mountain of the *me* [a 'me' is a related decree from a pantheistic deity] of magnificence, and Akkad, the land possessing all that is befitting, and the Martu land, resting in security—the whole universe, the well guarded people— may they all address Enlil together in a single language![49]

Constructing the temple facilitated the worship of Enlil in a common single unified language. Comparing that objective to the account recorded in the book of Genesis, the parallel similarities are astounding.

> And the whole earth was of one language, and of one speech. And it came to pass, as they journeyed from the east, that they found a plain in the land of Shinar [Sumer]; and they dwelt there. And they said one to another, Go to, let us make brick, and burn them thoroughly. And they had brick for stone, and slime had they for mortar. And they said, Go to, let us build us a city and a tower, whose top may reach unto heaven; and let us make us a name, lest we be scattered abroad upon the face of the whole earth. And the Lord came down to see the city and the tower, which the children of men built. And the Lord said, Behold, the people is

---

49. Ibid.

> one, and they have all one language; and this they begin to do: and now nothing will be restrained from them, which they have imagined to do. Go to, let us go down, and there confound their language, that they may not understand one another's speech. So the Lord scattered them abroad from thence upon the face of all the earth: and they left off to build the city. Therefore is the name of it called Babel; because the Lord did there confound the language of all the earth: and from thence did the Lord scatter them abroad upon the face of all the earth. (Gen. 11:1–9)

The eleventh chapter of Genesis now is at the very least a little more understandable and less obtuse. The author intended the requisite understanding of the Sumerian culture known in Palestine at the time of the writing. Those stories were told alongside the episodes and stories that eventually matriculated into the Torah. After the flood, the author specifically noted that the events took place in Sumer. The text of "Enmerkar and the Lord of Aratta" was known at the writing of the Torah. Both must be considered to understand the main point proposed by the Torah.

Before we can come to any established conclusion concerning the role of this specific *towlĕdah*, there is one other avenue that must be explored: the origin of writing! The epic suggests that discussion of Arrata's submission to the Enmerkar occurred over quite a few years. This required many trips by staff members of both sides going back and forth. The similitude of the messages did not significantly change. To move negotiations along, messaging introduced a technological breakthrough: writing. The invention of writing allowed for lesser rank representatives of the state to more efficiently be utilized at lower risk and cost.

The postmodern mind perhaps would gloss over that invention not fully considering its importance in the fate of these discussions in particular and within history in general. When Enmerkar delivered to the king of Arrata a message in writing, he was demonstrating the superiority of his ruling domain. It sent subtle messages regarding their inferior position. The development of writing in this instance was attributed to the seemingly endless verbal discussions. It moved negotiations along.

> His speech was substantial, and its contents extensive. The messenger, whose mouth was heavy, was not able to repeat it. Because the messenger, whose mouth was tired, was not able to repeat it, the lord of Kubala patted some clay and wrote the message as if on a tablet. Formerly, the writing of messages on clay was not established.[50]

The initial reaction by the king of Arrata to the transmission of a written message was recorded:

> The lord of Arrata received his kiln-fired tablet from the messenger. The lord of Arrata looked at the tablet. The transmitted message was just nails, and his brow expressed anger.

The response was just what one would have expected. Enmerkar attempted to show how smart he was by transmitting a written message from the newly developed methods in Mesopotamia. He was attempting to demonstrate their cultural and religious superiority over the backwoods king from the mountainous north. The king of Arrata despised the new technology because it appeared in his view to be "just nails." The king knew one thing: tablets carried no sword, but his militia was prepared to defend their territory and natural resources. His territory was equally prepared to defend the honor of their own way of life and city.

> At that moment, the lord worthy of the crown of lordship, the son of Enlil, the god Ickur, thundering in heaven and earth, caused a raging storm a great lion…He was making the mountains quake…he was convulsing the

---

50. "Enmerkar and the Lord of Aratta," accessed September 5, 2019, http://etcsl.orinst.ox.ac.uk/section1/tr1823.htm.

> mountain range...the awesome radiance...of his breast,
> he caused the mountain range to raise its voice in joy.[51]

We now have more context to understand the Tower of Babel episode. It now makes more sense in its relation to the Sumerian migration from the Mesopotamian region. Migrants were seeking to avoid becoming a casualty of war. But the story is recast in a Palestine version. Babel is introduced. The inhabitants were dispersed throughout the whole world. We now understand a plausible scenario why Terah would have wanted to leave Ur. The elements of mystery in the Bible can be explained in very reasonable terms. Just how did the Lord God disperse man? The armed conflict, or at least the potential for armed conflict, greatly disrupted the harmony of the civilization. It is no surprise to the postmodern to learn that the threat of war arose over the establishment of a religious shrine. The phenomenon of an unsettled society was attributed to the active interaction by God. Emerging out of that migration stood Abram, the father of many nations.

Our goal has been to establish that the chronology of the *towlĕdah* listed in the eleventh chapter of Genesis had a purpose other than the relation of a genealogical record. That is extremely clear when identified within the context of the oral tradition. It is essential to point out that it is not possible, nor does the Torah support a time line allowing for the first nine verses of Genesis chapter 11 to take place before the chronology listed in verses 10 through 32. In fact, just the opposite presumption must be made.

> Therefore its name is called Babel, because there the Lord confused the language of all the earth; and from there the Lord scattered them abroad over the face of the earth. (Gen. 11:9)

One easily concludes that chiaistic Hebrew writing forms require verse 9 and verse 32 to be considered within the same tandem timeline. In this case, Abram does not leave Ur 1800 BCE but instead over two thousand to three thousand years earlier than previously considered.

---

51. Ibid.

> And Terah took Abram his son, and Lot the son of Haran, his son's son, and Sarai his daughter in law, his son Abram's wife; and they went forth with them from Ur of the Chaldees, to go into the land of Canaan; and they came unto Haran, and dwelt there. (Gen. 11:32)

This specific *towlĕdah* allows us to conclude that it did not serve as a recorded chronological record. It supplemented an existing story line of the Torah. It rejected the premise that the egg came before the chicken. It promotes that rejection by identifying the founder of its religion as a Sumerian dedicated to YHWH, not Enlil. That message indeed elevates the boring chronologies to a substantial element that should excite our reading of the Bible based on its oral tradition.

Towlĕdah of Genesis 25:12

I have a couple of favorite episodes in the Torah. Cynicism and respect are two differing emotional thoughts I often exercise while reading the *towlĕdah*. Respect, however, guides this process of interpretive reading. Modern readings of the *towlĕdah* are often misguided adventures because the reader looks for genealogical connections. Reading the twenty-fifth chapter of Genesis as a reliable chronology is especially tempting because it contains all the flavor of a source document record. It however lacks the ability to be verified. It also produces a story line in contradiction to the reality of the day. That is exactly how faith is born. Faith is itself an element of evidence. This illustration becomes especially apparent in the most often overlooked miracle of Genesis.

Virility is a subplot as Abraham produces no less than six additional children after the birth of Isaac. We use the term "no less than" because the text indicates there were untold numbers. At a minimum, this would have taken at least seven complete years. Let's also be clear, Abraham was no spring rooster. The names of the children born are listed as Zimran, Jokshan, Medan, Midian, Ishbak, and Shuah. Jokshan and Midian are further singled out as fathering grandchildren to Abraham. That would have taken many more additional years untold in verse 6 of the chapter, it is also noted that Abraham had additional extramarital children not identified by name, but indeed family children that received gifts before sending them eastward, presumably toward the Mesopotamian plain.

Our goal in this segment is to demonstrate that the lists of births identified in this chapter perform a function other than recording a reliable record of births. The function of recording chronology is secondary to its main objective of supporting a story. Reviews of written genealogies are informed along two lines: (1) linear lists that impart knowledge of descendants and (2) segmented lists that serve in a more functional role to define ethnicity.[52] In short, linear lists impart knowledge of descendants while segmented lists serve in a more functional role to provide clarity to the story. We are interested in how a person heard the story (i.e., its functional role of support).

In the previous twenty-fourth chapter of Genesis, we observe a weakened Abraham. One not able to rise from his bed.

> And Abraham was old, well stricken in age; and the LORD had blessed Abraham in all things. And Abraham said unto his servant, the elder of his house, that ruled over all that he had: "Put, I pray thee, thy hand under my thigh." (Gen. 24:1–2).

As a hospice patient, he calls his servant to his bedside. Sworn to service, the chief eldest servant of Abraham personally journeys to the mishpacha of Abraham's brother. He was on a mission to secure a suitable wife to carry on the family seed. Confirming the oath, he placed his hand under Abraham's aging thigh. This was the very thigh from which the seed of Isaac originated.

One's mind immediately urges the servant to get on the road and return before poor old Abraham passes away. The unthinkable remains unrecorded. It becomes almost anticlimatic in scope. In the twenty-fifth chapter, Abraham experiences a dramatic recovery. What led to Abraham's apparent recovery? In the previous chapter, Abraham appears to be dying from his old age. Aging has a fatal effect on people. The chapter starts off with the most flavored prognosis. Abraham was

52. Yigal Levin, "Understanding Biblical Genealogies," *Currents in Biblical Research* BS9 (2001): 11–46.

old. Abraham was suffering from being old. Abraham revised his last will and testament. Abraham was dying, and he knew it. He had to provide for his son before it was too late.

> And Abraham gave all that he had unto Isaac. (Gen. 25:5)

Our protagonist recovers and takes another wife and fathers more children. The recovery was so successful he had even more uncounted numbers of children by concubines (plural). The primacy of Isaac had to be communicated in light of the multiple sons born to Abraham. We were introduced to Abraham's original designated heir, Eliezer of Damascus, in Genesis 15:2. This introduction is brought to us in the form of oral kvetching familiar to ancient Semitic thought processes. No additional information is revealed about Eliezer. Eliezer's adoption as an heir was not unusual for men lacking children from natural childbirth.

This kvetching was familiar and is presented as an unprompted response. We are never sure why this issue comes to the prominent role it assumes, except perhaps Abram had been mulling it over for quite some time. His experience was certainly not lining up with his expectations of what the divine was supposed to do for him.

> After these things the word of the Lord came to Abram in a vision saying: "Do not be afraid Abram I am your shield your exceeding great reward." (Gen.15:1)

Hebrew Word	*Pronunciation*	*Translation*
מָגֵן	mä·gān'	shield (figuratively the one who protects)

Gratitude would be a normal response from a pious soul upon learning he was the recipient of divine protection. Gracious gratitude over and above a normal sense of gratitude would also not surprise any reader. Instead of providing humble thanks to God, Abram kvetches that he has no heir.

> And Abram said: "O Lord God, what wilt Thou give me, seeing I go hence childless, and he that shall be possessor of my house is Eliezer of Damascus?" And Abram said: "Behold, to me Thou hast given no seed, and, lo, one born in my house is to be mine heir." (Gen. 15:2–3)

The complaint serves as an opening for a broader family discussion. Surely over time, in the intimate setting of the mishpacha, someone pointed out the obvious: what the heck happened to Eliezar? Why was Ishmael not given the favor of being the firstborn?

This was no small or insignificant point to establish. In time, Abram would come to have many potential heirs. So which heir gets the golden egg? How do we justify the Abram heir game of *Survivor*? Will the last person voted off the island be Eliezer? Or Ishmael? Or Isaac? Or Zimran? Or Jokshan? Or Medan? Or Midian? Or Ishbak? Or Shuah? Perhaps one of the children of Abram's many concubines would step up within the mishpacha to take over. This dilemma was created by the promise of God to be the father of many nations! The seemingly mundane chronology of Genesis chapter 25 answers that complicated problem in the oral tradition.

> Then Abraham breathed his last and died in a good old age, an old man full of years and was gathered unto his people. (Gen. 25:8)

In this episode that both Isaac and Ishmael bury Abraham. One must conclude that perhaps Eliezer was standing alongside the grave with tears in his eyes dreaming of what could have been. No mention at the funeral is made of Zimran, Jokshan, Medan, Midian, Ishbak, or Shuah. As the eldest uncle, Ishmael would have retained control of the mishpacha. However, the record indicates Isaac dwelt at Beer Lahai Roi, the family homestead.

More directly, the tradition is slanted in Isaac's favor when it is noted within the same context of the death of Abraham the following:

> These were the years of the life of Ishmael: one hundred and thirty-seven years. And he breathed his last and died and was gathered to his people. (Gen. 25:17).

The story line of the chronology was not established to record facts, but instead, explain why Isaac remained in charge. If this were a chronology to record lineage, then it also would have recorded the death of Isaac. That could not have happened. The chronology needed to relegate potential claims. We know that must have been the case because Abram promoted the status of Ishmael's mother from that of a mere slave handmaid to Sarai to that of a full-fledged wife.

> Then Sarai, Abram's *wife (אִשָּׁה 'ishshah/wife)*, took Hagar her *maid (שִׁפְחָה shiphchah/slave maid)*, the Egyptian, and gave her to her husband *(אִישׁ ish/husband)* Abram to be his wife *(אִשָּׁה 'ishshah/wife)*, after Abram had dwelt ten years in the land of Canaan. (Gen. 16:3)

Hebrew Word	*Pronunciation*	*Translation*
שִׁפְחָה	shiphchah	maid servant / slave (female)
אִשָּׁה	'ishshah	wife
אִישׁ	ish	husband
פִּילֶגֶשׁ	piylegesh	concubine

The promise of an heir to replace Eliezer was given ten years earlier. The slave attendant Hagar was given to Abram. Sarah gave birth to Isaac later at the age of ninety. The heir apparent at that point in time was Ishmael. For fourteen years, Ishmael carried the mantle of the firstborn.

Before this pregnancy, Sarah demonstrated an inability to bear children. She was barren. Yet Abram, at the age of seventy-five, was able to convince Sarai that they needed to have a baby. A command from God drove Abram's argument to at least attempt to have a baby. Most guys at this juncture would favor such a command. Sarai's response was one of laughter. Isaac's name was derived from the unfettered response of both parents. They laughed at the idea they would physically have a baby. But Abram seemingly never laughed during the ten years he attempted to have one.

Abram tried and tried and tried and tried. For ten years, Sarai, at sixty-five, accommodated the sexual requests of Abram to attempt reproduction. After ten years, one almost begins to sympathize with Sarai. Sarai left the tent one particular morning. The sheer exhaustion must have overwhelmed her. She concocted a scheme to find some personal relief in this exercise in futility. She pondered about the viability of introducing Abraham to her young slave. Clearly, Sarah had better things to do at night. Maybe in her heart of hearts, she privately considered the humiliation Abraham would experience if Hagar was unable to produce a child for him. Perhaps she must at least have understood it would still be a 50/50 proposition that a male child would be produced. Musing over her options, she sent the old man into the arms of the young girl. A clever device, and even a more clever plan, the young girl was an Egyptian.

Sarai considered herself too old to have a baby. After years of feeble attempts, she considered Abram too old to father a baby. Her plan was dangerously passive and deceptive. Sarai knew Abram could not keep up or satisfy the young *Egyptian.* All Sarai had to do was create an environment where the old man would be shamed for all the world to see. He could not father a child even with a young Egyptian slave.

That was the story line identified behind the text in the oral tradition of the chronology. How should we account for all the various claimants to the position of eldest *Dor* within the leadership of a highly successful wealthy mishpacha?

In this episode, Abraham died, Ishmael died, and all other stepbrothers were sent away.

> And Abraham gave all that he had to Isaac. But Abraham gave gifts to the sons of the concubines which Abraham had, and while he was still living he sent them eastward, away from Isaac, his son, to the country of the east [Sumer]. (Gen. 25:5–6)

The chronology fulfilled all the elements of what we do know about the role of toledots. They reflected the standing and rights of Isaac. It performed a telescoping function by singling out Isaac at the expense of other claims. It performed a role explaining the diffusion of other mishpacha(s) into other geographic regions. It recorded the complexity of ancient tribal migrations and customs. In short, it elevates the mundane to perhaps one of the most powerful stories in the biblical record of redemption.

Johnny Cash recorded a song entitled "A Boy Named Sue." Perhaps the punch line bears a striking resemblance to the original boy named Laughter.

> I got all choked up and I threw down my gun
> Called him my Pa, and he called me his son
> And I come away with a different point of view
> And I think about him, now and then
> Every time I try and every time I win
> And if I ever have a son, I think I'm gonna name him
> Bill or George! Anything but Sue! I still hate that name!
> Yeah.[53]

Isaac probably was teased as a young child by his peers. That name meant something. It had a meaning of derisive laughter. The English translation does not serve it well. Which begs the question, Why would a boy named Sue (laughter), then in turn, give his son the name Jacob (יַעֲקֹב) to supplant, circumvent; and not in a good way? The saga of Isaac, with such a beginning, allows for more stories in the oral tradition.

Towlĕdah of Genesis 36:1

Of all the *towlĕdah* listed in the book of Genesis, this particular account should receive significant attention. The spotlight in this instance needs to be preoccupied upon one of the daughters of Seir. Seir

---

53. Johnny Cash, "A Boy Named Sue" lyrics, accessed September 7, 2019, https://www.google.com/search?q=the+boy+named+su&oq=the+boy+named+su&aqs=chrome..69i57.4896j0j7&sourceid=chrome&ie=UTF-8.

was a Horite power figure that controlled what later became the country of Edom. Jewish Midrash provides some background to understand the complexity of this chapter. Twice the figure of Timna is named. We must ask; why was Timna such an elevated curious figure among rabbinic studies? Why would the author of Torah bother with such a woman? How could the Torah teach us anything of value about Timna? To answer that, let's first rediscover the title(s) and role(s) of women in the ancient Semitic cultures.

Women working alongside their mate in the Biblical texts normally took on one of the following titles:

Hebrew Word	*Pronunciation*	*Translation*
שִׁפְחָה	shiphchah	maidservant/slave (female)
אִשָּׁה	'ishshah	wife
אִישׁ	ish	husband
פִּילֶגֶשׁ	pilegesh	concubine
אָמָה	aw-maw'	female slave, handmaid, concubine

Concentrating within the oral tradition, it must be emphasized again how words would have sounded to the audience. The forcefulness of a pronunciation added emphasis to its context. The color of a word also added to its dimensional context. In Palestine, both the Hebrew and Aramaic languages allowed for various representations of the role of a wife. Usage of a foreign word intermixed within a story presented in Hebrew would have struck a deep chord in the audience. Timna was identified in the tradition as a concubine (פִּילֶגֶשׁ concubine). The story could have used an equivalent Hebrew word אָמָה aw-maw' but the desired effect to hate Timna would have been diminished.

> Now Timna was the *concubine* פִּילֶגֶשׁ (pilegesh) of Eliphaz, Esau's son and she bore Amalek to Eliphaz. (Gen. 36:12)

Identifying Timna as a פִּילֶגֶשׁ concubine was a purposeful marker because the author intentionally wanted the audience to hate her. This term was based on the low debased word of Greek origin.[54] Timna was the mother of Amalek of whom an additional special command resides in the Torah:

> Therefore it shall be, when the Lord thy God hath given thee rest from all thine enemies round about, in the land which the Lord thy God giveth thee for an inheritance to possess it, that thou shalt blot out the remembrance of Amalek from under heaven; thou shalt not forget it. (Deut. 25:19)

Antagonism dominated the history of relations between the offspring of Abraham's descendents. One such descendant became the evil figure identified in the biblical book of Esther. Serving the Persian King Ahasuerus (Xerxes 1) as a high-level interior political minister (circa 450 BCE), Haman devised a plan to kill all Jews living in the Persian Empire. Haman was an Amalekite. He generated such hatred that synagogues the world over remind themselves of his evil plan annually. Once a year the book of Esther is publicly read in an open service. When the hated name of Haman the Amalekite is read, the congregation must employ the noisy *graggers. Graggers* are a little toylike instrument that produces loud, violent noise. Haman sought to blot out the Jews. However, it is his name that has been blotted out for all eternity.

Timna should catch our eye because she is named four times in the ancient Hebrew Tanakh. Twice she is named in the Torah. Two times she is named in the opening chapter of the first book of Chronicles.

The Toledots as Purposeful Markers

The *towlĕdah* provides other purposeful markers. The editor of this passage borrowed from several sources to create an imposing narrative.

---

54. Gosta W. Ahlstrom, *The History of Ancient Palestine* (Minnesota: Fortress Press), 323–324. Ahlmstrom notes the origin of the word.

At least two sets of doublets are accessed culminating in a bookend narrative climax.

Our *towlĕdah* turns toward Esau, the firstborn son of Isaac. Esau perhaps could identify with his related half Uncle Ishmael who himself never benefited from his position as firstborn. In a move that he knew would upset his parents, Esau took his wives from the Canaanites. We are introduced to three: Ada, a Hittite; Oholibama, a Hivite; and Basemath, a family member from the clan of Ishmael. The first doublet introduced in this chapter comprises verses 1–8. The second doublet, verses 10–14, is worded differently but produces similar yet different information. This strongly suggests a common source with at least two separate scribal authors and at least one editor bringing the sources together. But why bring such disparate conflicting traditions into a single written [dis]unity?

This accounting is not a historical chronology. Can that be substantiated? Yes! In the first doublet, a reason is provided why Esau leaves Canaan. It records it as a voluntary exile based on the wealth acquired over time by Esau. The limits of the land could not support both Isaac and Esau.

Torah is efficient in its wording and does not entertain or allow for waste with extra superfluous words. The second doublet identifies a different story. The doublet exists in verses 1 –8 and then again 10–14 with additional material added, namely Esau's grandchildren. Verses 15–19 draw upon both of the doublets for a triplet and further adds some additional information into the text concerning the political influence Esau's descendants eventually exercise.

Introducing chapter 36 of Genesis, the outline is established. "These are the 'Toledot' of Esau, which is Edom." This is a scribal revision. We must get to Timna, perhaps the most evident character. First, she is identified in the Hebrew as a *pilegesh,* which is roughly translated as "less than a wife," an outcast wife. Clearly, she is someone possessing a single characteristic. She was important as a provision of physical, sexual interaction. She was a concubine, not a wife. There are other English words we could use to describe her if modesty were not an issue.

In order to contrast the status of Timna, the author needed an evident comparison. That contrasting balance is achieved in the wife of

Esau, the niece of Isaac, Basemath. Basemath conjures up the idea of a sweet smile. Esau, of course, was easily influenced by a pretty smile. He allowed his immediate needs often to overtake careful thought and planning. This is a powerfully important distinction in light of the fact that Basemath was a daughter of Ishmael. Ishmael was the son of Hagar, also a woman of less familial distinction. Hagar was the שִׁפְחָה *shiphchah* maidservant/slave (female) slave of Sarah. Esau took wives. Baked into the story of his wives are the type of women he liked. If Esau was this careless in his selection of women to associate with, would not the apple fall far from the tree?

The Hebrew designation for the word *pilegesh* occurs thirty-seven times in the ancient Hebrew Tanakh. It stands as a distinct word because it is not a Hebrew word of west Semitic origin. It derives possibly from a Greek origin. This type of word, *pilegesh*, would have served a post-Exilic audience (circa 450 BCE) by inflaming nationalism. Esau is Edom. They live on the other side of the mountain. The identification of Timna as a *pilegesh* was a concise use of language to serve as a double indictment. As a *pilegesh*, Timna lacked respect. For good measure to spice the story, indictments emerge against Ada, Basemath, and Ohlibama, the Canaanite, Hittite, and Hivite. This was not a chronology lesson. Chapter 36 clearly articulated inflammatory writing.

Scribal Edits Produce Ancient Revisionist Stories

So how is this inflamed writing pieced together? In Genesis 36:16, Korah is listed as a son of Eliphaz. His mother is Ada, the Hittite. However, in verse 14, Korah is identified as the son of Oholibama. This specific writing draws upon various circulating traditions. It also illustrates that this entire chapter was not the product of a single author. In verse 17, all the sons of Reul and Basemath are correctly identified, and in verse 18, Korah is listed as a son of Oholibamah. This agrees with verse 5 and contradicts verse 16.

The reader of this ancient text—or rather, the storyteller—likely would assume that the narrative was practical. Esau had an eye for the ladies. He had a particular eye for the Canaanite ladies, the Hittites, and Hivites. These are the girls that caught Esau's eye. Yet unanswered in this account is the most important question: why does Esau leave Canaan? Logistically it made more sense for Jacob to leave. After all, Jacob made his wealth outside of Canaan. A revision to the story demanded an accounting in order to facilitate the normal flow of questions within the mishpacha in the oral tradition. Disrupting Esau's life required an explanation. What better way to start that disruption than attack him where all men are weak: his sexual proclivities rendered him morally unsuitable to a favorable review.

Making sense of the story and the endless chronology of Genesis chapter 36 is now possible. Approaching it from the vantage of a story told around the campfire at night produces different vivid images. Esau was a ruinous character who littered the family with women of no reasonable character and background. For that reason, he had to go. There are two sides to every story. The Torah is not singular in its approach. The editors revised the episode's curious elements. Those elements focused on the nature of the people living on the other side of the river and mountains. Those people were not the type of people one normally would purposely associate with. They were however the type of people Esau would be comfortable living with.

The byline Genesis 36:20–30 invites the reader to a different view of the world. That view does not completely contradict the earlier points. Instead, it supplements that argument. What were the people like on the other side of the river Jordan before Esau moved over there? Enter Timna in verse 22. Nothing more needs to be said. Bad seed looks for bad seed.

In this separate account, Timna is not a pilegesh but instead the signal heroine daughter of the founder, Seir the Horite. She is specifically identified as the sister of Lotan. As a daughter of Seir the Horite, she was a prime candidate as a suitable marriage partner. In modern terms, she was a princess. But the editing has already been spoiled. The best a daughter of Seir can become is a *pilegesh* to the worst that Isaac has to offer.

The Horites ruled over land that comprised important commercial trade routes. Those routes facilitated the flow of commerce from Mesopotamia to Egypt. Trade was controlled by force of tolling and tax revenue confiscations. One paid for access. That required chiefs who caused and implemented patrols along the roads. Those patrols were feared for their viciousness and efficiency.

The second element of the doublet identifies each of the sons of Esau and his descendants as *alluwphs*. This Hebrew word is used to denote a "chief." The Esau clan was wealthy and ruled the territory that they occupied. It is never asked in the Bible how one merely moved unchecked from the Cis-Jordan region to the Trans-Jordan region? Resistance from the existing political structure in mountainous Seir would attempt to stop a migration that disrupted commercial and natural resources.

> These are the chiefs that came of the Horites: the chief of Lotan, the chief of Shobal, the chief of Zibeon, the chief of Anah,the chief of Dishon, the chief of Ezer, the chief of Dishan. These are the chiefs that came of the Horites, according to their chiefs in the land of Seir. (Gen. 36:29–30)

These chiefs/alluwph(s) possessed full rights of that classification. This is especially emphasized by the redacting scribe. There is a more fuller explanation contained within Genesis 36:31–39. Those *malachim* (kings) resided and reigned in Edom before any king reigned in Israel. We do not have a record related to any length of reign or acts performed during their reign. We do know that this list is differentiated from the list of the chiefs. Analyzing the meaning of the text is intimate with its contextual placement. Analyzing the exact content as data, or a genealogical record, in and of itself, would provide no productive information. It should be understood within the framework of ancient Near Eastern messaging and thought. The story needed a structural frame. The front end of the book in Genesis 36:29 reminds us of the chiefs of the Horites. Genesis 36:40–43 adds further structural framing into the analysis.

> And these are the names of the chiefs that came of Esau, according to their families, after their places, by their names: the chief of Timna, the chief of Alvah, the chief of Jetheth; the chief of Aholibamah, the chief of

> Elah, the chief of Pinon; the chief of Kenaz, the chief of Teman, the chief of Mibzar; the chief of Magdiel, the chief of Iram. These are the chiefs of Edom, according to their habitations in the land of their possession. (Gen. 36:40–43)

In this separate redacted version, we are treated one more time with a different version of the facts. In this instance, our heroine, the former *pilegesh* Timna, stands alongside Oholibamah as alluwphs (chiefs).[55] The chapter concludes with an emphatic declaration: "This is Esau the father of the Edomites." The intent of the scribes illustrates the desire to write a monologue along different terms. In this chapter, we should notice that no one dies except the *malachim kings*. This was a recognition that the true commercial power of the land resided within the alluwph structure. At the same time, it was a cunning jab at the kings on the other side of the river.

> Bela (v. 32), reigned and died
> Jobab (v. 33), reigned and died
> Husham (v. 34), reigned and died
> Hadad (v.35), reigned and died
> Samlah (v.36), reigned and died
> Shaul (v.37), reigned and died
> Baal-Hanaan (v. 38), reigned and died
> Hadar (v. 39), reigned and died

In the oral tradition, you would have taken notice of such a distinction. You would have curiously asked very probing questions. Why was it only the kings who died in this story?

Was life so fickle that even great chiefs were slandered after their deaths? Samlah died and Shaul of Reheboth by the River reigned in his

55 In the Hebrew text one would observe the insert of two different vowels in verse twelve and forty which are used in Timna's name. This scribal error is evident when the name of Oholibama is consistent in verses fourteen and forty-one. There is little doubt Timna is referenced.

stead. Someone dies, another reigns in his stead. The fate of fame and power is cyclical. The clarity of the original message as told was not lost.

Concluding Thoughts

The various redacted entries of Genesis 36 are important. They provide an important view because they contain antagonistic conflicting versions of the same story. They were edited into the written text to remind us how the story should be told. One would expect these differences. One particular flavor of the historical record suggests that Esau's migration was dominant over the existing power structure of the land. Perhaps this also is reflected in the labeling of Timna as a common *pilegesh*. Another flavor of the historical record in the same chapter refuted that account and labels both Timna and Oholibamah as equals and alluwphs. We could reasonably expect that a coterminous rule and coterminous existence prevailed. The dual identification of Timna as both a *pilegesh* and also as an *alluwph* perhaps represents the edited tension. Timna as a daughter of Seir was the prototype of a forged political alliance.

Ancient tales that emerge are colored with their own perspective. The color suits the dominant political thought of that day. While accounting for events, it also serves to glorify or condemn. At the same time, if moderns treat the text as one would treat a modern record looking to find evidence to support a narration, it quickly degrades into an exercise in futility. At best, it demonstrates that the oral tradition thrived within the mishpacha. Popular sagas emerged in the oral tradition. The stories were preserved in the eventual written tradition. They should not be used therefore as historical proofs. Yet they do survive and bring to life the color and flavor of the role chronologies played.

For example, in Genesis 36:22, the Bible in its silence suggests that there was significant acceptance of the migration by the existing polity. The Bible specifically identifies Seir the Horite, and his son Lotan. Seir must have been the political force that established power in the region since the mountain was named after him. Seir's daughter is mentioned in strict relation as a sister of Lotan (Gen. 36:22). There are two possibilities that emerge.

1) Esau ostensibly invaded Seir and occupied by force the region and reduced the daughter Timna to *pilegesh* status for the benefit of his son Eliphaz (highly unlikely) or
2) Esau migrated to Seir, and the daughter Timna was joined with Eliphaz as a marriage.

We wind up back at the beginning: what are facts, and what is truth? This chapter contains at least two, if not three or four, versions of events. The first of the doublets in verse 12 identifies Timna in the *pilegesh* status. The third version in verse forty identifies her as an *alluwph*. In verse 2, Oholibamah is identified as an *ishah*. More properly, the text conjugates the word correctly as third person אֶת־נָשָׁיו, "his wives." In the oral tradition, it was proper to identify the *ishah* Oholibama as a wife. This is an especially strong rendering since both verse 21 and 29 originated from separate sources and identified the status of the male line of Seir as *alluwphs*.

> These are the chiefs that came of the Horites, the children of Seir in the land of Edom. (Gen. 36:21)

> These are the chiefs that came of the Horites: the chief of Lotan, the chief of Shobal, the chief of Zibeon, the chief of Anah 30 the chief of Dishon, the chief of Ezer, the chief of Dishan. These are the chiefs that came of the Horites, according to their chiefs in the land of Seir. (Gen. 36:29)

The male line of Seir remained intact, and one must then conclude the same fate for the daughters of Seir. This renders the toledots not as chronology, but as mythical stories that teach morals.

PART III

THE ABRAHAM EPISODES

We are closer to God when we are asking questions than when we think we have the answers

Abraham Joshua Heschel

The Bible comes to us as a compiled edited whole. That compilation was completed after 450 BCE. The Torah then became a revision of many popular oral tradition stories. That revision was used to communicate and promote nationalistic pride.

That nationalism ultimately understood that the population demographic in Palestine was being reformed. Cyrus the Great conquered Lydia in Asia Minor and promoted a policy of rule there by local aristocrats. He issued edicts encouraging the Judeans to return to Palestine to rebuild there. The Judean nationalism sought a good cover story consistent with their memory of the past.

Effectively tracing that cover story back to an original person added credibility. Ultimately, that national hero had to be one of fame. Departing from the popular oral tradition was not an option. That history had intimate ties to the Akkadian/Sumerian/Mesopotamian tradition. Abram, unlike the desperate brigands, the Hapiru, was a wealthy migrant. Instead of fleeing to Canaan, he was directed by God Almighty to purposely move there. He was destined to end up in Canaan.

The oral tradition assigned a specific location from which Abram began the perilous journey to Canaan, Ur of the Chaldeans. The specific reference to Ur, as Chaldean city (Chaldean Empire circa 625–539 BCE) reminds the student of the Bible that this story originated at least a thousand years after Abraham died (if one generously dates Abraham ca. 1800 BCE).

> And Terah took his son Abram and his grandson Lot, the son of Haran, and his daughter-in-law Sarai, his son Abram's wife, and they went out with them from Ur of the Chaldeans to go to the land of Canaan; and they came unto Haran and dwelt there. (Gen. 11:31)

A current focus of the time period during 520 BCE was topical. Should those of Judean descent return from Babylon to Palestine? Many taken in exile died in exile. Many born in exile were already home! Why leave home to go somewhere only Mom and Dad talked about? This problem is also topical in America in the twenty-first century AD. Immigrants coming from other countries often live in small, mostly low-cost housing communities. The children observe their parents posting the national flag of a land they barely remembered, if it was remembered at all. The purpose often is to remind their children who they want them to be, not who they will be. The old country is spoken of in glowing terms that in many instances reflected a fabricated fantasy. Cheers ring out during sporting events for those other national teams in their common tongues. This environment creates an isolation among the children. They struggle to become part of the mainstream and never really connect with the former land of their parents or the current land within which they reside. Depression creeps in. Over time marriages intermingle and new cultural ties emerge. Once, Grandpa used to be simply "Grandpa," now he is either Grandpa or *Abuelo*, depending on many factors.

To understand the message that was communicated it is important to break down the various story lines of the episodes. That is important because the story lines were not related sequentially in the form that the Bible is currently presented. The oral tradition considered all the various episodes within the context of the values contained in the story line during the evening discussions. Questions were asked concerning God's ability to properly administer justice. The present condition of the Judean in Mesopotamia demanded such an inquiry. That demanded one set of facts for the discussions at hand. This encouraged one type of story.

Major Episodes of Abram the Sumerian/Akkadian Migrant

Bible Pericope	Story Line	Summary
Genesis 11		Toledot (genealogy) of Abram tracing Hebrew lineage back to Mesopotamia
Genesis 12:1–9		Call of YHWH for Abram to leave his country of birth (Chaldean territory) and moved to the Judean mountains east of Bethel. A promise was made to Abram to give to his descendants the land (Judeans left Babylonian exile initiated under the Chaldean ruler Nebuchadnezzar).
Genesis 12:10 –20		Abram journeys to Egypt; passes his wife off as his sister; pharaoh attempts to claim her as his wife until he finds out she is Abram's wife
Genesis 13:1–18		Abram and Lot return to Canaan; Lot separates from Abram to establish a separate mishpacha in the plain of the Jordan River overlooking Sodom and Gomorrah; Abram settles in the Hebron area south of Jebus (Jerusalem).
Genesis 14:1–24		Abram pursues and overtakes the Sumerian Army.
Genesis 15:1–17		Promise of an heir within the context of covenant; marked by promise of slavery in another land.
Genesis 16:1–16		Abram given Hagar as a wife; Ishmael born
Genesis 17:1–8		Abram at age ninety-nine received a vision and a covenant in the land in which he was a stranger. This call was when he was already in Canaan.

Genesis 17: 9–27		Abram's name changed to form a deviation plural form Abra*ham* and the Hebrew vowel *hey* was added to his name and Sarah's name. Isaac will be called Laughter (obviously, this is a different version of the account in Genesis chapter 18). Covenant related with Semitic practice of circumcision was added to the Hebrew tradition. Ishmael replaced by Isaac as beneficiary of the promise before he was even born.
Genesis 18:1–18		Three men visit Abraham and Sarah, and one of the men predicts Sarah will have a child in a year. Sarah laughs in the tent.
Genesis 18:19 –33		A question of morality is discussed: will God slay the righteous with the wicked? But the story line is introduced in the context that Abraham will provide an orderly command to his children to live as righteous.
Genesis 19:1–38		Chapter dedicated to Lot
Genesis 20:1–18		Abraham journeys to Gerar and Abimelech takes Sarah. Morality questions focus on God's ability to assign sinful conduct to the right person/party: Can a sin be ascribed to hands that entered the process as clean hands?
Genesis 21:1–8		Yet another account of the naming of Isaac, "God has made me laugh and all who hear will laugh with me"
Genesis 21:9–21		Hagar placed the boy (fourteen years of age) under a shrub; moral of the story: he was a wild boy, an archer, destined for the wilderness of Paran
Genesis 21:22–34		Swear to me you will not deal falsely: the well was beer-sheva well of oaths
Genesis 22:1–14		Testing of Abraham; offering of Isaac; God will provide

Genesis 22:15–24		Milcah and Nahor, eight kids; Reumah and Nahor, four kids (twelve)
Genesis 23:1–20		Death and burial of Sarah at 127; he purchases a cave among the Hittites in Kirjath Arba (Hebron). City of the four (Arba): Abraham, Isaac, Jacob, and Adam (first man) were all buried there.
Genesis 24		Abraham is elderly and called his servant to return to the dwelling of Nahor and obtain a wife from his brother for his son Isaac; Isaac marries Rebekah, his relative from his cousin Bethuel. These two likely were not compatible in age.
Genesis 25		Death of Abraham; Isaac dwells at Beer Lahai Roi
Gen. 16:14 Abram; 24:62 Isaac; 25:11 Isaac		Well of the one who lives and sees me

CHAPTER 1

ABRAM PROMISED HE WOULD BE MADE A GREAT NATION

Fate of the exiles living in Babylon in 520 BCE was a current topic of interest. Should the Judeans remain in a political exile, or should they venture back home? This question predicated parts of the various Abram episodes. To what extent were the Hebrews different from all others? If they were no different, then one needed merely to stay in the land of their birth, Babylon, their ancient homeland associated with Abram. The oral tradition invited many different views regarding this vital debate. Abraham, the great protagonist, lived many lives and represented the emergence from a society dominated by differing plural deities.

A most interesting question must now be asked: exactly what was the promise given to Abram? For that answer the English translation serves no reliable help.

> Now the Lord said to Abram: Get out of your country, from your family, and from your father's house, to a land that I will show you. I will make you a great *nation* *(גּוֹי / gō'·ē / nation)*; I will bless you and make your name great; And you shall be a blessing. (Gen. 12:1–2)

The promise of the Lord (יְהוָה) was to make Abram a great nation. It would be one thing if that nation existed within the pure form of a specific patrilineal descent. The author of Genesis never intended such an approach.

Tracing a story constructed from a genealogical perspective was not realistic.

There were several words to choose from if the author intended for the emergence of a nationalistic body with a common bloodline. The words in Hebrew reflecting the concept of nation are set forth below.

Hebrew Word	*Pronunciation*	*Translation*
גוֹי	gō'·ē	nation/people/usually non-Hebrew people
מַמְלָכָה	mam·lä·kä'	kingdom (sovereign territory)
עַם	am	nation/people

The word עַם, pronounced "am," most closely refers to a unified people as a nation. In the oral tradition of Hebrew, it would have been the word that associated a sense of unified nationalism. It is first used in the Torah referring to the Sumerians at the Tower of Babel.

> *And the Lord said, "Indeed the people are one* and they all have one language, and this is what they begin to do; now nothing that they propose to do will be withheld from them." (Gen. 11:6)

וַיֹּאמֶר יְהוָה, הֵן עַם אֶחָד

The English translation of *people* in the New King James Version presents an interesting dilemma. The word translated as "people" actually is better translated as "nation." But the essential meaning is correct. The descendants of the Sumerians from Shinar were both a people and indeed represented as a collective nation aggregated from competing city/states. Over time competition turned into antagonistic territorial disputes. Control of commercial markets dominated the process despite a shared common heritage. The word עם occurs 1,862 times in the written Hebrew Bible and is the common word associated with Israel as a tribal confederated nation.

The promise of the Lord however was not to make Abram a great עַם (am); instead, the promise of the Lord was to make Abram a great גּוֹי (gō'·ē, nation). This word was associated and reserved usually for non-Hebrew people. That promise would have made perfect sense in either Babylon or Palestine after 520 BCE. In that day it would have been a current topic of debate. Imagine two young star-crossed lovers, one family intends to migrate back to Canaan. The other family intends to remain in Mesopotamia. Families, lovers, friends, businesses would have been torn over the ultimate choice to leave the stable present for an unknown future simply because Grandpa once lived there. The various collective עַם am(s) would have constituted the reality of the land comprised of גּוֹי.

For the modern, the question of Jewish identity is a riddle still seeking to be solved. Is Jewishness an ethnicity or is it a religion? The term *Semitic* is often used to describe Jewish ethnicity. Yet that word is unique in that it describes cognate verb language unity, not ethnicity. That lingering question originates from its founder who did not establish an *am* but instead founded a *gō'·ē*. We should be asking: what is the nature of that nation.

Exactly Who Was Abram the Father Of?

So who was Abram the father of? Technically, he was the father of Isaac and Ishmael. We must explore exactly what that meant to the people who first heard those stories and compare them with how those episodes are related today.

With an interesting twist of the oral tradition, God changes Abram's name by adding a vowel, the Hebrew letter *Hay* (ה) as a final vowel, then adding a plural form ending after the final form vowel. This vowel was not a letter available in the time period ascribed to the life of Abram, circa 1,800 BCE. It is an indicator for us to understand that the figure of this legend perhaps was also the subject of nationalistic revisions after the eighth century BCE. The change of Abram's name was a curious distinction in the post exilic world that would have meant much more than simply changing someone's name, from something like Tom to Thomas. Abram emerged as a legendary figure in the oral tradition. The story of the name change, employing a unique Hebrew addition to the tradition, had such a significant impact that Abram lost his Akkadian/Sumerian identity and became a father of the Habiru/Hebrews.

In the Torah, we have observed and accounted for Toledots, which seemingly provide a chronological history. These chronologies pose a difficult problem when attempting to tell a story in our own day about our own religion. To what extent are the Toledots our history, or even a reliable history? Possessing the form of a chronology, these records come up short in their explanation as a credible source document relating chronological information. One such example relating to unreliable chronology is aptly illustrated in the life of Abram. That life originates within a *towlĕdah* in Genesis chapter 11.

Stories of Abram that are presented in the Torah arise out of the oral tradition. They should not be considered as a single continuous narrative. Forms the stories take present dynamically clear intentions. Those intentions are obscured when they are intermixed by the well intentioned seeking a continuous narrative.

There is an unusualness in the story lines related in the Torah. Abraham had two sons: Ishmael and Isaac. Isaac, not the firstborn, received a preferential status over Ishamel. This needed an accounting.

Isaac had two sons: Esau and Jacob. Jacob received a preferential status over the firstborn. This needed an accounting.

Jacob had twelve sons, six by his wife Leah: Reuben Simeon, Levi, Judah, Issachar, Zebulon. His second wife, Rachel, gave Jacob two sons: Joseph and Benjamin. Jacob had four sons by two concubines: Gad, Asher, Dan, and Napthali. In all, he had twelve boys. But these twelve did not constitute the traditional twelve tribes of Israel. Levi was eliminated from this count in order to perform a function related to serving all of the other brothers.

> But unto the tribe of Levi Moses gave not any inheritance: the Lord God of Israel was their inheritance, as he said unto them. (Josh. 13:33)

Joseph was the firstborn son of perhaps the favorite wife of Jacob, Rachel. Jacob's uncle Laban was Rachel's father, and it was for her hand that he diligently labored within Laban's mishpacha. After he thought he was marrying Rachel, he awoke from his sleep in the marriage bed to discover it was occupied by her older sister Leah. This followed the long tradition of biblical explanations: the man simply was too drunk to realize who he was in bed with. Lot was too drunk to know his daughters visited him at least for three or four months. Of course, the girls got away with it. Noah was so drunk he ended up cursing his grandson who was not even involved with the incident in question.

Joseph, however, poses a problem. We never know why in the Bible that the house of Joseph was not included as one of the twelve tribes to which land parcels were distributed. That distinction fell to Joseph's two sons, Ephraim and Manasseh. The mother of Ephraim and Manasseh was Asenath. Asenath was the daughter of the Egyptian priest Potiphera who controlled Egyptian religious cultus from Heliopolis (On). Asenath's name indicates she was dedicated to the Egyptian goddess Neith, an original cocreator of the universe who governed by fate all the cosmos.

The presence of Asenath as a mother to two of the twelve tribes becomes even more complicated if one considers the dual religious entanglements combined with nationalistic sensitivities. In that regard, there is a direct Egyptian connectivity with the named tribes. Rabbinic explanations that later emerged explain but in no way diminish the problem. For example, one set of teaching suggests Asenath was the child born to Dinah as a result of her rape in Genesis 34:1–2 by the Hivitie named Shechem.

> And Dinah the daughter of Leah, whom she had borne unto Jacob, went out to see the daughters of the land. And Shechem the son of Hamor the Hivite, the prince of the land, saw her; and he took her, and lay with her, and humbled her. (Gen. 34:1–2)

Another rabbinic explanation in circulation suggests Asenath converted from her dedication to Egyptian gods and goddesses in favor of Judaism as a convert.

In either scenario, there is no direct pathway to the origin of the twelve tribes as distinctly Hebrew within the construction of עַם (nation/people) people without considering the reality of a broader classification of non-Hebrew people גוֹי (gō'·ē).

Hebrew Word	*Pronunciation*	*Translation*
גוֹי	gō'·ē	nation/people/usually non-Hebrew people
מַמְלָכָה	mam·lä·kä'	kingdom (sovereign territory)
עַם	am	nation/people

At best we can say the established history connects the עַם Israel as consisting of both Semitic and non-Semitic lineage. The fact that there is no rabbinic consensus should also instruct that the issue is neither settled nor universally held. For our purposes we build on that lack of consensus. If any doubt existed in the population of the fifth century BCE, the antagonistic debates would have been kindled among that population. There would have been internal squabbles among those who thought they knew arguing with those they presumed not to know.

The presence of Midrash concerning Asenath suggests such a debate took place. The fact that there is more than one explanation for Asenath indicates the issue was never settled. In that environment, two people hearing the same story would have reached two different conclusions.

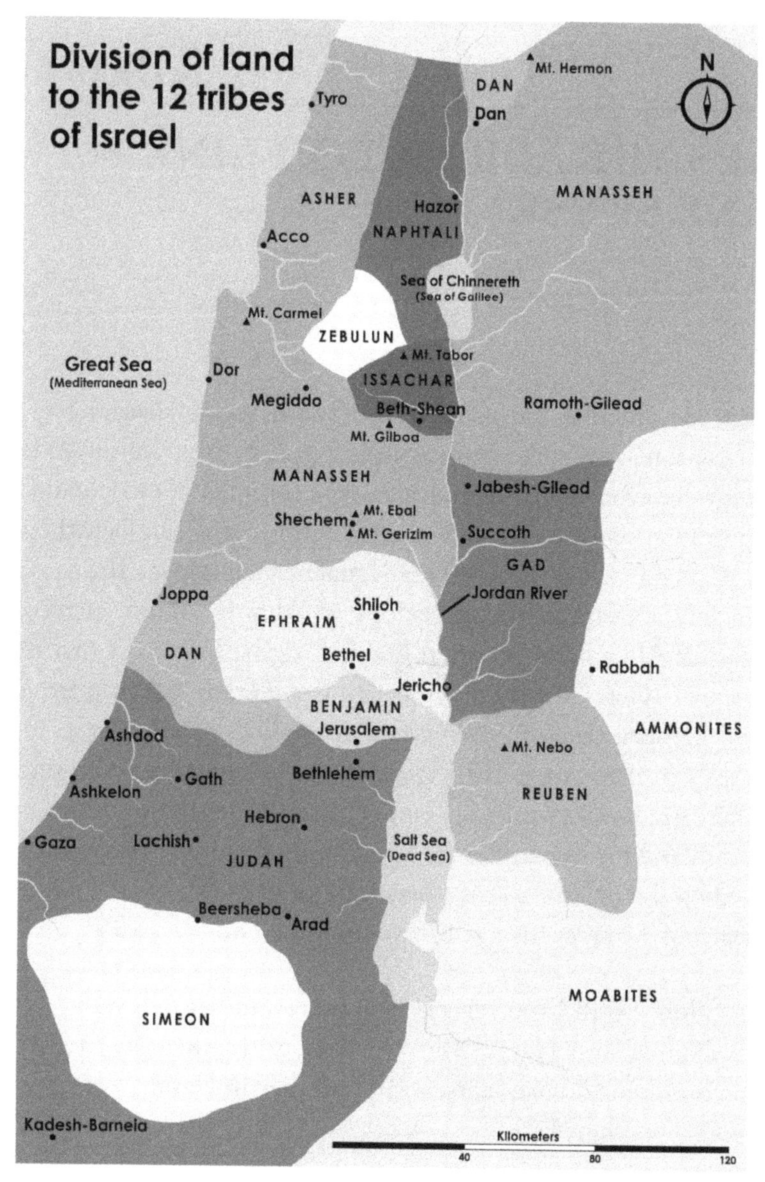

Twelve Tribes Of Israel

CHAPTER 2

DOES THE ABRAM TIMELINE MAKE SENSE?

The various timelines provided in the Torah appear disconnected for a very good reason: they are disconnected! They were not intended as an integrated whole needing midrash type commentary to explain how the contradictions are not really contradictions at all. In fact, there are many years for which there are inadequate explanations. The first such inadequacy appears in the genealogy of Abram. Abram is recorded as being of Akkadian/Sumerian lineage originating out of "Ur of the Chaldeans" (Gen. 11:31b). To identify the Abram as being from the city of Ur was an attempt by scribes in the fifth century BCE to add legitimacy to their story. Their founder was of ancient legit lineage!

There are two key markers enumerated in Genesis 11 with respect to Abram and his father, Terah. The first marker indicates Abram was born when Terah was seventy-five years of age. The second marker is the death of Terah at the age of two hundred and five years.

> Now Terah lived seventy-five years and begat Abram, Nahor, and Haran...So the days of Terah were two hundred and five years, and Terah died in Haran. (Gen. 11:26; Gen. 11:32)

A literal reading now places Abram in Haran (now southeast area of the country of modern Turkey). Abram would have been 130 years old at his father's death. The text suggests but does not explicitly state that Abram resided with his father through his death. If this was writing to demonstrate history in the sense of its western usage then the separation by Abram from either his bet-ab or his mishpacha would need an explanation. However, the episode in the eleventh chapter of Genesis should be read as a separate story line. This episode sets up the separate Southern Palestine oral tradition concerning the origin of the group of Semitic people living in Judah. It was a romantic backward-looking exercise. It placed the origin of the Hebrews at a time consistent with our modern understanding of Neolithic man. After the great flood, men migrated to Shinar.

> And it came to pass as they journeyed from the east, that they found a plain in the land of Shinar [Sumeria] and they dwelt there. (Gen. 11:2)

The episode in that sense confirms what we have discovered in the west about Sumer being the cradle of civilization. The narrative is consistent with Hebrew chiastic poetical thought processes. Two bookends contain the value of the story in the middle.

> A: Civilization emerges when men built cities
> B: Geneology of Shem culminating in Abram
> A: Men (Terah) migrates from Sumer to other cities

This model was helpful. It was an easy way to explain why the Judeans would need to voluntarily leave Mesopotamia (former Chaldean territory) to return to Judah after the Babylonian captivity.

> Now the Lord (YHWH) had said to Abram: Get out of your country, from your family, and from your father's house, to a land I will show you. (Gen. 12:1)

That story line was needed since it would have been understood that Abram walked the path before them. He too originated from a society with an established religious hierarchy and pantheon of gods. Abram distinctly heard God's call to leave and go to Canaan.

In this rendering, there is no background information added about this call from YHWH. This assumes that Terah departed Ur and intended to go to Canaan and at some point changed his mind and continued a westward journey and settled in Haran, a commercial trading partner with the larger city of Ur. Perhaps Terah never reached his destination, Canaan. The question is: when did Abram embark on that journey?

The Hebrew text is at least ambiguous at best. This is partly since it was not intended as a chronological history, but instead was used in oral discussions.

> וַיֹּאמֶר יְהוָה אֶל-אַבְרָם, לֶךְ-לְךָ מֵאַרְצְךָ וּמִמּוֹלַדְתְּךָוּמִבֵּית אָבִיךָ
>
> Now the Lord had said to Abram: *Get out of your country, from your family, and from your father's house...*

Exactly where was Abram coming from? The Hebrew term וּמִמּוֹלַדְתְּךָ *mowledeth* (and from your *mowledeth*) is the word used Genesis 12:1, not the word for "clan," *mishpacha*. The word has a deep context with a birth related to a specific land. A better translation might be

> YHWH said to Abram leave the country [land] of your birth from your father's house (Gen. 12:1)

A *mowledeth* is a referent to a birthplace. Abram's *mowledeth* would not have been Haran. It would have been the Mesopotamian city of Ur. There is an immediate disconnect between the closing chapter of Genesis 11 and the introduction to Genesis chapter 12. The disconnect can be easily explained, oral tradition! Separate stories have separate beginnings and endings. They teach a lesson unto themselves. We can begin to examine the separate lessons.

An important question for any Hebrew living either in Mesopotamia or Canaan after 520 BCE would be rather obvious: How did we get here? How do we convince others to leave and return to Canaan?

Several versions of the story arose around the central figure of a man who acquired wealth in the big important Mesopotamian city of Ur. That man, Abram, was a transcendent figure who ignored the voices of the various deities prominent in the Akaadian tradition and eventually focused on the single monolithic figure later known as יְהֹוָה (YHWH).

Genesis chapter 11 circulated a tradition in response to that central question: the Hebrews originated from Sumer.

> Now the whole earth had one language and one speech. And it came to pass, as they journeyed from the east, that they found a plain in the land of Shinar (Sumer), and they dwelt there. (Gen. 11:1–2)

The movement of man after the episode recorded as the great flood in the Bible is at least consistent with what is known about the origin of civilization.

Historians ascribe the Mesopotamian plain as the cradle of civilization. The biblical record does not identify a specific time period, merely general notations. A specific time period is attempted in rabbinic and Christian tradition by counting back chronologically through the recorded *towlĕdah*. The problem with that approach is that the *towlĕdah* does not establish chronology, but something else altogether different.

CHAPTER 3

GET UP AND GO

In a previous chapter, we discussed a doublet episode mirroring the actions of Isaac with his father Abram. In that doublet both disguise the nature of their marriage. But there are two episodes in Abram's life where Abram himself conceals his relationship with his wife. In Genesis chapter 12, the first episode occurs as Abram leaves Canaan and journeys to Egypt. The second episode is located in Genesis 20:1–18.

The circumstances of Abram's venture into Egypt has a reasonable story line. Abram is concerned for his safety. One begins the story with Abram commenting that his wife is fair to look upon. This presents a problem for him since now once men observe how beautiful she is, they will kill him. Once this beautiful maiden is free of any marriage constraints, she would be free game for any Egyptian to pursue their own affair with her. In this scenario, there are three principals: Abram, Sarai, and any Egyptian male. In Abram's mind, this story ends badly for at least one of the principals. But is that really the story that would have been heard in the oral tradition?

Reading the story in a straightforward univocal context misses the plot completely. There are some elements that we already accept. Sarai is sixty-five. Age must have been an issue with the Abram episodes since it was the driving concern surrounding Sarai's barren condition and Abram's lack of an heir. Modern readers of the Torah begin the fanciful speculation about Sarai's beauty. Her beauty in Bible readings allows the most vivid discussions. For example, I once attended a Sunday school class where the main topic was introduced based on this account: "Is it proper to lie to protect yourself?" It was an ironic discussion. Sunday-morning coffee, doughnuts, fellowship—all centered on lies to maintain our credibility and status quo. But was that the lesson from the Bible?

Over the years, I should have been as worried as Abram travelling across the country. My wife is more than equally beautiful to Sarai. In my entire adult life, I never once allowed for lies to protect myself just because I was married to a pretty girl. So the story must be about something else. It is easier to address what this story is not about. Then by eliminating what it isn't, we can explore its true message.

Attractiveness is an elusive concept. Young males generally find young females attractive. Within the concept of what causes attraction, there are some truisms that dominate. One such truism is opposites attract! Another truism is, the heart wants what the heart wants! It is unlikely for one female to be an attraction to all males. Young males invariably prefer young women of childbearing age as sexually attractive. It is most uncommon for young males to be universally attracted to women over the age of sixty-five merely because they are fair to look upon. While looking upon Grandma Sarai, young males may comment on something like, "Not bad for her age!"

In the Torah, it teaches us by the questions it raises. Therefore, we must remember first to look for the question raised in the discussion. The text preserved those questions to support the conversations that needed to take place. The question raised by Pharaoh in this story is profound.

> What is this that you have done to me? Why did you not tell me that she was your wife? (Gen. 12:18)

In this instance the story line addresses a lie. But this is a different kind of lie. We are not really certain why this episode exists, unless Sarai really was so attractive that the laws of attraction did not apply to her. Since the story appears incomplete, we have to look elsewhere to see if there is any other tradition with Abram and his wife that may provide other illustrative insight.

> And Abraham journeyed from there to the South, and dwelt between Kadesh and Shur, and stayed in Gerar. Now Abraham said of Sarah his wife, "She *is* my sister."

> And Abimelech king of Gerar sent and took Sarah. But God came to Abimelech in a dream by night, and said to him, "Indeed you *are* a dead man because of the woman whom you have taken, for she *is* a man's wife." But Abimelech had not come near her; and he said, "Lord, will You slay a righteous nation also? Did he not say to me, 'She *is* my sister'? And she, even she herself said, 'He *is* my brother.' In the integrity of my heart and innocence of my hands I have done this." (Gen. 20:1–5)

Abram's initial reservations about men in general need to be dismissed as a central operating theme. Even in ancient societies, marriages enjoyed certain social protections. It was clear that Pharaoh understood that principle, and Abimelech, king of Gerar, understood that as well. Therefore, we can dismiss the folly of Abram's lie under the byline of self-preservation. In fact, it is more likely that one of the two doublets was a corruption of the other. In this instance, it makes sense to conclude that the doublet first encountered, Genesis 12:10–20, is a corrupted version of the more complete oral tradition of Genesis 20. Abimelech's response to Abram in Genesis 20 was similar to the response of Pharaoh:

> And Abimelech called Abraham and said to him, "What have you done to us? How have I offended you, that you have brought on me and on my kingdom a great sin? You have done deeds to me that ought not to be done." Then Abimelech said to Abraham, "What did you have in view, that you have done this thing?" (Gen. 20:9–10)

In Genesis 20, however, the question of Abram's offense was contextualized within God's judgement of the righteous and the wicked. Ironically, in both instances in the Bible, Abram was the wicked one and the Pharaoh of Egypt and the king of Gerar, a Philistine, were the righteous ones. The question was never about Sarai's beauty. That discussion would take less than a minute. Some would think she was;

others would have preferred another type altogether. The real meat and potatoes of these episodes would have been consequential back and forth among all audience participants regarding who exactly was righteous. In this instance, it was not Abram.

The great question of the day was focused on a personal application of one's ability to trust God. To what extent does God ignore the righteousness of a man? Does God equally slay the righteous along with the wicked? If I have clean hands why am I being punished? These would have been the great questions around the family meal of the mishpacha in the evening. If God is all knowing, does He not know that my father sinned and I am not my father? If God punished my father by exiling him, why should I even bother going back to Judea? Some would even have argued that God apparently couldn't tell the difference between the righteous and the unrighteous.

This observation aids us in understanding what made Abram such a failed hero in Genesis 12:10–20. Portraying Abram in such a negative, dishonest light allows the story to resonate with the audience. The protagonist is unclean, and yet he is still the hero. The story under any other condition would have made little headway among the audience. How would the story have ended if Abram was truly victimized, murdered, and discarded in an Egyptian field? It would not have taught any lesson. The audience understood the absurdity in Abram's characterization of the morals in that day. Men did not randomly kill others as a daily activity then or now.

Abram's failings opened the door to question God's ability to know the difference between right and wrong and apply that to his dealings with all men.

> But God came to Abimelech in a dream by night, and said to him, "Indeed you *are* a dead man because of the woman whom you have taken, for she *is* [a]a man's wife." But Abimelech had not come near her; and he said, "Lord, will You slay a righteous nation also?" (Gen. 20:3–4)

The lamenting bellowing cry once raised in the house of Abimelech, still resounds in the ear of all men in every nation: "Lord, will You slay a righteous nation also?" If God exists, then why does he allow crime and destruction? If God promised after the flood to no more destroy all flesh, then why does he allow hurricanes to wipe out coastal communities? If God really cared for man, then why does he allow mad men filled with hate to take guns in public to shoot the innocent?

The story of Abram created an environment to discuss not the righteousness of Abram, instead, Genesis chapter 12 and Genesis chapter 20 place on trial God's ability to discern the righteous from the unrighteous. This is no small matter. The Torah provides guidance in those discussions. Pharaoh returned Sarai to Abram. Abimelech returned Sarah to Abraham.

Pharaoh and Abimelech proved their righteousness. In this matter, Sarai did not exactly enter the stage of the story with clean hands. She certainly was a party to the deceit of the story. The response of Abimelech, the righteous party in this episode, therefore is all the more compelling. Abimelech is recorded in the New King James Version as concluding the affair in this manner:

> Then to Sarah he said, "Behold, I have given your brother a thousand pieces of silver; indeed this vindicates you before all who are with you and before everybody." Thus she was rebuked. (Gen. 20:16)

So why was Sarah rebuked? The various translations of this situation differ. Some translations say she was justified, or perhaps better stated, her virtuosity/integrity was kept restored since this was all Abraham's doing. Which makes the double entendre wordplay in the oral tradition all that more special. The word translated that indicated Sarah was "rebuked" was the Hebrew word יָכַח, pronounced "yä·kahh'." This specific word could be employed as either an insult or a compliment. This punch line extends and promotes a profoundness that captures everyone's attention. The reference to Abram as Sarah's brother, after the jig is up, would have been a juicy ending. Abram and Sarah both remained flawed! The villains were heroes! God's ability to determine right from wrong received a proper discussion.

CHAPTER 4

ALL IN THE FAMILY

Genesis 13 contains an interesting story regarding the dissolution of the mishpacha controlled by the eldest uncle, Abram. One must assume that Lot ventures with Abram and Sarai into Egypt as recorded in the twelfth chapter of Genesis. What is specifically told in this story is that the mishpacha migrated from Egypt back to the Negev, a wilderness not necessarily suited for the maintenance of cattle. Abram decides to establish a residence in a portion of land suited for the cultivation of trees that produce pistachios. Abram built an altar there.

A potential conflict is not the object of the story in Genesis 13. The story instead addresses the fate of the two sons of Terah. So for now, we will identify the conflict and allow that issue to remain unresolved for the moment. At question would be who actually controlled the land at this point in time. In Genesis 23 we learn part of the area is controlled by a Hittite clan led by Ephron. Abraham had no specific right to that land and needed to purchase a plot to bury Sarah. The original audience understood a more practical problem was at hand: too little land, many competing assets for limited resources.

"Facts" merely muddle the story line and are inconsequential. Abram's mishpacha migrated from Egypt and is apparently rather wealthy. Abram was very rich in livestock, in silver, and in gold (Gen. 13:2). As the leader of the clan, he had authoritative rights to administer his property. This would have been completely understood in the original setting. What would have been unusual was the specific way this administration was carried out. The location Abram settled in was for the most part mountainous and not specifically cultivable. As he pondered the fate of the mishpacha, the obvious problem stood out. How can so much wealth survive under such limited conditions?

Bartering and horse trading now appear to be a specific skill set Abram possessed. Those skills identified allow for an exciting twist. Lot was being set up to accept a bad deal painted as a good deal. The Lot affair contains irony and humor. As told from Babylon in the fifth century BCE the punch lines delivered a wallop. Abram stands with Lot one day and says, "Look at how pretty and cultivated that land is!" Despite the land being thirty miles away on the other side of the Dead Sea, Lot acknowledges that it appears to be more fruitful and productive than the initial location the mishpacha selected as a residence. Lot most certainly had very good vision.

Abram proposes a family split! "Listen, Lot, there is no reason why we should both contend for the few spots of shade. I will let you decide." Perhaps the TV show *Let's Make a Deal* arose under different conditions, but the appeal was the same. "Lot, would you like what is behind door number 1? Plush meadows, easy access to water, green fields? Or would you like to choose door number 2, living 3,300 feet above sea level, dirt, rocks, and limited rain?"

Lot chooses the only door that made sense. The wealthy mishpacha would not survive under such burdening conditions. Lot moved on, and the mishpacha was split.

> And Lot lifted his eyes and saw all the plain of Jordan, that it was well watered everywhere (before the Lord destroyed Sodom and Gomorrah) like the garden of the Lord, like the land of Egypt as you go toward Zoar. Then Lot chose for himself all the plain of Jordan, and Lot journeyed east. And they separated from each other. Abram dwelt in the land of Canaan, and Lot dwelt in the cities of the plain and pitched his tent even as far as Sodom. But the men of Sodom were exceedingly wicked and sinful against the Lord. (Gen. 13:10–13)

Lot could not have known what was in store for his new home in the future. He was focused on his present condition: surviving. That story line struck a chord with the audience. Did it make sense to look beyond the present conditions and accept what seemingly was tough? Or should one live life pursuing that which was easy?

The story lives because it accomplishes many objectives. It describes how Terah's family immigrated and evolved from Shinar (Mesopotamia).

It does paint Lot in a narcissistic corner. Abram appears generous. Faith was explored under the premise of a future domination not simply a limited shady grove. Reminding a population in exile, if they simply reside in Babylon, no one can predict what the future will bring. Since the Chaldean empire had already fallen, the transitory nature of political stability prompted the Judeans to carefully consider their future. Remaining in Babylon was the moral equivalent of Lot's personal greed. The Torah illustrated that God promised Canaan to Abram. To choose that which appears to be more profitable over that which does not appear productive has its pitfalls.

The land on the other side of the Jordan was just like the Garden of Eden. That specific reference to the garden of the Lord presents a picturesque state.

> And Abram said unto Lot: "Let there be no strife, I pray thee, between me and thee, and between my herdmen and thy herdmen; for we are brethren. Is not the whole land before thee? separate thyself, I pray thee, from me; if thou wilt take the left hand, then I will go to the right; or if thou take the right hand, then I will go to the left." And Lot lifted up his eyes, and beheld all the plain of the Jordan, that it was well watered every where, before the Lord destroyed Sodom and Gomorrah, like the garden of the Lord, like the land of Egypt, as thou goest unto Zoar. (Gen. 13:8–10)

The tenth verse was a notorious reference. The fruit of the tree possessing knowledge of good and evil was beautiful to look at and tasted like perfection. Yet its end was destructive. The story informs the audience of Abram's duplicitous intention, after the fact. The land indeed was fruitful before the Lord destroyed Sodom and Gomorrah!

If anyone thought that it was an option to merely remain on the other side of the Jordan, outside the defined political map of Palestine proper, then the story of Lot served as a strong reminder of how quickly and often geopolitical, social, and even natural resources are exploited and drained. That message resonated after the fall of the Chaldean empire.

Twice in this story, Abram calls upon the name of יְהוָה the Lord (that name possessing the three unique vowels introduced in the eighth century BCE by the Hebrews). Calling on that name, and not the traditional northern name associated with God, *Eloheim* אֱלֹהִים, was a nationalistic call to return to Judea. If the men of Sodom were exceedingly wicked, then it followed that the men of Babylon were exceedingly wicked. The story was now framed: life has no guarantees!

This produced a counterintuitive conclusion. If there are no guarantees, then why would it make sense to move from Babylon to Judea? If things are bad there, what would it be like if they suddenly got worse? That answer was driven by a religious sense of identity. Indeed, it may be worse, but it is a "worse" centered within the protective cloak of יְהוָה the Lord.

The promise of the Lord was to make the seed of Abram as the dust of the earth. Lot eventually received another type of promise. Lot was a family member of the seed of Terah, but he was really from the other side of the family, the seed of Haran. Abram's seed was yet another seed, different from his brother, though related. But that distinction evaporated when the mishpacha ended. Lot chooses a course different from the land of promise. Lot singularly selected the plushest immediate residence. He now would secure for himself perhaps that which he desired, the ability to lead his own mishpacha. He would embark on the most obvious path and create his own destiny. No one needed to cry for what would eventually overtake Lot. He was also the product of his own hands.

CHAPTER 5

HOT PURSUIT

Forget about the war going on for the moment. It will be discussed! Who is Abram? Abram the Sumerian must have felt like two men.

> Then one who had escaped came and told Abram the Hebrew, for he dwelt by the terebinth trees of Mamre the Amorite, brother of Eshcol and brother of Aner; and they were allies with Abram. (Gen. 14:13)

In this episode, Abram is identified as a Habiru and an economically displaced man living on the fringe of society, causing and wreaking havoc for established authorities.

Recreating the sense of connection between the past and present is a tendentious activity. Suppose an American were to move from New York to a small country in Central America because the tax and political climate of the day seemed advantageous at the point of the decision. Several years pass and what once was politically stable has been the subject of upheaval. The refugee suddenly notices an unstable environment. The government then sends troops to calm the disorder.

Abram's persona is under revision in this valuable narrative. Abram is a Hebrew. In ancient Palestine the term *habiru* represented a violent tax-evading migrant. It was a moniker you called someone in anger. Yet it is a term many consider to be the origin of the name later identified in Hebrew as עברי, which means "Hebrew." The little consensus that exists over this name suggests it was a crude slang term used for slaves and the economically distressed. Perhaps if you hated another person, you would have ended up referring to them in the language of colorful slang derision. *Habiru* then would have been a term that matched your vocalized intent.

We know from other stories that Abram would have likely identified with Amraphel, king of Shinar (Sumer). The land to which Lot moved exhibited a sense of political stability since it paid tribute to Amraphel. That tribute resulted in peace. Economic toll roads served as highways along the eastern coast of the Salt Sea. The Jordan River promoted prosperity and peace. The residents were fine with that arrangement. But in a certain year, the evil men of Sodom and Gomorrah, with the assistance of the smaller municipalities of Admah, Zeboiim, and tiny insignificant Zoar, decide it was their appointed time to change the taxation landscape.

Returning to the war, this tax rebellion set forth a chain of events. Amraphel led a coalition of what would have been the most strategic military expedition at that time upon the face of the earth. The action involved Sumer, the Chaldean city of Larsa (Ellesar); Elam (Southern Iran/Persia); and the Hittite warrior Tudhaliya תִּדְעָל, pronounced "Tidal." Amraphel swept through the plush plains of the Jordan River to restore the former order. For his trouble, Amraphel does what all armies do to raise immediate cash: he confiscates as much plunder as possible. Securing revenue streams by forcing slavery upon rebels was a norm. The slaves would have been sold in distant distant markets.

The particulars of the story add some delightful commentary to the discussion. Everybody likes revenge against overzealous governments. In ancient worlds, the taxing authority of governmental bodies was seen as both necessary and hated. Tax-collecting power was vested in active agencies proficient in confiscating wealth. Balancing enough strength to enforce while not instigating full mass population rebellion required skill.

This episode represents some popular myths of the ancient Hebrews. It also answers the question: was Abram really one of us? Abram was a rich man. The Habiru were poor. Abram negotiated! The Hapiru stole! Abram received respect. The Habiru instilled fear. Abram lived out in the open! The Habiru lived in the deep wooded hilly areas of the northern provincial regions.

Promoting the incredible man versus the governing authority. An age-old saga was revisited. Our forefather overran an entire military machine to take back what was his. There are several indicators that the story has color in its purpose.

> And the king of Sodom, the king of Gomorrah, the king of Admah, the king of Zeboiim, and the king of Bela (that *is,* Zoar) went out and joined together in battle in the Valley of Siddim against Chedorlaomer king of Elam, Tidal king of nations, Amraphel king of Shinar, and Arioch king of Ellasar—four kings against five. (Gen. 14:8–9)

Futility against fighting this militia is emphasized. The four kings were able to overcome the strength of five kings. That numerical reference was inserted to demonstrate a point of the story. This army was invincible. The futility was also emphasized by the lack of success. The kings fell and those that were able fled to the mountains. All who listened in knew the fate. Foreign despotic kings enslaved to raise revenue streams. Who could stand against such a force?

The story would be told at night after dinner. "Children, gather round. Let me tell you the real truth about the famous Abram. People want you to think he was some fancy highbrow with wealth. No, forget about everything you have ever heard. Abram was just like us, a dirty, mean, nasty Habiru. In fact, forget about all those stories where he received riches from Pharaoh. No, Abram would never do that. He didn't receive from the government, he gave!"

> But Abram said to the king of Sodom, "I have raised my hand to the Lord, God Most High, the Possessor of heaven and earth, that I will take nothing, from a thread to a sandal strap, and that I will not take anything that is yours, lest you should say, 'I have made Abram rich'—except only what the young men have eaten, and the portion of the men who went with me:

> Aner, Eshcol, and Mamre; let them take their portion."
> (Gen. 14:22–24)

The questions around the campfire would flow at night. "Uncle, I always heard that Abram received riches from Pharaoh because Sarai was so beautiful!" The uncle would purse his lip in anticipation of the great debate that night. "True, true, true, Sarai was indeed a beauty. But Abram was not the kind of guy who sat around and traded his circumstances for riches." The real Abram was revealed to the audience: "Our forefather was actually a very powerful man who secured his position in life just like you and me. He was not the kind of guy who was a sympathizer with the government of his birth. No! In fact, when mean old Amraphel came down here to collect some prisoners to sell, he tangled with the wrong Hebrew. Abram divided up his men and went after the old koot Amraphel! Chased him clean out of Canaan! Abram took alongside him some of his best friends, the Amorites. I got to tell you…so listen close…many people want you to think he hobnobbed with the Hittites. No, my friend, Abram was a first-rate Habiru!"

Capturing the hearts of the northern population living in the exiled south required some accommodations. Abram paid respect to the ancient king, Melchizedek. Melchizedek also was a priest, not of the Lord, יְהוָה, but instead, a more familiar name to the Habiru: אֵל El. This northern name was not identified as Eloheim; instead, it was identified as אֵל עֶלְיוֹן, El Elyon, God Almighty. But the story was not about God, the story was about this guy, just like you and me. You can tug on Superman's cape, you can spit in the wind, but you simply cannot mess around with Abram.

CHAPTER 6

PROMISES

The most significant and compelling affair about Abram arises out of his need for an heir. The entirety of the warp and woof of all theology and religion in both Judaism and Christianity focus on the central figure of Abram. It would have been extremely beneficial had the matter been addressed in a more systematic process. For example, causing Sarai to bear a child in her ninetieth year of life was miraculous and unprecedented. But the issue of an heir was only settled in that manner after much anguish. Before we get to that point, Abram, in a customary manner, appoints Elieazar of Damascus as an heir.

The name is important. The name Eliezar is a compound word constructed as a name. El refers to the God named El. The second part of the name is comprised of three Hebrew consonants עזר Ayin-ZayinResh, denoting the meaning of help. There is an eerily similar sounding word derived from the consonants Ayin-Tsadeh-Resh עָצַר meaning to restrain.That word is used in 1 Kings 18:44 at a time that God has directly restrained the rain from watering the land of Israel during Ahab's reign. With the right twist and tone one begins to notice the double meaning and its impact. At issue during the evening discussion: God's ability to deliver on His promises. Wrapped inside that dialogue are our hopes and dreams.

After these things the word of the LORD came unto Abram in a vision, saying, "Fear not, Abram, I am thy shield, thy reward shall be exceeding great." And Abram said, "O Lord GOD, what wilt Thou give me, seeing I go hence childless, and he that shall be possessor of my house is Eliezer of Damascus?" (Gen. 15:1–2).

One could imagine hearing this as a conversation between Abram and God.

> GOD: Abram, Fear not I have your back and your reward will be huge
>
> ABRAM: Dude, I have no children and my heirs name is El עֵזֶר ezer [עָצַר aw-tsar You restrain], i.e., It's your fault!

Abram has been identified as a man of faith in both Judaism and Christianity. Special attention is attributed to that faith in the Christian New Testament's book of Hebrews:

> By faith Abraham obeyed when he was called to go out to the place which he would receive as an inheritance. And he went out, not knowing where he was going. By faith he dwelt in the land of promise as in a foreign country, dwelling in tents with Isaac and Jacob, the heirs with him of the same promise; for he waited for the city which has foundations, whose builder and maker is God. (Heb.11:8–10)

We actually have no record in the Torah where Abram waited for a city that has no foundations. So it is fair to conclude that the waiting involved a metaphor. The metaphor was one of faith. The entirety of Abram's faith began as the substance of things hoped for.

That hope itself was used by the Christian author of Hebrews to describe the term *evidence*. Usually evidence is something tangible. As a mild example, if police seek evidence in a murder, something like a weapon used would then be submitted as evidence. Even better if the gun is smoking. With this example in the Torah faith itself is 'evidence' which is rewarded by God.

The episode instead allows the picture to unfold in a much different manner. The most relevant questions for consideration are: Was Abram justified in kvetching with God to the point of insolent anger? What do we do when we seemingly are upset with God's plan? Do the accounts of faith recorded in the scripture line up everything we think should happen? Or stated another way: does the Torah signal for all generations and all people everywhere the tool of faith? And if the Torah does demonstrate such a signal, exactly what would that signal "sound" like? If the Torah was derived from an oral tradition, the messages that resounded in the ear of its audience must have been clear. Those messages took an equivocal double entendre, and that is absolutely illustrated in the exasperating study of Abram in the fifteenth Chapter of Genesis.

There is a short word study that must be performed:

Hebrew Word	*Pronunciation*	*Translation*
בֶּט nun bet tet נָבַט	bei't	to look
בֵּיִת	beit	house
רָאָה	rä·ä'	to visually look at

The word בֶּט (bei't, to look) is unique especially in its spoken form with the *segol* vowel. With only a slight twist of the tongue, it could be made to sound similar to the Hebrew word *house* בֵּיִת.

The introduction to Genesis 15 is surprisingly dull in English. It begins with the common religious intonation. The word of God comes to Abram in the customary religious clothing. "Don't be afraid I am both your shield of protection and your great reward." If that particular message would have come to anybody else, it would likely be met with very humble cries of gratitude. Not so with Abram!

Dispensing with the niceties, Abram gets down to brass tactics. The translated image appears disconnected with the previous promise. He is immediately blaming God for having such a dumb plan, and in order to remedy it, Abram is now taking matters into his own hands.

> But Abram said, "Lord God, what will You give me, seeing I go childless, and the heir of my *house (*בֵּיִת pronounced *"beit")* is Eliezer of Damascus?" Then Abram said, "Look, You have given me no offspring; indeed one born in my *house (*בֵּיִת pronounced *"beit")* is my heir!" (Gen. 15:2–3)

Let's turn the table around and examine the response of God to Abram's unusual rant.

> Then He [God] brought him outside and said, "Look *(בֵּט pronounced "bei't," to look)* now toward heaven, and count the stars if you are able to number them." And He said to him, "So shall your descendants be." (Gen. 15:5)

In the oral tradition, if one would have wanted someone to view something, then the verb נָבַט *navat* could be used. In fact it is used over sixty times in the Hebrew scriptures. Most importantly, it is predominantly used in connection with a context of faith.

Another word that could have been used as a verb *to look* would have been the Hebrew word רָאָה *ra-a*, which occurs over 1,300 times and almost exclusively within the context of a purely physical action (i.e., somebody looking at something).

On the one hand, *bei't* could be used with no context of a faith action, but is doubtful. On the other hand, is the teaching of the Torah revealing to us that the encounter in Genesis 15 must be understood in the context of faith? If this is a reasonable context, we should be able to locate this usage in other settings in the Hebrew text. There are many examples of such usage.

Predominate among those usages is a Hebrew text found in the book of Psalms that includes both the verb *bei't* and *ra-a* side by side in sharp distinction.

> The Lord *looks (הִבִּיט pronounced "he"beit")* from Heaven He **sees** *(רָאָה pronounced "ra-a")* all the sons of men. (Ps. 33:13)

מִשָּׁמַיִם, הִבִּיט יְהוָה; רָאָה, אֶת-כָּל-בְּנֵי הָאָדָם

The response to God of Abram's rant deserves close analysis. If read under this light God's response includes the double entendre involving the words *look* and *house*. Both present themselves as similar-sounding words. The response therefore demands an entirely new translation.

Abram was worried about his house on earth, and God reminded him of his "house" which is in heaven.

> Then He [God] brought him outside and said, "Look at your house *(בֵּט pronounced "bei't," to look)* in heaven, and count the stars if you are able to number them." And He said to him, "So shall your descendants be." (Gen. 15:5)

The promise of God was always to make Abram a great nation ("גוֹי, gō'·ē). Do we suppress our true reaction when God's plan does not go as we think it should go? In this instance, the double entendre focuses on faith. The writer of the book of Hebrews explicitly understood that. Abram began his rant focused on his earthly house. Yet the Bible does not settle for God to respond to Abram's earthly rant.

The Torah reminds Abram, and by extension all who will hear, that our house is not on this earth, but instead we must consider the heavens (*ha' Sh'mayin*) when we first begin to think about things on the earth. For that reason alone, the episode in the Bible performs a great service to how we think about God's promise to us. It shreds any possible conclusion that there is a link between righteousness and birthright.

> And he believed in the Lord, and He accounted it to him for righteousness. (Gen. 15:6)

The righteousness accounted to Abram was one of faith. Had the text intended it as a birthright, then the wording would have been absolutely different. The oral tradition retains that meaning. Had it been any other way then the response would have been to Abram:

> *Then He [God] brought him outside and said,* "Look (רָאָה pronounced "ra-a," to look) *now toward heaven, and count the stars if you are able to number them." And He said to him, "So shall your descendants be."* (Gen. 15:5)

That did not happen, instead the word for look, sounding like house in its oral form was used to accentuate and inspire the audience.

It seems counterintuitive, but that is the only scenario that makes sense. By linking both similar sounding words *house* and *look*, we can understand more fully the meaning of the story. The best possible literal translation thousands of years after the fact simply fails. How does one account for faith?

The Covenant

With the Torah, one must struggle. Teaching and learning at times requires a struggle. Covenant is the focus of Abram's actions. When the ancient Sumerians cut a covenant agreement with a god in the Mesopotamian plain, it involved a situation similar to the scene outlined in the story in Genesis 15:7–21. Asking and identifying questions allows one to get to the heart of the matter.

The Lord proclaimed to Abram that He [God] indeed was the one who commanded and brought him forth from Mesopotamia, the city of Ur. Specifically, Abram was brought in order to inherit the land. That should have been quite a concern for Abram. There were people already living in the land, and he was the migrant newcomer. Examine this from Abram's perspective. First of all, he was eighty-five years old. The Lord promised him that he would have a son of his own seed to inherit his accumulated wealth. Secondly, not only would he be a proud father to a baby at his age, he would in fact possess political power all the way from the Nile river in Egypt up to the Euphrates river. This revelation causes Abram to ask the boldest of questions: "Lord, how shall I know that I will inherit it?" In other words: Talk is cheap! Give me proof!

Passing his own wealth down to a son involved an "inheritance." Having the land transferred to his control involved another type of inheritance altogether. Abram must have said to himself on more than one occasion: "This is crazy talk! I am eighty-five! The only way to confiscate this land that I know of is by force, and I am not willing to fight for the land at my age."

When Abram died, all that he owned in the land was a cave that contained the body of his dead wife. The issue of inheritance dominates the theme of this story line. So Abram did what any good old-fashioned Sumerian would have done. Abram engages in a Sumerian based cultural worship involving the cutting of animals on an altar to establish a covenant. But this covenant is not with Marduk, this covenant is with the Lord יְהוָה.

Again, this story is different from other stories. Looking at the response of Abram will not aid in understanding the message. We must look at the response of the Lord. God requires Abram to perform an act that he likely performed with other gods many times as he searched for guidance. But this time, God is having nothing to do with Abram's sacrifice. Abram performed the ritual perfectly, and there was no response. Abram got really tired in the process of driving wild animals and birds away and fell asleep waiting for God's response. This was a shocking development to the audience. Sumerian gods responded to these types of covenants, and if not, perhaps the priests in those jurisdictions had ways to move the scene along. Abram could not risk moving the scene along and waited, and waited, and waited. All the while, vultures flew overhead, eyeing their next dinner. Abram waited and started dozing off. The vultures saw their opening and swooped in for a free meal. Abram jumped to his feet, awakened by the clatter, and intervened because he thought God abandoned him.

He stood before the Lord with dead animal carcasses. Now he was beside himself. He left Sumer to go someplace where he wasn't really wanted. When he reached out to the God who called him, he was left with no response. The message of the Torah is clear: you cannot treat the Lord (יְהוָה) as if he was another common deity of a particular עַם (am/ nation/ people). This message was communicated very vividly to its audience. Perhaps children laughed as Abram awoke in vain, swinging his arms, swooshing away the vultures. Now he was on his own, left with no answer, merely a hope in faith, waiting for the city that has foundations, whose builder and maker is God. That was the message sent to Abram. The Lord is a different God!

Torah goes even further in its unique perspective of how an individual will interact with this God. The initial response of God was a powerful message marked by a no response. God could not be coerced to respond. If one imagines that faith in this God will be all spectacular beds filled with roses, then the second response would have been even more contemptuous. The descendants of Abram would in turn become migrant slaves in a foreign land for four generations, and Abram would die in this land among the inhabitants of Canaan. The most obvious question prompted during this story time left many wondering, *Exactly how do we know when God will demonstrate to us that He approves and will fulfill his plan for our lives?* Abram moved at an elderly age from the country of his birth. Had he made a mistake?

The perspective of this account should be worrisome. Not only was a promise given, but along with the promise appear contradictory conditions. The recipient (Abram) never actually experienced the benefits of the promise. This is the message of this story. Not only a promise, but conditions under which one would not see their fulfillment. As we return to the New Testament author of Hebrews, the role of faith stands front and center. Faith is evidence. Faith is not seen and likely not experienced. Why is that so? Because if we had fulfillment in this present world, then we would not need faith. Abram represented the man to whom the promise was given. Even Abram died looking forward in faith to that promise.

At this point, perhaps we have forgotten exactly how this chapter opened! God initiated the conversation with a declaration. He declares Himself to be Abram's shield and exceedingly growing reward. But the declaration in fact is much more than a reward. The word שָׂכָר, pronounced "sa-kar," is employed. That word had an entrenched foundation in compensation due as a benefit of either an employment hire or wealth obtained from work. Abram, however, over his lifetime, learned that there was nothing he could do to enforce the payment from God. This demonstrates the power of irony. Believing was a sign of faith, despite all the events going on around him. When our Creator speaks to our hearts, what are we to do?

CHAPTER 7

ABOUT LAST NIGHT

An obligation to state the dramatic reality despite its favor or disfavor leads the difficult venture of Genesis 16: 1–6.

Hebrew Word	*Pronunciation*	*Translation*
גּוֹי	gō'·ē	nation / people / usually non-Hebrew people
גֵּר	gār	inhabitant in a country with limited rights
ה	hay	fifth letter of Hebrew alphabet. Serves as a definite article *the*
עָנָה	ä·nä'	afflict / browbeat

The usage of the Hebrew matres lectionis *hay* was introduced as a vowel to aid in reading. Originally, it was predominantly used as a final form letter, meaning, it ended up at the end of a written word. The Hebrews expanded the usage of vowels during the first millennia BCE, and the *hay* eventually became a definite article affixed to the noun it modified at the front of a word.

Hagar, as a name, presents a curious venture into what was heard and what was written. Like others in the written text before her, the name means almost everything to the story. Even if the name of Hagar was an innocent name given to a cute baby girl born to Egyptian parents, the coincidence seems uncanny. To derive the name of Hagar in the Hebrew form, the person would have added the definite article to a noun. In this instance, the noun was pronounced "ger," which meant an inhabitant living in a country with limited rights. No more adequate description could be affixed to this story.

1. Abram was the promised by the Lord that he would be a nation (גּוֹי, gō'·ē, i.e., a nation/people/usually non-Hebrew people).
2. Abram received Sarai's mistress as a wife. Her name was Hagar (הָגָר, pronounced "ha-gār," meaning the stranger/inhabitant in a country with limited rights).
3. To Abram and Hagar was Abram's firstborn beautiful baby boy named Ishmael, meaning "God has heard." Specifically, what God heard was the afflicted anguish of the young woman. Hagar fled from the tormenting affliction imposed by a third person, the very beautiful on the outside first wife of Abram, Sarai.

Questions must be realistically centered. Does this story have a moral message that would have been understood by the original audience? If so, can that message be clearly identified?

Hagar was elevated from the maid-servant role of Sarai as introduced in this story.

> Then Sarai, Abram's wife, took Hagar her maid, the Egyptian, and gave her to her husband Abram to be his wife, after Abram had dwelt ten years in the land of Canaan. (Gen. 16:3)

Is this then a story about Sarai's barren condition? Is this perhaps a story about Hagar's youthful ability to provide Abram an heir (with all the sexual tension poured into the tale being told)? If the answer to both questions is no, then what moral message does the story provide? That answer is found in the key verb עָנָה ,pronounced "ä•nä'," which means to afflict or engage in battering and browbeating of another. It corresponds as a double entendre with a similar word meaning to respond or answer עָנָה (aw-naw').

Everyone at some point in their life intersects with another person that they simply cannot please. Perhaps we perceive that if we get into the good graces of that person, then they will like us. So we try and try and try! Inside, we feel somewhat inferior to the person of our admiration. Yet we push back on that notion in hopes that one day we will strike an amicable chord and become friends.

This story of Hagar perhaps meets all the conditions of the oppressed who in vain try to please another. In English, the phrase "no good deed goes unpunished" rings a bell. In trying to go out of our way, the person who benefits repays the other person with shame.

> And when Sarai dealt harshly (וַתְּעַנֶּהָ) with her, she fled from her presence. (Gen. 16:3)

Sarai's harsh treatment of the foreigner who could do nothing right caused Hagar to flee to a wilderness. Inconsolable weeping and emotion captured the attention of her Creator.

The Angel of the Lord said to her, "Return to your mistress, and submit (וְהִתְעַנִּי which uses the root עָנָה as a weakened submission) yourself under her hand. (Gen. 16:9)

Only once in the Torah does the Hebrew word עָנָה possess the connotative meaning of a "weakened submission." Messaging in the Torah serves to remind a very common word that meant one thing, in its equivocal usage actually meant the opposite. It also serves to illustrate the sovereignty of the Creator. Our Creator knows of our circumstances.

Our Creator recognized in our lives there would be moments exactly like this. The questions prompted by the orator keep the audience engaged. How does one run away from life? It is impossible to run from our problems. Happiness and security in life are created by the individual dealing with each personality in their own sphere of influence.

CHAPTER 8

THERE'S A NEW KID IN TOWN

The seventeenth chapter of Genesis stands uniquely on its own in the various ways in which it differs from all previous conversations between God and Abram. In this particular dramatic moment, we learn that God reveals himself by the name El Shaddai. The word *Shaddai* is often translated as "God Almighty." It however had a much more emphatic emphasis as an adjective. It is derived from a Hebrew word focused on violent destruction. The root word suggested a terrifying notion. Yet God introduces himself in this episode as the God of destruction.

The question arises as to why God is identified as El Shaddai. In this chapter, there appears to be no destruction. The riddle is intimately tied to the intricate development of doublets and story fragments circulating in the oral tradition. Over time stories are modified to address specific interests of the current generation. The seventeenth and eighteenth chapters of Genesis can be viewed as a laboratory of that process.

The common theme in the naming of Isaac includes information about exactly who laughed. Abram laughs in the seventeenth chapter. Sarah laughs in the eighteenth chapter. There are different reasons for why both of these figures laugh. Laughing however was never the punch line of the story. The laugh was incidental to the moral lesson that was taught in the oral tradition. Focusing on the laugh, and using the instance of the fact of a laugh, misses entirely the moral lesson of both episodes that relied on a common corpus of material.

Genesis 17:6 is almost capricious in one way in particular. The promise is reiterated that Abram shall be a father of many nations (גוֹיִם),

and we know that verse has a broader application than the single nation that later became the Hebrew confederated state of Israel.

> I will make you exceedingly fruitful; and I will make nations of you, and kings shall come from you. And I will establish My covenant between Me and you and your descendants after you in their generations, for an everlasting covenant, to be God to you and your descendants after you. Also I give to you and your descendants after you the land in which you are a stranger, all the land of Canaan, as an everlasting possession; and I will be their God. (Gen. 17:6–8)

One must ask, if Abram was the father of Ishmael, would that promise have extended both to the elder Ishmael as well as Isaac? Does God not hear the afflicted or the displaced? The answer to such a challenge would significantly alter how we approach understanding this story in particular and also how we approach God.

This incident in this story is not so much about Abram. Instead, it teaches why Isaac received benefits not available to his older brother. It teaches why Isaac was favored with precision. Poor Abram! This traditional story is set in the following scene: God came to him when he was ninety-nine years. God declared himself as the God of destruction and further declared that his descendants after him will inherit Canaan. Abram must have been fuming inside himself during this meeting with God. He had this same exact conversation with God many times over the past thirty five years.

First, Abram favored Eliazer. Eliazar was eventually disinherited. His heir, Ishmael, was named after God (that seemed about right). What more could God expect or want? Why didn't God resolve this issue thirty-five years ago when he called him forth from Mesopotamia? Abram is almost one hundred years old. Sarah stopped becoming his sexual partner at the age of seventy-five. Abram must have been thinking about that when he fell down on his face and started laughing. How was he ever going to get Sarai to agree to such an arrangement? She threw him out of the tent after ten unsuccessful years of trying to appease him.

The favor of Isaac over Ishmael occurs after what appears to be rudimentary ritual religious recitations. The rite of circumcision became a necessary oblation to receive the inherited promise. It differentiated the line of Ishmael and Isaac. Ishmael was born of a union wherein circumcision was not an accepted practice. Isaac was the first of the Hebrews born after the demonstrated ritual of circumcision.

Richly flowing with instruction, this was differentiated from other stories in circulation throughout Palestine. In this dialogue, Isaac is named Laughter because Abram laughed at God. In the next chapter, we are treated to similarities in circumstances of circulating versions. In that setting, Isaac received his name because Sarah was laughing at God.

> And He said, "I will certainly return to you according to the time of life, and behold, Sarah your wife shall have a son." (Sarah was listening in the tent door which was behind him.) Now Abraham and Sarah were old, well advanced in age; and Sarah had passed the age of childbearing. Therefore Sarah laughed within herself, saying, "After I have grown old, shall I have pleasure, my lord being old also?" And the Lord said to Abraham, "Why did Sarah laugh, saying, 'Shall I surely bear a child, since I am old?' Is anything too hard for the Lord? At the appointed time I will return to you, according to the time of life, and Sarah shall have a son." But Sarah denied it, saying, "I did not laugh," for she was afraid. And He said, "No, but you did laugh! (Gen. 18:10–15)

The tradition of any version would have required somebody to laugh. That was the name of the boy. Yet that particular story line does not even mention circumcision. The reason for the climax reaches toward obviousness. Previously introduced to the God of destruction, we soon learned that there was virtually no destruction in the episode. The setting however in Genesis 18 was filled to the brim with destruction. In the oral tradition, it was highlighted by a question: is there anything too hard for God?

This chapter also employs clever tidbit sound bites. If Abram follows and walks before God he will be תָּמִים, pronounced "tamiym." That word is applied to select men. It was first applied to Noah in Genesis 6:9. Noah was perfect, or tamiym. The second use is now relating to Abram. If Abram walks before God, he will be blameless, or tamiym. Abram received this revelation perhaps as many as thirty to thirty five years after he first decided to follow the direction of God and leave Mesopotamia. The timing of such a statement is in itself a good point for discussion.

Occurring ninety-one times in the Tanakh, it is no small consideration to note that almost half of the time that its usage is found in the Torah. The word *tamiym* is found in forty-one verses of the Torah. Thirty-seven of the forty-one times it is used is focused on the type and condition of an offering that will be presented to God.

The word is used within the instructions for Moses in preparation of the first Passover meal. The lamb must be perfect and without blemish (Exod. 12:5). The first Passover did not differentiate. One could use either a lamb or a goat. This was not a rushed process. The sacrificial lamb or goat was selected by the family on the tenth day of the month. Instructions were to hold it in a special place for four days until the fourteenth of the month. The entire household was then to participate in destroying the animal. It was killed at twilight, and the blood was sprinkled on the doorpost of the house. The animal must meet the condition of perfection (tamiym) in order to qualify for the Passover meal.

Below is a record of each use of the word in the first five books of the Bible. For our purposes, the stories of the seventeenth and eighteenth chapter of Genesis were fragmented in order to allow the family to engage in moralistic conversations that were passed from generation to generation. If the mishpacha was to survive, it needed a mechanism to tie future generations to the past.

Exodus 12:5; 29:1

Leviticus 1:3; 1:10; 3:1; 3:6; 3:9; 4:3; 4:28; 5:15; 6:6; 9:2; 9:3; 14:10; 22:19; 22:21; 23:12; 23:15; 23:18; 25:30

Numbers 6:14; 19:2; 28:3; 28:9; 28:11; 29:19; 28:31; 29:2; 29:8; 29:13; 29:17; 29:20; 29:23; 29:26; 29:29; 29:32; 29:36

Another use of this word occurs in the book of Deuteronomy. It describes a characteristic of God in the song of Moses.

> *He is* the Rock, His work *is* perfect [תָּמִים, "tamiym"];
> For all His ways *are* justice,
> A God of truth and without injustice;
> Righteous and upright *is* He.
> (Deut. 32:4)

The fragmented story involving Sarah and her laughter illustrates the true power of El Shaddai. It was alluded to in the previous version. This story was not about inheritance, or even why the children of Isaac were better than the generations of Ishmaelites. This story focused on the destructive power of El Shaddai. Would the righteous become incidental casualties of God's terrible power employed against the unrighteous? Immediately one would understand those persons to not be tamiym. Beyond that obvious question lingered an anger against a God who was supposed to be a personable God yet at times seemed absent to the oppressed. The oppressed cried to and seemingly received no response.

Confronting this was Abraham's task. He knew the type of men who lived in the area of Sodom and Gomorrah. They were dedicated to anything but walking blamelessly before God. In the fragmented story, El Shaddai, has set his course to right wrongs not too far removed from Abraham's campsite. Abraham attempted to restrain God from his proposed actions through a well-designed argument.

Informing Abraham of his intent to employ destruction, set forth are explicit terms. Abraham was to be the father of a great and mighty nation (גוֹי gō'·ē). He stood before God seemingly wanting to argue his case for the protection of these nations. Abraham surely had to wonder, *Who could stand blameless (תָּמִים, tamiym) before God?* Very few people could meet that standard of perfection. Everyone listening to the story at night would have asked that same question: "What will happen to our city? If only fifty people in a city met the established condition of perfection would it be fair to destroy them? What was the fate of other inhabitants?

At least the bar was now set. If fifty righteous people were found in the city, then El Shaddai would simply move on. Abram does not end the discussion because those who would listen to the story needed to know exactly how low that bar could descend. The comedic tragedy of the story is established. Abraham begins the process of negotiation.

> Far be it from You to do such a thing as this, to slay the righteous with the wicked, so that the righteous should be as the wicked; far be it from You! Shall not the Judge of all the earth do right? (Gen. 18:25)

Colorful commentary was initiated by Abraham. To what extent shall the Judge of all nations show mercy on the nations? Abraham needed to know the answer to that question. If he was going to be the father of these nations, now was the time to determine exactly how that father status would be manifest. The bar was lowered from fifty over the course of six separate iterations down to ten.

Perhaps Abraham was comfortable in his negotiations. He knew that Lot was there. Lot had a wife. Lot had four daughters and two of them had husbands. Lot also had two other daughters living with him. By Abraham's count, he knew of at least eight righteous people living in that area. All he had to do was bet on the farm that there would be at least two people in the entire region that attempted to live a righteous life before God. Those would be odds that even the most careless bookie would accept a wager upon. Abraham folded his cards and assumed his position of the negotiator in chief of the nations (גּוֹי gō'·ē).

These stories reveal the connections between the northern Israelites after their migration to the South. Similar stories emerged as fragmented doublets within the Jewish tradition. Those stories stretched into different discussions. The discussions provided the foundation for the establishment of personal faith in the mishpacha setting.

The fate of Sodom and Gomorrah represented an opportunity for deep social family interactions. Lot escaped ss El Shaddai was raining fire down and destroying the wicked. He pleaded to go to this little insignificant city on the other side of a mountain. Fleeing, he heard behind him all of the destruction. Lot's wife turned around to look upon the historic event. In that moment, she is transformed into a pillar of salt. Did she defy the command of God? Or was the overwhelming compassion she felt for those whom she knew too much to bear?

CHAPTER 9

ROMANCE

Ancient writings were often communicated in forms as weaponized political, ethnic slurs. The agenda at times was obvious while appearing as hidden in plain sight. One such example of this type of ancient writing involved Lot, the nephew of Abraham. Both shared the same heritage. Yet a fifth-century-BCE scribe felt compelled to differentiate between Lot and Abram, despite their common heritage. These stories matriculated through specific regions of the country designed to impart distinct national pride. Abraham's brother, long since dead, left a son under the care of Abram. As a *dor* certain familial obligations existed. The two daughters of Lot find themselves alone with their father living in a cave afraid to go to any town. At first, that is a pressing consideration in light of the recent destruction of Sodom and Gomorrah.

> Now the firstborn said to the younger, "Our father is old, and there is no man on the earth to come in to us as is the custom of all the earth. Come, let us make our father drink wine, and we will lie with him that we may preserve the lineage of our father. So they made their father drink wine that night. And the firstborn went in and lay with her father, and he did not know when she lay down or when she arose. (Gen. 19: 31–33)

Speaking to the younger sister, the eldest daughter took control of the situation. "Last night I went into Dad. Tonight is your turn." So for the second night in a row, the dutiful daughters sought to preserve their father's lineage. They were taking one for the team, so to speak. This resulted in both daughters becoming pregnant and giving birth to two young boys.

What exactly does the recording of these two births do to advance any moral training? Were these records the result of a careful pen-preserving events in chronology? The concept of *ya'lad* (giving birth) is without doubt a major event in this episode. But in any society, that set of facts raised one's brow as an aggressive insult. Imposing this story under its original oral tradition produced shrieks and groans. The context is almost semi-lost in translation.

The firstborn gave birth and named the little baby Moab. The second daughter gave birth and named the baby Ammon. These were not just mere names to be memorized in a geography or history test. These were names of insults. *Moab* is translated as "from the father." *Ben-Ammi* is translated as "son of my people." What daughter would tell the whole world she conceived a baby with her father and a son was born? That is what the eldest daughter of Lot did. What daughter would tell the whole world Moab's cousin was also the product of a sexual encounter with Dad? That is what the youngest daughter of Lot did.

The purpose of the text was to drip bias into the tradition of the origin of two countries. In fact, such a story, as related in the oral format, sparked a deep sense of pride among those living in Palestine. The others who lived on the other side of the Jordan may have been related, but they certainly had different moral compasses than us over here. The mutant incestuous Moabites and Ammonites lived over there. It was proper to hate them. They were the product of questionable sexual origin and inherently not to be trusted. Young children would have responded appropriately, "Yuck!" The fact that the meaning could have been veiled to reflect something else altogether made the story enduring.

CHAPTER 10

LAUGHING OUT LOUD

Abraham begins a journey. At the close of our last encounter with Abraham, he was settled in a grove of trees in Mamre near Hebron. There are several wordplays contained in this story. One struggles initially to figure out why Abraham would move from the grove of trees near Hebron to Gerar. In the oral tradition, there is no mystery at all. It is not at all doubtful that the story gained popularity due to its employment of mnemonic devices.

And Abraham journeyed from there to the South, and dwelt between Kadesh and Shur, and stayed (גּוּר gür, "dwell/ stranger") in Gerar (גְּרָר Gerar).

> Now Abraham said of Sarah his wife, "She *is* my sister."
> And Abimelech king of Gerar sent and took Sarah.
> (Gen. 20:1–2)

Cleverly employing the two words *stayed* and *Gerar* alerted the audience to pay attention.

Hebrew Word	*Pronunciation*	*Translation*
גּוּר	gür	dwell/ stranger / stand in fear
גְּרָר	Gerar	city ruled by Abimelech

But this word גּוּר/*gür* possesses some special auxiliary meanings beyond the verb *to dwell.* The location of the dwelling was in a place with a similar sounding word to that of *gür*. Yet attention is drawn by the secondary use of this word. Eleven times the word is used as defining *fear*. So, the atmosphere created in the opening monologue sets the stage for the message. At this point in the story those who were inclined would grasp each other's hand tightly.

Studying this doublet previously we know Abraham had a deal already worked out with Sarah. No matter where they went, Sarah was first introduced to strangers as his sister. This arrangement presumably allowed Abraham a level of security. He would stand by and allow other men to secure the favor of Sarah. Abraham, in exchange for the lie, would enjoy the privations of safety from all harm.

Of course, Sarah would then be subjected to either the abuse of other men or marriages. It is in this arrangement that the postmodern reader often settles their interpretation of the text. Supposing the story is about Abraham's safety and God's divine intervention, the message is inverted and perverted. The message of the Torah as a teaching despite this episodic twist is contained within the questions and emotion posed by Abimelech. The questions are posed respectively to God and then to Abraham. These questions are a variant twists of previous questions from the most recent encounter with Abraham.

Question Posed by Abimelech to God

"Lord, will You slay a righteous nation also?" (Gen. 20:4b). We saw this question with a slight variation in Genesis 18. God purposed and revealed to Abraham his plans for the destruction of Sodom and Gomorrah. This information was passed on during a quick stop at Abraham's tent along the way to engage that action. Abraham looked up, and found in front of him the Lord and two men. Abraham discovered what their end goal was and posed a series of questions.

"Would You also destroy the righteous with the wicked?" (Gen. 18:23b). Noticing there is a common theme, the differences are highlighted. In the previous teaching, there was a presumption that God's justice dominated over human personal conduct. At issue was the central problem of accidentally destroying the few righteous. In this instance, the variation focuses on a more deliberate set of circumstances. Will God destroy a righteous nation?

Abraham is normally considered to be a protagonist. In this story, Abraham is exactly the opposite. He is a weak man filled with fear. The fear is implied in the special word גּוּר *gür*. There is an inclination to favor Abraham in this episode simply because he is Abraham. Yet the reality of such a standing dissolves under careful scrutiny. This story intentionally begs and leads the audience to see Abraham in a less favorable light. It facilitates the discussion. One must next consider the questions posed by Abimelech to Abraham.

Questions Posed by Abimelech to Abraham

> What have *you* done to us? (Gen. 20:9b)
>
> How have I offended you, that you have brought on me and on my kingdom a great sin? (Gen. 20:9c)
>
> What did you have in view, that you have done this thing? (Gen. 20:10b)

God visited Abimelech in a dream. That dream was filled with fear. God acknowledged the most important point. Abimelech was a man of integrity within his heart. The command therefore given to Abimelech to return Sarah was incidental to the outcome. There was never any real question as to whether Sarah would be returned. Abimelech's actions would demonstrate the proof that he was righteous. Otherwise, the story has no meaning at all. The fulfillment of the story occurs after the questions posed by Abimelech to Abraham. Abraham suggested that he was concerned for his life, but that concern does not stand up to examination. It is a red-herring clue meant to distract with the intention to reveal the fundamental argument.

The issue remained: would God also slay a righteous nation? That point is clarified in all of the questions presented to both God and Abraham. Abimelech, a Philistine king, was righteous. As a righteous man, he was incensed that the actions of another would be a burden on his doorstep. Stimulated by anger directed toward Abraham, he cried out, "What have you done? What have I done to offend you that you brought a great sin into my kingdom? Why in the world did you do this? Did you see something that suggested this was the best course of action for you to take?" These were questions of fear!

Will God accidently slay the righteous in His role of reeking vengeance upon the sinner? Will God slay righteous nations if they are not Hebrew nations? Ultimately, two major questions would come up within the mishpacha setting:

1) Who is righteous?
2) To what extent is there a fear of YHWH among a non-Hebrew mishpacha?

Those were important issues that needed to be resolved. In this episode, Abraham was not righteous. He was acting in a way to preserve himself. Concerned only for his own safety, he placed all the others around him at risk. Sarah was placed in harm's way. Abimelech was placed in harm's way. The servants of Abimelech were placed in harm's way. At every turn fear of the unknown drove the conversations.

Abrahams answer to Abimelech reveals the story line. "I did not think that in this place there was a fear of God." In his own mind, the result of that situation ended with him dying and his wife being given to another man. The most outlandish action conceivable occurred. Abraham simply gave his wife away. To conclude that Abraham acted righteous is contrary to the story line. The oral tradition conveys perhaps the most sarcastic retort contained in the Bible.

To explain that retort, we first come to the terms of the response. The oral tradition reminded the audience Abraham stayed (gür) in Gerar and linked that word by implicating the stay with the double entendre. Not only did he stay there, his stay was intimate with fear. To convince the audience that Abraham was not acting in good faith in this episode his wife Sarah is characterized in legal language.

Hebrew Word	*Pronunciation*	*Translation*
אִשָּׁה	ish·shä'	wife (Eve was the ish·shä' of Adam)
בָּעַל	bä·al'	wife/ dominion / rule over

> But God came to Abimelech in a dream by night, and said to him, "Indeed you *are* a dead man because of the woman whom you have taken, for she *is* a man's *wife* (בָּעַל bä·al')." (Gen. 20:3)

The biblical account did not identify Sarah as Abraham's *ish·shä.* Eve was characterized as Adam's *ish·shä.* The word *ish·shä* occurs over 780 times in the Bible. Over 750 times, it is used in connection with the denominator as either a woman or as a man's wife. Only once is בָּעַל used in the book of Genesis to refer to a woman as a man's wife. The purpose of its use is clear. The story line wanted all to be put on notice that there was a legal relationship at play. So why is that element important? The importance comes to fruition when Abimelech finally confronts Sarah.

Presented in a weak condition, Abraham attempts a justification of the absurd. He responds to Abimelech that technically Sarah is his stepsister. This type of justification reveals in teaching that when you are caught in a lie, just accept responsibility and move on. To the ear, any further justification only digs the hole a little bit deeper. When someone attempts to cover a lie with technical information, our natural response is further disdain and disgust for the liar. The Bible student then is faced with an ethical conundrum: should I accept Abraham's technical explanation and move on?

Biting on that piece of the apple would be the wrong thing to do. The episode purposely paints Abraham in a negative light because the overriding question needed to be resolved. Are the Philistines righteous? What is righteousness? Can the righteous engage in sinful actions? When the righteous engage in sinful actions what is God's response? When the righteous engage in sinful actions what should be our response? The Philistine was righteous.

CHAPTER 11

A NICE COOL DRINK OF A LAD

> Then God remembered (tzacar) Noah, and every living thing, and all the animals that *were* with him in the ark. (Gen. 8:1a)

> And it came to pass, when God destroyed the cities of the plain, that God remembered (tzacar) Abraham... (Gen. 19:29a)

> Then God remembered (tzacar) Rachel, and God listened to her and opened her womb. (Gen. 30:22)

There are a couple of facets opened in this account of Abraham that include Sarah. The first issue is the remarkable way in which God either remembered or visited Sarah due to her barren condition. So let's first be introduced to the word *paqad* to set the scene in motion. It could mean to visit or remember. The word tzacar is more frequently used for the word remember.

Hebrew Word	*Pronunciation*	*Translation*
פָּקַד	paqad	visit/remembered
זָכַר	tzacar	remember
צְחֹקָה/צָחַק	tsä·khak'	to laugh
יִצְחָק	yits·khäk'	Isaac/from laughter

It is a word that occurs fifty-nine times in the Bible when it is translated as "visit." Paqad could possess the double meaning of remember. It could mean one thing and intend another. In the Torah "God remembered (זָכַר) tzacar remembered) Rachel, and God listened to her and opened her womb" (Gen. 30:22). That God visited Sarah and remembered Rachel may or may not be a difference. Clearly, the oral tradition reminds us that the miracle with Sarah was distinct from the young Rachel who was of childbearing age. Rachel giving birth would have been hardly noticeable. Sarah giving birth at her age was something to take note of.

We often seek God to simply remember the natural course of the affairs of our life. In those instances we want God to remember us. Even during some events in our life, all we want is a more "normal" course to prevail. We would even accept a lesser acknowledgement from God that he is indeed on our side. For example, in Genesis 50:24, as Joseph lay upon his deathbed, he proclaimed that God will surely visit his brothers and lead them out of Egypt. Joseph's brothers entered Egypt to escape the severe conditions of Palestine. Would it take a miracle sometime in the future to send them back? It was merely a two to three days journey back home.

In Exodus chapter 3, God spoke to Moses. He instructed him to call the elders of Israel and inform them he had visited them. God had seen all the oppressions they were experiencing in Egypt. There is no doubt that the Hebrew words *paqad* and *tzacar* had distinct differences. God visited Sarah, and God remembered Rachel.

A second facet of this particular story hints at a separate tradition in the naming of Isaac. For this reason, Genesis 21:1–8 must be either a separate story, totally unrelated to the saga of Hagar and Ishmael in Genesis 21:9–21, or it is a perfectly fitting constructed introduction. In the first eight verses of chapter 21, Sarah entertains the audience with a remarkable revelation. She provided Abraham with a son when he was one hundred years old. This was so remarkable that Sarah exclaimed, "All who hear of this will laugh on my account."

Why would this be considered as a different circulating story from the other popular versions of the naming of Isaac? An analysis of those other versions will shed some light on the discussion. That tradition stems from an episode contained in the seventeenth chapter of Genesis. Abram was enjoying the company of his thirteen-year-old son, Ishmael. Suddenly, the Lord appeared out of nowhere. A linguistic device in the oral tradition is employed. God changes Abram's name to Abraham. There are many nuances to the importance of this act. The most important is set forth here. Abram of Akkadian/Sumerian lineage is now fully aligned as a Hebrew. The addition of a Hebrew vowel and pluralization of his name accomplishes that.

A covenant was both declared and reaffirmed. The reaffirmation is driven by the act of circumcision. God declared that Sarah would provide Abraham with a son. Abraham then dropped to his knees. One would suspect Abraham dropped to his knees to worship God for this promise; however, nothing could be further from the truth. Abraham found this promise to be so hilarious that he could not let his real reaction be known. He fell to his knees in order to hide his face while he laughed at God.

> Then Abraham fell upon his face, and laughed, and said in his heart: "Shall a child be born unto him that is a hundred years old? and shall Sarah, that is ninety years old, bear?"...Then God said: "No, Sarah your wife shall bear you a son, and you shall call his name Isaac (laughter)." (Gen. 17:17 and 19a)

This chapter presents the variant version of an already popular story. It attempted to account for the weird name attached to the son of Abraham. It is humorous in the oral tradition because in the Hebrew oral tradition, man's response to God results in a permanent reminder. Issac (laughter) is now the boy's permanent name. Yet oral tradition provided a third variant accounting as to the origin of Isaac's name. In one tradition, the name is ascribed to what people will do when they hear the story. In another tradition, it reflected Abraham's response to God. In yet another variation, it retold the story from Sarah's point of view.

CHAPTER 12

THE WELL OVER THERE

Establishing a story line is evident in the passage in the Bible after the naming of Isaac. Perhaps it is linked in the Bible as a segue since it involves some familiar characters and also some familiar background. It is misunderstood when it is taken as a historical lesson. If the banishment of Hagar teaches us a lesson, what might that lesson be? That it is okay to be mean as long as God justifies your basis in your own mind? Of course not, that would be both a silly conclusion and a poor application of righteousness.

In oral tradition, the episode prompted questions around the family meal. An outline of the story is required. The story in the translation is not complicated. Sarah becomes extremely jealous of another woman and her son. Unilaterally, Sarah determines the best course of action within the family mishpacha. Banishment is decreed for both to a certain poverty, if not death. No more extreme measure could have been considered.

Abraham allowed for this decision after weighing the personal peace he would enjoy with Sarah. Arising on a certain morning, he provisions Hagar with a container of water and bread. She would be exiled from the only family she has known as an adult. Ending up in the wilderness of Beersheba, her life is crumbling. Unable to watch the lad die, she places him under a bush and then walks a good distance to cry.

There is no indictment for the cruel treatment of a stranger such as Hagar. That is why we know that the lesson is about something else. So what does the Torah teach? Either the rules of civility always apply or they don't apply at all. Discerning what is being taught is understood from both the context and the message. The context is clear. This episode originated out of oral tradition. It was designed to spark and ignite discussion deeply ingrained in the morality of the mishpacha.

To arrive at the message requires a more coherent translation. Embedded in the language are obvious clues.

Hebrew Word	*Pronunciation*	*Translation*
מְצַחֵק	me-tsä·khak'	scoffing/making sport/(a word derived from Isaac's actual name)
רָעַע	raw-ah'	displeasing/grievous/evil/ ill/ harm
רַע	rah	evil/bad/disagreeable/wicked
בְּאֵר שָׁבַע	Be·ār'shä·vah'	name of a town/Beersheva
בְּאֵר	be·ār'	well from which water is stored
שָׁבַע	shä·vah'	swear an oath
קֶשֶׁת	keh'·sheth	bending a bow for shooting
מַיִם	mah'·yim	water

> And Sarah saw the son of Hagar the Egyptian, whom she had borne to Abraham, scoffing (מְצַחֵק*/me-tsä·khak'*/ scoffing/making sport/ a word derived from Isaac's actual name). Therefore she said to Abraham, "Cast out this bondwoman and her son; for the son of this bondwoman shall not be heir with my son, *namely* with Isaac." And the matter was very displeasing (יֵרַע ye'rah'; displeasing/grievous/evil/ill harm) in Abraham's sight because of his son, (Gen 21:9-11)

The entirety of the matter is introduced. The eldest son of Abraham was scoffing and making sport. That would not be unusual for a boy of fourteen. Ishmael was not an infant. Ishamel was sprouting as a young man. Possessing the height and weight of a young man, he still maintained the vulgarity of a teen boy. Teens back then were not much different than today. Teens test the waters, so to speak, of acceptable behavior. Ishmael's actions in light of his age are consistent.

There is some solace as we attempt to work through the obvious issues. Abraham was not initially on board with the decision to banish Hagar. We are treated to the ruse of the episode as Abraham talked with God. In fact, God appears to be perfectly fine with the plan.

> But God said to Abraham, "Do not let it be displeasing in your sight because of the lad or because of your bondwoman. Whatever Sarah has said to you, listen to her voice; for in Isaac your seed shall be called. Yet I will also make a nation of the son of the bondwoman, because he *is* your seed. (Gen. 21:12–13)

Perhaps Abraham said something like, "God, this is just not the right thing to do!" We are not sure if he said this, we just simply know it is a gut reaction we have when we read this story. That is the exact type of response the Bible wants to cultivate. We should instinctively and rationally apprehend that which we ought to do. We should know right from wrong. We should know that which Abraham and Sarah did was wrong.

> So Abraham rose early in the morning, and took bread and a skin of water; and putting it on her shoulder, he gave it and the boy to Hagar, and sent her away. Then she departed and wandered in the Wilderness of Beersheba (בְּאֵר שָׁבַע *Be·ār'shä·vah*/name of a town /Beersheva). And the water in the skin was used up, and she placed the boy under one of the shrubs. Then she went and sat down across from him at a distance of about a bowshot (קֶשֶׁת *keh'*·sheth / bending a bow for shooting) for she said to herself, "Let me not see the death of the boy." So she sat opposite him, and lifted her voice and wept. (Gen. 21:14–16)

In the span of one paragraph, we have moved from a healthy fourteen-year-old doing what strong healthy teens do best to a limp baby on the verge of death (unless, of course, that is not what the story is about). The banishment of Hagar and Ishmael as an event read in a modern language is extremely difficult to digest. Reacting to this episode places one in the crosshairs of different moral decisions than when originally told. It becomes difficult to untangle the web because we want to love Abraham and Sarah.

We justify the account seemingly because God appeared to justify Abraham. We convince ourselves that since God justified the banishment, who are we to question the outcome. In the oral tradition imagine if you heard that story for the first time. The number of follow on questions sparked from such a sinister story line would be as numerable as the stars in the sky.

1. How do we react when people intend evil for our lives? This was a huge question in light of the close similarity to the two words placed at the center of the story. Both words would have sounded eerily similar, composed with the right accentuation.

רָעַע	raw-ah'	displeasing/grievous/evil/ ill/ harm
רַע	rah	evil / bad / disagreeable / wicked

2. Why was Abraham a willing conspirator in something evil?
3. Why does God acknowledge an action as evil, but since it is destiny, do it anyway?
4. How do we react when someone as influential as Sarah intends evil for our lives?

The story line of the episode, after the tale was told, would have focused on the four questions identified above. In postmodern Bible studies, we focus on the genealogy of Abraham instead. The story serves little instruction under the latter model. The tales come to life within the mishpacha when it is time to discuss right versus wrong. Interacting with a less-than-perfect Abraham provides a powerful baseline from which morals are identified and discussed.

The episode explodes with powerful imagery useful in remembering how to ignite conversations. Hagar sat down a *bowshot* away from Ishmael. That is more than a weird usage of the word.

> So God was with the lad; and he grew and dwelt in the wilderness, and became an archer (קַשָּׁת *keh*'·sheth).
> (Gen. 21:20)

> וַיְהִי אֱלֹהִים אֶת-הַנַּעַר, וַיִּגְדָּל; וַיֵּשֶׁב, בַּמִּדְבָּר, וַיְהִי, רֹבֶה קַשָּׁת

The story line became memorable since Ishmael was placed a bow (קֶשֶׁת) shot away. He then become an archer (קַשָּׁת). That nuance was evident to the audience. It illuminated and allowed the story to be easily introduced when it was time to discuss morals. The story contained a mnemonic device to facilitate the conversation.

Was it essential to place Ishmael a bow shot away from his mother? Of course not. Then why introduce that fact? The answer lies in the nature of oral tradition. It facilitated the story so that it could be communicated across many different venues with a degree of consistency. What would never change though would be the reaction of the audience.

Was it indispensable for Abraham to be troubled grievously? Of course! It ignited and moved the discussion. It colored the audience's reaction against a person of a heroic nature. Allowing such an action against Hagar, Abraham became relatable. But the character flaw was not the story. Of course, Abraham was grieved and that grievous condition was by its nature evil, bad, and disagreeable. The episode became a perfect cover story for the most important questions: Is God ultimately in control? What can man do against us that has not been ordained by God who protects us individually?

The promise given by God to Abraham is instructive. From Ishmael, a nation will also be born for he was of Abraham's seed. When God made the initial oath to Abraham, he encouraged him. In him all the families (mishpachas) of the earth shall be blessed. In Genesis 15:5, God told Abraham to look up to the stars. His seed/descendants would also be innumerable.

This story line is only halfway told. The author of the book of Hebrews listed both Abraham and Sarah appropriately as pillars of faith.

> By faith Abraham obeyed when he was called to go out to the place which he would receive as an inheritance. And he went out, not knowing where he was going. By faith he dwelt in the land of promise as in a foreign country, dwelling in tents with Isaac and Jacob, the heirs with him of the same promise; for he waited for the city which has foundations, whose builder and maker is God. By faith Sarah herself also received strength to conceive seed, and she bore a child when she was past the age, because she judged Him faithful who had promised. Therefore from one man, and him as good as dead, were born as many as the stars of the sky in multitude—innumerable as the sand which is by the seashore. (Heb. 11:8–12)

It is therefore reasonable to ask: Does the Bible also depict Hagar as a woman of faith? Clearly, she was a woman of the promise since God declared her son would rise to be a great nation. But of faith?

The story line gives us more than a hint that was the case. Abraham provided Hagar with a bottle of water and sent her out to Beersheva. The name Beersheva is composed of two Hebrew words בְּאֵר שֶׁבַע. The word בְּאֵר literally means "well." The word שֶׁבַע literally means "oath/ promise." All the school-age children listening to the story would have interrupted the tale and screamed out ecstatically, "Look at the well!" Sarah runs out of *mayim* (water) right next to the well of promise. When God opened her eyes, she saw a well. The only well she could have seen there was the established בְּאֵר at Beersheva.

Is it a stretch to establish Hagar as a woman of faith? Many of us feel as if we are on the outside looking in and can relate with Hagar. Sarah in her imperfections is relatable. Abraham in his imperfections is relatable. The singer/songwriter B. J. Thomas moves us when he sings:

So please play for me a sad melody
So sad that it makes everybody cry-why-why-why
A real hurtin' song about a love that's gone wrong
Cause I don't want to cry all alone
Hey, won't ya play another somebody done
somebody wrong song
And make me feel at home while I miss my baby,
while I miss my baby

The banishment of Hagar is relatable. We can look to her also as a woman of faith. She alone sat on the verge of death unable to see what was in front of her. Through faith and the promise to make her son a great nation, she survived.

CHAPTER 13

SEVEN LAMBS AT THE WELL

"Swear unto me that you will do unto me as I have done unto you." This principle of fair treatment was taught in the Torah. Yet the teaching comes from an unlikely source in an unlikely setting. The king of the Philistines, Abimelech, uttered this phrase to Abraham.

> Now therefore, swear to me by God that you will not deal falsely with me, with my offspring, or with my posterity; but that according to the kindness that I have done to you, you will do to me and to the land in which you have dwelt (Gen. 21:23).

The setting for Genesis 21:22–34 most assuredly has been edited into the biblical record at a seemingly suspect location. It follows the episode of the banishment of Hagar from Abraham's mishpacha. The story of Hagar takes place at the well of Sheva. That well produced water. We are informed of that in this pericope. We learned that Abraham himself dug that well. The episode either confirms the Hagar affair previously recorded or it serves an entirely different function.

That function is not hidden. It relates an alternate version of how בְּאֵר שֶׁבַע *(Beersheva)* actually got its name. The story takes an innocent turn immediately after Abraham affirms to Abimelech that he will extend to him fair treatment. That turn had to occur. Without the turn there is no story.

> Then Abraham rebuked Abimelech because of a well of water which Abimelech's servants had seized. And Abimelech said, "I do not know who has done this thing; you did not tell me, nor had I heard *of it* until today. (Gen. 21:25)

There really appears to be no apparent predicate event necessitating Abraham's rebuke of Abimelech. In the previous verse, Abraham swore an oath.

Hebrew Word	*Pronunciation*	*Translation*
שָׁבַע(אִשָּׁבֵעַ)	shä·vah'	I swear an oath
שֶׁבַע	sheh'·vah	seven

To consummate that oath, Abraham performs a Mesopotamian custom known to him.

> So Abraham took sheep and oxen and gave them to Abimelech, and the two of them made a covenant. And Abraham set seven ewe lambs of the flock by themselves. Then Abimelech asked Abraham, "What is the meaning of these seven ewe lambs which you have set by themselves?" And he said, "You will take these seven ewe lambs from my hand, that they may be my witness that I have dug this well. (Gen. 21:27–30)

Hearing this account in the oral tradition without benefit of the next sentence produces a startling conclusion. Abraham took seven (שֶׁבַע, *sheh'·vah*/seven) ewe lambs and cut a covenant invoking the blessing of God. One suspects that the name of the well to which Hagar found God's promise over time became a point of dispute. Was the name of the well בְּאֵר שָׁבַע or was the proper name for the well related to the number of sheep Abraham offered in cutting his covenant with Abimelch? One easily imagines that over time a dispute occurred between political and religious factions over the proper pronunciation. Was it *pronounced* "Be·ār'*sheh'·vah*" or "Be·ār'shä·vah"?

This was more than a nuanced religious argument. It struck to the heart of the pride established within families seeking to protect the tradition. One easily suspects that a later editor completely wanted to eliminate a religious controversy. "Therefore he called that place Beersheba, because the two of them swore an oath there" (Gen. 21:30). The ending could have as easily been settled as, "Therefore he called that place Beersheba, because the two of them swore an oath with seven ewe lambs."

We will never know the intent of the scribe. It is perhaps logic or misguided conjecture to suggest that there was even a religious controversy. Yet the story stands in stark contrast to its opening verse. Abraham is mild and humble while swearing an oath promising to be fair. Instantly, he rebukes the person to whom he has sworn an oath. A second oath is performed. For what reason? Two oaths within one story certainly tells us that something is amiss. The detraction is apparent when the conclusion is laid out. The origin of naming the well.

Abimelech as a Philistine king was in a similar situation with Abraham on a previous occasion. Abraham passed his wife off as his sister (Gen. 20:1–16). It is unlikely that Abraham moved away from Gerar just to establish a spat with Abimelech over a previously dug well. Therefore, we can conclude this story is edited into the text for a specific purpose. It arrives in the text immediately after the banishment of Hagar, and Hagar is not even mentioned, it's textual location in the Torah creates an association with Hagar. Since it involves a unique name, the text becomes highlighted and possibly an attempt to show the other side of a story.

CHAPTER 14

MY DARLING CHILD

Abraham once again comes under the microscope of scrutiny in a fantastic episode wherein Abraham is "tested." In this narrative, the traditional extraction focuses on the holistic commitment of Abraham to the promise and provision provided by God. That promise placed in question Abraham's faith. Seemingly, if he passes the test he will be rewarded. But first, he must obey the command from God to slay his son. That implausible command does not make sense even within the context of faith. The underlying story emerges. Abraham spent eighty-six years of his of his life with no biological heir. If he slays his son, then what will become of God's promise? Faith emerges as one hopes for a positive outcome for Abraham. Since the outcome was already known, it is fair to ask if that was really the story?

> And He [God] said: "Take now thy son, thine only son, whom thou lovest, even Isaac, and get thee into the land of Moriah; and offer him there for a burnt-offering upon one of the mountains which I will tell thee of." (Gen. 22:2)

God laid down the bar of faith: slay your only son to prove your faith in me! Except for one simple fact. Isaac was not Abraham's only son. Also, there were previous-designated heirs. The audience now is involved in a humdinger.

Hebrew Word	*Pronunciation*	*Translation*
יָחִיד (root יָחַד)	yä·khēd'	only (other translations provide a different meaning: darling; only child, desolate, solitary)
יָחַד	yä·khad	to unite or become one

Variants of the root are listed in their grammar based form as follows:

> Genesis 22: 2, (יְחִידְךָ) your only son
> Genesis 22:8, (יַחְדָּו) together

Genesis 22:12, (יְחִידְךָ) your only son
Genesis 22:16, (יְחִידֶךָ) your only son
Genesis 22:19, (יַחְדָּו) together

The Hebrew word as a root word יָחַד appears five times in the twenty-second chapter of Genesis. The three times it is used in the Torah in the form of yä·hēdekah' it appears exclusively in the twenty-second chapter. Those verses are 2, 12, and 16. The only other time the root form of yä·khad is used is in the forty-ninth chapter of Genesis. Jacob laid upon his death bed reminding his family of the evil performed by Simeon and Levi. That pronouncement by Jacob sanctioned Simeon and Levi by declaring they would be "dispersed" in Israel, not united in Israel.

The original story had very little to do with the testing of Abraham. It is not in dispute that the story line revolves around a test. Nor is it in dispute that Abraham passed the test. What is in dispute is that Abraham did not offer his "only son." Isaac had an older brother. Ishmael reached a majority age before Isaac was born.

Is there a better translation to the word יְחִידְךָ ("your only son"). The answer is yes!

Abraham offered his "darling" son, not his only son.

> Deliver my soul from the sword; my darling [precious] from the power of the dog. (Ps. 22:20 NKJV)

> Lord, how long wilt thou look on? rescue my soul from their destructions, my darling [precious life] from the lions. (Ps. 35:17 NKJV)

Replacing the translation of "only son" with "darling son" restores the integrity of the text. It also elevates the accuracy in light of everything we know about Abraham. Yet there is one special thing accomplished in the text that indeed serves to unite the story.

Relegating the test and Abraham's response to God as a secondary element of the story line serves to introduce the most important teaching of the Torah. The Torah does not emphasize the faith of Abraham as much as it elevates the faith of those around him.

> And it came to pass after these things, that it was told Abraham, saying, Behold, Milcah, she hath also born children unto thy brother Nahor; Huz his firstborn, and Buz his brother, and Kemuel the father of Aram, and Chesed, and Hazo, and Pildash, and Jidlaph, and Bethuel. And Bethuel begat Rebekah: these eight Milcah did bear to Nahor, Abraham's brother. And his concubine, whose name was Reumah, she bare also Tebah, and Gaham, and Thahash, and Maachah. (Gen. 22:20–24)

Chiastic Hebrew poetry pairs together two ideas with a variant as an illustration. There is no doubt that Abraham was a man of faith. It was a miracle that Abraham fathered a son at the age of one hundred. Overlooked has been the remarkable story of Abraham's brother, Nahor. We know of Abraham and Sarah's infertility. We overlook that Nahor, his brother, left Mesopotamia with Abraham. We are never told that his wife, Milcah, was barren. Yet that indeed was the case. Huz was the firstborn of Nahor and Milcah. Since he was born after Isaac, perhaps this represented an even greater miracle. We can only assume Sarah and Milcah were about the same age.

> And Abram and Nahor took them wives: the name of Abram's wife was Sarai; and the name of Nahor's wife, Milcah, the daughter of Haran, the father of Milcah, and the father of Iscah. (Gen. 11:29)

Milcah is identified as Nahor's wife during the time that he resided in the ancient city of Ur. Abram and Nahor were approximate in age. They were brothers. Abraham, Sarah, Nahor, and Milcah most assuredly would have known each other and participated in feasts within the mishpacha. They would have shared dreams, family stories, and the hardships of being unable to produce offspring. Their mutual infertility would have served as a bond as they admiringly looked upon others.

The connecting thread between Genesis 22:1–19 and Genesis 22:20–24 is now revealed. The boy Isaac and the girl Iscah.

Hebrew Word	*Pronunciation*	*Translation*
יִסְכָּה	yis·kä'	sister of Lot and Milcah
יִצְחָק	yits·khäk'	Isaac

Concerning the pronunciation of יִסְכָּה (yis·kä') and יִצְחָק (yits·khäk'), we must turn. Iscah (Yis·kä') is a feminine name. With the right accent, it has the flavor of the name associated with Isaac. Iscah is introduced well before the birth of Isaac. Perhaps she represented a name tribute to her cousin. Or perhaps somebody wanted to embellish a good story to gain a few laughs from the audience. Lost in the episode are the miraculous births attributed to Nahor and Milcah. Sarah had one son. Milcah had eight.

It was not enough that Abraham believed. The Torah teaches us a more important lesson than Abraham's personal journey of faith. Singling out Nahor was important. Nahor was never specifically provided with the promise given to Abraham. Today, we read of God's promise to Abraham. The Torah teaches us however to have the faith of Nahor. Nahor heard of the promise given to Abraham and against all odds hoped for his own promise to come true. We live and struggle in a world of religious confusion. We look to the Abrahams of our day, those seemingly blessed with fulfilling faith. We live as Nahor and Milcah, out of the limelight.

In Genesis 22:20, it was told Abraham that his brother just had a baby. This suggested that there was close communication between the brothers. It is easy to conclude that Nahor had to provide some comfort to his wife. In future family gatherings, the old subject of being barren was sure to come up. If for no other reason, the presence of Isaac at the family meal would serve as a curious needle piercing Milcah's heart. Milcah had to fight the pervasive curse: "How could God remember Sarah and forget me?"

Nahor had to deal with this. His wife was hurting and struggling, asking God, "Why have you forsaken me?" She was well past the age of bearing children. That message stimulated discussions in the oral tradition. Did God favor Sarah over Milcah? Does God favor others over us?

We live a life, like Nahor, watching the blessings of God bestowed upon others around us. Nahor comforted his aged bride: "Have faith! Have faith! Don't look at that which happens to others! Keep in focus that God has created you and is watching over your daily care." In the end, was Milcah's faith rewarded? Do you have the faith of Milcah? Despite all that goes on around you, do you trust God?

Nahor's faith was complete. Not only was he the father of eight, God's blessings knew no limit. Milcah gave over a concubine to Nahor as she was unable to fulfill all of Nahor's vigor. To Nahor's concubine was born an additional four children. This Nahor was something else.

The amazing episode of Abrham's faith therefore served as a chiastic bookend to cement the story line of one's personal journey of faith. Abraham never offered his only son. That translation makes no sense. Had Abraham actually gone through with the slaying of Isaac, he could always rely on Ishmael to carry on the family name. But Nahor had no Ishmael to rely upon.

Has God only remembered Abraham and forgotten us? Milcah teaches us that is not the case. Rely on the promise our Creator has spoken to us personally. In faith, we fulfill his intent for our life.

CHAPTER 15

SARAH

The death of Sarah dominates the twenty-third chapter of the book of Genesis. It also reminds the reader of a critical problem. For all of God's promises, to reward his faith by giving him possession of the land, Abraham remained landless throughout most of his life. Sarah's death necessitated a burial plot. Ancient Semitic burials within Palestine followed a similar yet geographical deviant pattern from Mesopotamia. Perhaps the deviations arose because dwellings in Mesopotamia were more urban. In Palestine, burials in specific gravesites are recorded on family plots outside of the home. Abraham however was a migrant stranger. He possessed no property.

This episode must be analyzed within specific parameters. First and foremost is the self-identification by Abraham that he is a foreigner

(גָּר/gar). The second element that is to be parsed is the response to that self-identification.

> And the sons of Heth answered Abraham, saying to him, "Hear us, my lord: You are a mighty prince among us. (Gen. 23:5–6a)

That response came from the sons of Heth. One easily imagines that involved in this discussion was a regular guy named Heth. That however was not the case. The Hittites were the people among whom Abraham is recorded as living among. Ephron was the son of a man named Zohar that owned a specific piece of land in what later became the city of Hebron.

Hebrew Word	*Pronunciation*	*Translation*
קָבַר	kä·var'	bury/ grave/ to be buried
בְּנֵי-חֵת	beni-Het	sons of Het
חִתִּי	khit·tē'	plural form of (חֵת) meaning the Hittites

The acknowledgment by the sons of Heth was not an acknowledgment of a single family led by the patriarch Heth. Instead, the episode was recast within the oral tradition acknowledging an equality between the economically displaced Habiru living in the isolated remote highlands and the prevailing Hittites. The interior demographic population of Palestine was dominated for a period of time by the Hittites.

The Hittite empires abounded in the Levant beginning around 1600 BCE. They were centered within what is now central Turkey. It is easy to imagine Hittite migrations during the mid-second millennia BCE into Palestine since the distance would not be all that extensive.

The Hittities, through their acknowledgment, preferred to just give the land to Abraham. Insisting that the land be sold, the tradition relates that the acquisition of the land was based on a legal exchange. Consideration flowed to both parties of the agreement.

> Abraham weighed out the silver for Ephron which he had named in the hearing of the sons of Heth, four hundred shekels of silver, currency of the merchants. (Gen. 23:16b)

The field and the cave were now the legal possession of Abraham. One must ask: why did Abraham wait so long to legally acquire property? We are entreated to multiple stories of his wealth, yet in all of his life, he was a landless migrant.

> This *is* the sum of the years of Abraham's life which he lived: one hundred and seventy-five years. Then Abraham breathed his last and died in a good old age, an old man and full *of years,* and was gathered to his people. And his sons Isaac and Ishmael buried him in the cave of Machpelah, which *is* before Mamre, in the field of Ephron the son of Zohar the Hittite, the field which Abraham purchased from the sons of Heth. There Abraham was buried, and Sarah his wife. And it came to pass, after the death of Abraham, that God blessed his son Isaac. And Isaac dwelt at Beer Lahai Roi. (Gen. 25:7–11)

Curiosity within the oral tradition led to the most important discussion. Is this really our land? That question would have been front and center circa 450 BCE as the Judeans pondered whether or not they should leave Mesopotamia. That central question needed to be explained to a displaced citizenry returning from exile. How could Abraham be both a foreigner in a land and a father of a nation in that land? A bridge had to be built.

CHAPTER 16

ABRAHAM

How is the premise tested: how could Abraham be both a foreigner and a father of a nation in a land in which he only owned his own burial plot? After Sarah's death, Abraham remarried. In the preceding twenty-fourth chapter of the book of Genesis, Abraham is old and well stricken with age. We will not discuss that chapter in this book. Arguably, one could consider it not as an Abrahamic episode, but instead more closely associated with Isaac. However, key factors from that story were understood and are borrowed for illustration.

In the twenty-fourth chapter Abraham was well advanced in age and his death was imminent. He made his eldest servant swear an oath to go to the land of his father's house, unto his mishpachah, to secure a wife for his son. That dialogue included some very practical questions. What if I find a young woman and she does not want to migrate to Palestine? Should I take your son and migrate back to Mesopotamia? Those were important questions. They struck at the very heart of a national ideological debate. In the view of Abraham's eldest servant migrating back to Mesopotamia had its merits. First, from Shinar (Sumer) to Palestine. From Palestine to Egypt. From Egypt to the Negev, the desert southern confines of Judah. From the Negev to the Gaza coast populated with Philistines. From the Philistine territory back to the Hebron interior of Judah. One leaves the twenty-fourth chapter of Genesis observing a feeble man lying on his death bed.

Enter the maiden Keturah, a lass promising to revive even the most docile levels of male testosterone production. Keturah reinvigorated Abraham for at least a period of seven years, giving birth after their courtship and marriage to Zimran, Jokshan, Medan, Midian, Ishbak, and Shuah.

Upon the death of Abraham, all that he had was singularly given to Isaac. At the age of 175 years, Abraham died. Before he died, he gave gifts to the children of his concubines and sent them away to Mesopotamia.

> And Abraham gave all that he had to Isaac. But Abraham gave gifts to the sons of the concubines which Abraham had; and while he was still living he sent them eastward, away from Isaac his son, to the country of the east. (Gen. 25:5–6)

The message of the text was clear. Ishamel was already living away from Isaac. He need not be accounted for in this story. Other children were given gifts of inheritance and sent away to allow for his son Isaac to remain as a rightful heir. In a fascinating twist, Isaac does not take possession of the field in which his mother and father were buried. Instead, Isaac dwelt at Beer Lahoi Roi.

Beer Lahoi Roi is the translation of "The well of the living one who sees me." This living one was God. It was not a property owned by Abraham; otherwise, he would have buried Sarah on or near that property. Yet for all its ignoble character, the location of Beer Lahoi Roi as the dwelling of Isaac is perhaps the most unlikely and equally ironic in biblical history.

Beer Lahoi Roi was the location to which Hagar fled when she was pregnant with Ishmael the elder brother of Isaac. Upset that Abraham actually conceived a child after a decade of failure with Sarah, Sarah imposed harsh cruel conditions upon the pregnant Hagar. Hagar in distress flees from Sarah to a remote location. At that location, Hagar was visited by an angel. The angel declared unto Hagar some interesting promises:

> Behold, you are with child,
> And you shall bear a son.
> You shall call his name Ishmael,
> Because the Lord has heard your affliction.
> He shall be a wild man;
> His hand shall be against every man,
> And every man's hand against him.
> And he shall dwell in the presence of all his brethren.
> (Gen. 16:11b–12)

The promise given by God to Hagar seems at first glance to be compensatory in nature until the sixth and seventh line of the poem are revealed. It is easy to understand how such a wild man should have his hand against every man. It is also easy to understand that consequently every man's hand would be against him. In irony, the possessor of the land that perhaps was to be initially associated with Ishmael, now becomes the dwelling of Isaac. This tradition has been lost in translation and context, yet was not lost to the original audience.

Abraham's death closed the story line on faith and inheritance in Palestine. The land of promise, the people of promise, the people of destiny had to reconcile hard facts. The Abraham episodes serve to remind us while these stories are among the greatest never told, the theology behind them is nothing if it does not create a connection with our Creator. L'chaim!

BIBLIOGRAPHY

Ahlstrom, Gosta W. *The History of Ancient Palestine*, edited by Diana Eldelman. Minneapolis, MN: Fortress Press, 1993.

Altar, Robert. *The Five Books of Moses: A Translation with Commentary.* New York, NY: WW Norton & Company, 2004.

Berlejung, A. "Twisting Traditions: Programmatic Absence—Theology for the Northern Kingdom in 1 Kings 12:26–33 (The Sin of Jeroboam)." *Journal of Northwest Semitic Languages* 35 no. 2 (2009): 1–42.

Brisco, Thomas V. *Holman Bible Atlas: A Complete Guide to the Expansive Geography of Biblical History*. Nashville, TN.: Broadman & Holman Publishers, 1998.

Brown, Francis, et. al. *The Brown-Driver-Briggs Hebrew and English Lexicon*. Peabody, MA: Hendrickson Publishers, Inc. 2001.

Carr, Edward Hallet. *What is History?* New York, NY: Random House, Inc., 1961.

Dalley, Stephanie, trans. *The Epic of Creation in Myths from Mesopotamia: Creation, The Flood, Gilgamesh, and Others*. New York, NY: Oxford University Press, 2008.

Finkelstein, Israel. *The Forgotten Kingdom: The Archeology and History of Northern Israel.* Atlanta, GA: Society of Biblical Literature, 2013.

Finkelstein, Israel, and Amahai Mazar. *The Quest for the Historical Israel: Debating Archeology and the History of Early Israel*, edited by Brian B. Schmidt. Atlanta, GA: Society for Biblical Literature, 2007.

Finkelstein, Israel and Neil Asher Silberman. *The Bible Unearthed: Archeology's New Vision of Ancient Israel and The Origins of Its Sacred Texts*. New York, NY: Simon and Schuster, 2001.

Heschel, Abraham Joshua. *The Sabbath*. New York, NY: Farrar, Straus and Giroux, 2005.

Hoffman, Joel M. *In the Beginning: A Short History of the Hebrew Language*. New York, NY: New York University Press, 2004.

King, L.W., trans. *Enuma Elish*, http://www.sacred-texts.com/ane/enuma.htm.

Kramer, Samuel Noah. *The Sumerians: Their History, Culture, and Character.* Chicago, IL: The University of Chicago Press, 1963.

Kramer, Samuel Noah. *Sumerian Mythology: A Study of Spiritual and Literary Achievement in the Third Millennium B.C. Revised edition.* Philadelphia: University of Pennsylvania Press, 1972.

Longman III, Tremper. *How to Read Genesis*. Downers Grove, IL: Intervarsity Press, 2003.

Mitchell, Larry A. *A Students Vocabulary for Biblical Hebrew and Aramaic.* Grand Rapids, MI: Zondervan, 1984.

Noth, Martin. *The History of Israel, 2nd ed.* Translated by Dr. P. R. Acroyd. New York, NY: Harper and Row Publishers, 1960.

Satlow, Michael L. *How the Bible Became Holy.* New Haven, CT: Yale University Press, 2014.

Snell, Daniel C. *Religions of the Ancient Near East.* New York, NY: Cambridge University Press, 2011.

Sproul, Barbara C. *Primal Myths: Creation Myths Around the World.* New York, NY: Harper Collins, 1991.

Strong, James: *The Exhaustive Concordance of the Bible: Strong's Concordance with Hebrew and Greek Lexicon*, https://www.blueletterbible.org/lang/lexicon/lexicon.cfm?strongs

Van De Mieroop, Marc. *A History of the Ancient Near East ca. 3000 to 323 BC 2nd Ed.* Malden, MA: Blackwell Publishing, 2007.

Van der Toorn, Karel. *Family Religion in Babylonia, Syria and Israel.* Atlanta, GA: SBL Press, 1996.

Walton, John H. Edited by Terry Muck, et. al. *Genesis: The NIV Application Commentary, From Biblical Text...To Contemporary Life.* Grand Rapids, MI: Zondervan, 2001.

Walton, John H. *The Lost World of Genesis One: Ancient Cosmology and the Origins Debate.* Downers Grove, IL: Intervarsity Press, 2009.

ABOUT THE BOOK

The Torah is the first five books of the Hebrew and Christian Bible. *Torah* means "to teach." It is fair to ask exactly what does the Torah teach? Scholars agree the Bible evolved from an oral tradition to its written form. This book examines the messages of the book of Genesis, the first book of the Bible, based on what those messages would have sounded like to an audience in the original oral tradition.

The episodes of Creation and the twenty-one separate stories of the iconic figure of Abraham are recast under the microscope of the prevailing Near Eastern context of their birth. The reader is invited to experience the vivid world of antiquity and for the first time hear *The Greatest Story Never Told.*

ABOUT THE AUTHOR

Vincent M Krivda is the executive director of Education Directions. With over thirty-five years of experience writing and negotiating contracts, Vincent now serves as an adjunct professor in the disciplines of ancient religions and business/finance. Vincent is a 1984 graduate of Lee University and has completed graduate degrees at American Graduate University (Master of Contract Management, 2008) and Liberty University (Master of Arts Theological Studies, 2012). Vincent currently teaches at Oakstone Academy in Westerville, Ohio, as an adjunct of Ohio Christian University. Vincent resides in Pickerington, Ohio, with the beautiful wife of his dreams, Coty. Vincent and Coty have three grandchildren: Lucy, Reagan, and McKinley.

CPSIA information can be obtained
at www.ICGtesting.com
Printed in the USA
BVHW081318160921
616889BV00001BA/158